D0428765

Their
Turf

Their Turf

America's Horsey Set & Its Princely Dynasties

BY

Bernard Livingston

ARBOR HOUSE
New York

 Published in the United States by Arbor House Publishing Co., New York, and simultaneously in Canada through Musson Book Co.

Library of Congress Catalog Card Number: 73–82188

ISBN: 0–87795–068–7

Manufactured in the United States of America

Because of Barbara Berger . . .

Contents

Contents

List of Illustrations

ERRATA: F. (not J.) Ambrose Clark Award, page 154; Mrs. Cloyce Tippett (not Tippet), page 247; Elliott (not Elliot) Burch, page 249, 250; Alfred G. Vanderbilt died in the sinking of the Lusitania in 1915 (not the Titanic in 1912), page 100; Mary Lou Hosford (not Hanford), page 75; Cornelius Vanderbilt Whitney bought his racing stable from his father's estate (it was not inherited), page 77; also page 77, there are no riding horses at Mr. Whitney's Adirondacks camp, nor have wolves or mountain lion ever been shot there; and Mr. Whitney does not have residences in Long Island, South America, Mexico and River House in Manhattan.

Acknowledgments

FIRST THE FRIENDS—and they were many and helped in many ways. Dr. Barbara Berger lightened the burden of countless heavy evenings not only with culinary wizardry on alfalfa, oats and hay, but also with valuable tips on human motivation. Nina Martin always got in line at the "Win" window when the odds were longest, Joan Wile phoned in enough action to create a "minus pool," and my full sister, Mrs. Beverly Solomon, was ever willing to muddy *her* thoroughbred legs ponying me in workouts on sloppy tracks. Phyllis Flaxman, Barbara Harkins and Barbara Bauer compiled the data for my Racing Form charts. Charlotte Kogan and Rose Moselle not only fed, watered, "cooled me out," and sat up late preparing me for the big ones, but also, between the two, made a rooting section more vocal than the hundreds of Venezuelans that cheered Canonero II to his Derby victory. Then there were my loyal backers at the track on Madison Avenue where I sometimes run: Tracy de Kruif, Fred Druzba, Shirley Irons, Hortense Nash, Joe Rickard, Jay Siskin, Suzanne Smoot, Ben Weiss and Sidney Matthew Weiss, in addition to Frank Allshouse and Paul Moser, who laid it on the line for me at the OTB office in Woodside, Long Island. And, finally, my trainer, Donald ("Sunny Jim") Fine, whose wise, if sometimes vociferous, instructions—together with the care of assistant trainer Judith Sachs, and of Wendy Nicholson, Belle Blanchard, Angela Miller, Joseph Grabois and the rest of the staff at Arbor House Stable, helped get me to the wire in world-record time.

In addition, those many wonderful people in thoroughbred racing: in management, on the farms, in stables, on the track, in media, libraries, sales and service. My thanks to each and every one who lent a hand.

But most of all, to Secretariat and Sham and Bold Ruler and Seabiscuit and all the rest of the thoroughbred heroes whose examples gave me the heart to see this challenge through.

The following books, publications, and organizations have been of invaluable help in the preparation of *Their Turf:*

American Magazine (Thomas Sugrue, 1936)

Charles Scribner's Sons, *The American Scene,* by Henry James, 1946

Charles Scribner's Sons, *Meditations on Hunting,* by José Ortega y Gasset, 1972

Holt, Rinehart & Winston, *The Hudson,* by Carl Carmer, 1968

New York *Herald-Tribune* (Eugenia Sheppard, Red Smith)

The Saturday Evening Post (Joe E. Palmer)

Country Life (George T. F. Ryall)

Sports Illustrated

The Blood-Horse

Prentice-Hall, Inc., *Saratoga, Saga of an Impious Era,* by George Waller, 1966

The Thoroughbred Record

The Daily Racing Form

Time

Life

The Washington *Post*

New York *Post*

Fortune

The New York Times

The Maryland Horse

The New Yorker

New York Sunday *News*

New York *Daily News*

Newsweek

G. P. Putnam's Sons, *Without Drums,* by Peter A. B. Widener, 1940

The Jockey Club

The Saratogan

Louis Sherry, Inc.

Sears, *Peacocks on Parade,* by Albert S. Crockett, 1931

Nevins, Alan (Editor) *The Diary of Philip Hone,* 1927

Simon and Schuster, *The Fireside Book of Horseracing,* 1963 (Grantland Rice)

The *Morning Telegraph*

Business Week

Foreword

SOME YEARS AGO, in the middle of a career spent photographing Roosevelts, Trumans, Rockefellers, MacArthurs and other V.I.P.'s for United Press International, I received a note from a Mr. John A. Morris: would I come to the offices of The Jockey Club in New York to talk with him, as chairman of the club's Thoroughbred Breeding Bureau, about the production of a documentary film?

Something of a thoroughbred himself (his racing silks are among the oldest on the American Turf), Mr. Morris had been impressed by a horse-racing promotion film I had put together on my free weekends. Could I do something similar for The Jockey Club, he wondered?

From that moment on my view of the world made an abrupt about-face. Until then I considered that, spending my days as I did at camera-length from presidents, generals and tycoons, I was observing American life at the very top. I soon discovered nothing was farther from the truth.

There is in this country a group that is above presidents, generals, and tycoons. Many of its members, indeed, would not indulge in such mundane pursuits as politics or commerce. In its fashion, this group is not unlike the British Monarchy: it endures while prime ministers, political parties and parvenus come and go. It is the Establishment's Establishment. Popularly, it is known as the "horsey set."

When I started work for Mr. Morris on the film, "The Jockey Club," I was able to observe the world of the horsey set from behind the scenes. And I went on to make other films involving Phippses, Whitneys, Wideners, Vanderbilts and Woodwards. I was in communication with DuPonts, Mellons, Klebergs and Aly Khans; I had a close look at their homes, their stables, their breeding farms, their inner sanctums. I watched them at work and play. Since my mission had to do with the phenomenon they treasure most—the thoroughbred horse—essentially no place was off limits to me. In a word I became what might be called the film Boswell of the horsey set, with the important difference that my eyes and ears often recorded what my camera did not.

This book attempts to describe and document the inside story of that world—a world which, though it may seem far removed from the average American's life, is in fact a most profound influence on the lives and fortunes of every one of us.

If, for instance, we look at nothing more than the intricate tax write-off system by which the horsey set has managed to shift the cost of its pleasure onto the back of the American people, we can see something of how our fortunes are affected. If, additionally, we examine how this group of Americans, of immense economic and social power, has suceeded in sustaining their aristocratic way of life right at the center of our democracy, we can further begin to understand how our society is fundamentally affected.

—Bernard Livingston

CHAPTER 1

The Original Horsey Set

God forbid that I should go to any Heaven where there are no horses!

—Robert Bontine Cunningham-Grahame
in a letter to Theodore Roosevelt

NEARLY 2,500 YEARS AGO Herodotus, the first reporter to cover the horsey scene, jotted the following item in his notebook: "Just outside Athens, beyond the road called Through the Hollow, Cimon (father of the great general, Militiades) lies entombed, together with the two mares which won him three Olympic races."

If Herodotus were making the rounds today, he might have ferreted out a parallel item: just outside Lexington, Kentucky, on Greentree Farm, the thoroughbred Twenty Grand (which won the Kentucky Derby and Preakness for the Whitney family) lies entombed. Here the two items would diverge, for Twenty Grand sleeps alone in the tomb, at least for the moment. John Hay Whitney, Greentree's present owner, has not yet shaken off his mortal coil. Moreover, should he decide to be interred with his horses, "Jock" Whitney would have, besides Twenty Grand, the choice of Tom Fool, Capot, and any number of his other famous thoroughbreds. While waiting for his master to make up his mind, Twenty Grand reposes under a tombstone appropriate to the high regard in which he was held.

These two items spanning two-and-a-half millennia point up the fact that mankind has always had what is known as a "horsey set." Of all the various kinds of "sets" into which society seems disposed to fragment—art lovers, auto racers, stamp collectors, dog showers—the one that revolves around the horse has had the longest continuous history, and, without question, the most fabulous.

There is something about the "fun" of racing (*racing*, not betting) horses that, as the Spanish philosopher José Ortega y Gasset points out in his *Meditations on Hunting*, published some thirty years ago, has a special meaning for man, particularly the rich man. Ortega demonstrated how throughout history, in his free time, man "has always done the same things: raced horses, competed in physical exercises, gathered at parties . . . engaged in conversation, and hunted." Man, and particularly aristocratic man—who has had the necessary freedom—has done this because, for the most part, his jobs (the very terms describing man's occupations derive from the Latin word *tripalium*, which originally meant instruments of torture) are things he would never do by choice. "In the sweat of thy brow shalt thou eat bread," decrees Genesis.

Thus man has always sought to lighten this terrible curse by escaping into sports, where he labors not by necessity but for pleasure, and the crushing burden of time disappears. And, in all societies and in all times, it has been hunting which has been elevated to the level of the premier sport, particularly for the noble class, the group that was able to make leisure a way of life.

The reason why hunting achieved such status, stated Ortega, is because it artificially reproduces a situation that is highly archaic, nostalgic and pleasurable: that early state when man still lived within the orbit of animal existence.

"When one is fed up with the troublesome present, with being very 20th century," he says, "one takes his gun, whistles for his dog, goes out to the mountain and, without further ado, gives himself the pleasure, during a few hours, of being Paleolithic. And men of all eras have been able to do the same without any difference except for the weapons employed. Thus does man succeed in renewing the primitive situation."

And horseracing, in those areas where horses existed, has always performed something of the same function, chiefly, however, by vicarious means. Apart from being an outdoors activity like hunting, horseracing provides man (and for women, who have never hunted, this is especially significant) with the opportunity of relating to an animal in a situation that also gives release to his primitive drives. Moreover, it offers the possibility of cloaking the expression of those animal instincts with the veneer of civilization and legality. By identification

On May 13, 1845, people from all over the country arrived at the Union Race Course on Long Island to watch Peytona and Fashion race for a purse of $20,000. Tremendous interest had been built up in the race. It was considered a contest between North and South with Peytona, who won the two heats in the race, representing the South. Estimates of attendance ranged from 80,000 to 100,000.

Not far from what is now Aqueduct, the "Big A" of American racing, Crown Colony Governor Richard Nicholls established what is generally considered the first formal race course in the New World in 1665. On Salisbury Plain in Long Island, the British colonists would gather on holidays to race their best horses and wager, just as they did in the Old Country.

with a horse that you have bred (or even are merely betting on) you can take the club to a rival and demolish him. This is what winning a race means, especially for the aristocracy, which has little concern for the cash value of a winning bet. It means destroying the "enemy" in the "cave" over the hill; it provides release for the profoundest aggressive wishes and all in a gentlemanly (or ladylike) manner. William Collins Whitney admitted this when he set out to "get" James Keene, his Wall Street rival, on the racetrack.

The horsey set has always been presided over by royalty, its present liege lady being Elizabeth II of England, who, besides owning thoroughbreds, can actually ride one. In America, where there is no official noble class, the horsey set, particularly as it relates to thoroughbred racing and breeding, is synonymous with great wealth. Among the American rich, the sport of kings has always been a status symbol, or in the words of Thorstein Veblen, a vehicle "for conspicuous consumption" of surplus wealth. To say nothing, of course, of a loophole for the writing off of taxes.

Despite the absence of an official peerage, the sport has managed, in a peculiarly American way, to generate its own version of a feudal system in this country.

At the top of this system, as always since colonial days, sits The Britannic Majesty. But Elizabeth II has only sentimental sovereignty for the American horsey set. The real power is held by the wealthy First Families. Not just any kind of wealth, but old established wealth: DuPont, Mellon, Phipps, Whitney, Morris, Widener and Vanderbilt wealth. This top stratum, sheltered in a kind of Camelot of exclusionary "clubs," has always been off limits to those of certain religious, social or ethnic background, no matter how rich or powerful, a situation that still prevails today.

At the bottom of the hierarchy sprawl the "serfs," a nameless miscellany of grooms, hot-walkers and stablehands, who service the superstructure, often with a kind of sentimental loyalty to the manor house.

In between is a bustling corps of bourgeois. These are the nouveau riche owners of racetracks and stables, administrators, concessionaires, trainers and jockeys—some of them quite rich. They give the structure a façade of democracy (on the racetrack a member of this thoroughbred community may address a Whitney as "Jock" or a Vanderbilt as

"Alfred"—but not outside). However, no matter how great their professional achievement or how large their bank accounts, they never get an invitation to sit in the Royal Enclosure.

The roots of this seemingly feudal structure go back to the first English colonists who brought horses to the New World. There were no horses this side of the Atlantic when the English arrived. The species had survived in the Western Hemisphere for a million years, and then mysteriously disappeared 10,000 years before the English arrived—perhaps victims of the Great Glacier. A number of Spanish *caballos* survived the rigors of Columbus's second voyage to the West Indies, but there is no record of what happened to them after landing. In 1610, a consignment of seven English horses disembarked at Jamestown. This time it was the Virginia horsey set rather than the glacier that disposed of them—as table food during the hungry winter of that first dreadful year.

When the English booted the Dutch out of New Amsterdam a half century later the horsey set got its real start. Peter Stuyvesant, who presided over 1,600 staid Hollanders that were never particularly interested in the racing qualities of their placid beer-type horses, retired to his Bouwerie Farm. He was the last Dutch governor of New Amsterdam. The new master, Colonel Richard Nicolls, immediately set about to "improve the breed."

This he did with typical British dispatch by laying out the first formal racetrack in the colonies, which he named Newmarket, after the fashionable English course that operates to this very day. Its superlative qualities for racing were described by a contemporary reporter in language that might well have been written by Audax Minor, racing reporter for *The New Yorker* Magazine:

> Toward the middle of Long Island lieth a plain sixteen miles long and four broad, upon which plain grows very fine grass that makes exceeding good hay; where you shall find neither stick nor stone to hinder the horse-heels or endanger them in their races, and once a year the best horses in the Island are brought hither to try their swiftness, and the swiftest rewarded with a silver cup, two being annually provided for the purpose.

That first racetrack was located not far from the present Belmont Park where, as the New York subway posters have it, the "improved" descendants of Colonel Nicolls' animals outspeed the cheetah nine times a day.

The horsey set was still very much in embryo in those days, for established wealth had not yet arrived on the scene in numbers great enough to make a clique. Even so, that did not prevent class from having its impact felt even in the Virginia of 1674 where, the York County records report:

> James Bullocke, a Taylor, having made a race for his mare to runn with a horse belonging to Mr. Matthew Slader for two thousand pounds of tobacco and caske, it being contrary to Law for a Labourer to make a race, being a sport only for Gentlemen, is fined for the same one hundred pounds of tobacco and caske.
>
> Whereas Mr. Matthew Slader and James Bullocke, by condition under the hand and seal of the said Slader, that his horse should runn out of the way that Bullocke's mare might win, w'ch is an apparent cheate, is ord'ed to be putt in the stocks and there sitt the space of one houre.

The more serious crime was not that of fixing a race but rather the audacity of the tailor, Mr. Bullocke, in making a race, something that was the exclusive prerogative of gentlemen.

It was inevitable that, as the leisure class grew larger and more prosperous, its lusty scions would begin to succumb to a traditional outlet of the very rich: the racing of the fast horse. Throughout the colonies incipient horsey sets began to appear. Racing at Williamsburg became so popular with the aristocratic students of William and Mary College, to the detriment of their studies, that the authorities passed the following regulation:

> Ordered y[t] no scholar belonging to any school in the College, of what age, rank, or quality, soever, do keep any race horse at ye College, in ye town—or any where in the neighborhood—y[t] they be not in any way concerned in making races, or in backing or abetting, those made by others, and y[t] all race horses kept in ye neighborhood of ye College, & belonging to any of ye scholars, be immediately dispatched and sent off & never again brought back, and all this under pain of ye severest animadversion and punishment.

It is a testimony either to the perennial narrowmindedness of academic authority or to the perserving hold that horses have on the mind of the very rich, that as a student young Alfred G. Vanderbilt, current president of Belmont Park, suffered the same admonishing for sneak-reading the Racing Form in Latin class while he was at St. Paul's School.

At the beginning of the eighteenth century the infant horsey set was already on its way to getting a foothold in the New World. In 1730, Bull Rocke, the first "bred horse," was imported to Virginia from England. By 1757 there were racetracks in Jamaica, Long Island, and Greenwich Village, New York. A few years later, the wealthy DeLancy family, which imported several blooded horses to New York, built its own running track on the Bouwerie with stables on what is now Chrystie Street and a paddock on the present Forsyth Street. On the very eve of the Revolution, a London racing paper reported that "the Hempstead Newmarket Course in Long Island is celebrated for its races throughout all the colonies and even in England, being held twice a year for a silver cup, to which the gentry of New England and New York resort."

Throughout the colonies everybody who was anybody was racing. George Washington was a steward in 1761, at a race meeting in Virginia; in 1772, his diary notes, he plunged for the sum of one pound, six shillings, at Annapolis; during the Revolution he managed to absent himself from Valley Forge long enough to acquire a stallion that caught his eye at a vendue.

An even more passionate member of the early horsey set was Andrew Jackson. He was said to have inherited $1,500 from his grandfather when he was sixteen, and to have lost it all at the Charleston races. He helped to establish the first race course in Nashville, Tennessee. During his campaign against the British at New Orleans, he found time to lay bets on matched horses in Tennessee, by mail and messenger. When he became President of the United States in 1829, Jackson continued to own and train a string of racehorses in Washington. The man who would not hesitate to shut down the Bank of the United States certainly would think nothing of adjourning Congress and going off with his legislative friends to catch a horserace at the Maryland Jockey Club in nearby Baltimore.

At the same time the beginnings of a professional "serf" stratum in the burgeoning feudal structure of the horsey set was developing in a manner that was uniquely American. In the South black slave boys were often used for jockeys. Some horsemen actually bred slaves for small size just as a hunter might stunt a dog for tracking badgers, or a sultan might create a eunuch for a harem. One of the first American jockeys to make a national reputation was a hunchbacked slave four feet, six inches tall, named "Monkey Simon." Later, after the Emancipation, the blacks rose to a high point as professional trainers and jockeys. One of them, Isaac Murphy, became the greatest rider in American history but was segregated back to anonymity and meniality by the end of the century. Except for stable hands, water-boys and hot-walkers, the professional end of the field was left entirely to the whites.

At this point in history, racing was still a sport rather than a business. Bookmaking was nonexistent; whatever wagering there was took place between the individuals concerned. Every gentleman owned a large stable which he sent to the races simply because he was a gentleman and not because he was a gambler. Races were held simply to prove that one man's horse had more speed than that of his rival. The ladies, decked out in their most seductive finery, watched the contest from the side lines while sipping coffee spiced with rum, or ice creams, blancmange and cookies. The gentlemen moved about on horseback showing off for the ladies. The stakes were put up by the contestants and their friends, and few days passed without some kind of hotblooded brawl or swordplay.

Most of the important races of that period were match races between the North and South. There were at that time no such national sports such as baseball, football, or even prize fighting and these match races became regional contests that, considering the absence of modern electronic media, generated a public interest that was every bit as intense as the current World Series in baseball or the heavyweight championship contest.

The Diary of Philip Hone refers to one of these match races on Long Island at Union Race Course in 1842, on the morning of which the eight-mile road from New York was covered with horsemen and a triple line of carriages and the track jammed with over 60,000 spectators:

> GREAT MATCH RACE. The great match race took place yesterday on the Union course, Long Island, between Fashion, a mare be-

> longing to Mr. Gibbons of New Jersey, and Boston, a horse belonging to Col. Johnson and Mr. Long. It was in many respects similar to the great race between Henry and Eclipse: North against South, the Southern horse—the favorite before the race—beaten by his Northern competitor, the amount of the stakes exceedingly large (in the present case $20,000 a side, besides great bets outside). I went over in the barouche with Mr. Phelps and Robert, and at Brooklyn we took up Mr. John C. Stevens. The day was favorable, and so far as circumstances can combine to make a race exciting and interesting they did on this occasion. But the crowd and the dust and the danger and difficulty of getting on and off the course with a carriage are scarcely compensated by any pleasure to be derived from the amusement. . . . The tens of thousands of the sovereign people who wished to see this race made their arrangements to go by the railroad from the South Ferry, but the numbers were so great that the locomotives refused to draw. They balked and would not go ahead; the mob who had provided themselves with tickets, finding it was "no go", became riotous, upset the cars, placed obstructions on the rails, and indulged in all sorts of violence, in which some persons were hurt.

That was thoroughbred racing in America up to the time of the Civil War. After the war, the foundation was laid for modern horse racing, with its huge public wagering, its great financial investment in plant and breeding and racing stock, its political directorates, and its First Family domination. Bookmaking now emerged as a component part of the sport and grew swiftly. The nation's oldest racetrack, Saratoga, opened only a month after the Battle of Gettysburg. The first major racetrack, Jerome Park, was launched on Long Island a year after the war, with a special clubhouse set aside for betting. The sport of kings spread throughout the country, even to California, where Leland Stanford raised horses on an 11,000-acre ranch that is now part of Stanford University. Elias J. Baldwin built Santa Anita racetrack where he hit it big in the Comstock lode. For the great American fortunes it was the era of the spinoff into horseracing. It was the time of Lorillard, Phipps, Whitney, Widener, DuPont, Vanderbilt, the founding sires of the modern American horsey set. It was the birth of the American bluebloods.

CHAPTER 2

The Jockey Club (1894-)

The public be damned!
—William H. Vanderbilt, (1821-1885),
reply to a newspaper reporter
(circa 1883)

BEFORE THE END OF THE CENTURY, racetracks and the business of breeding and racing thoroughbreds had grown to represent a major capital investment. Racing also evolved into the sport of kings for the more lusty of the American barons.

In 1894 The Jockey Club was born, an organization without parallel in American history in terms of political power. It was created, writes Walter S. Vosburgh, in *Racing in America,* "at a meeting at the Fifth Avenue Hotel in New York City, with Mr. James R. Keene, as owner of one of the leading stables, taking a conspicuous part. In an address Mr. Keene took the ground that the time had arrived for the organization of a jockey club, that the Board of Control was unequal to dealing with the exigency that had arisen, owing to its defective organization. . . . A jockey club similar to that of England should be formed. . . . The Jockey Club should have the power to allot the dates for meetings, the licensing of jockeys and trainers, enforcement of the forfeit list, revision of the rules, the appointment of officials, and constitute a final court of appeal in the interpretation of the rules and with power to discipline all persons under its jurisdiction."

That jurisdiction came eventually to comprise practically all of the many thousands directly connected with the business of breeding and racing thoroughbreds (a business that currently has a dollar volume of several billions) in addition to the millions of citizens indirectly connected with the sport as patrons of the tracks.

At the outset many of The Jockey Club's objectives were useful and no doubt well-intentioned. Racing was a frightfully disorganized sport. Many tracks were lax about punishing violators. Others arbitrarily set their own racing dates, often in destructive competition with tracks in the same city. There was no way of guaranteeing the identity of horses, so that "ringers" were a common hazard; naming of horses frequently resulted in haphazard duplication that created an appalling confusion of misleading names—to say nothing of the fixing of races.

So a group of tycoons of industry and finance recruited mostly from the Social Register stepped in to remedy the situation. They wrote their own Rules of Racing, interpreted and enforced them as a court of last appeal. They licensed owners, trainers, jockeys, racetrack employees (a purely state prerogative), allotted racing dates and took over publication of the *American Stud Book.* Any individual who failed to swear fealty to The Jockey Club's authority, or any horse that was not registered in its *Stud Book*, was classified as "undesirable" and outlawed from its recognized tracks. It was an awesome concentration of public authority in private hands, while official state government cooperatively looked the other way.

Today, the average person who looks at a racetrack program and notes among its roster of officials a listing that reads: "Invited Member of The Jockey Club, John Hay Whitney," or perhaps "George H. Bostwick" generally doesn't give it a second thought. "Must be some kind of club for jockeys," John Average remarks to himself.

George H. "Pete" Bostwick, a member of a family that owns a large chunk of Long Island and a good piece of Standard Oil, is certainly no jockey, except when he is mounted on one of his $50,000 polo ponies at Bostwick Field, or on a fine thoroughbred in a "gentlemen's" race at Aiken, South Carolina. And John Hay Whitney may be called "Jock" by friends such as Queen Elizabeth, but that's merely the Scottish form of "Jack" used out of affection, and in no way due to his riding abilities. In fact, many of the members of The Jockey Club would be inconceivable on any horse, let alone a racehorse. No, The Jockey Club is a center of immense power, wielded quietly but effectively from behind the scenes; a kind of silk-stocking Mafia or an American version of the old British Cliveden set.

Webster's New International Dictionary, 2nd. ed.—lists this entry:

> *jock'ey* (jok'i), n. Dim. of *Jock,* Scot form of Jack.
> *1.* One who rides or drives a horse; now, a professional rider of horses in races. *Hist.* A wandering minstrel, a vagabond.—v.t. *1.* To cheat, outwit or overreach. *2.* To manage with skill; esp., to treat trickily; to effect, put or the like, by tricky dealing.—v.i. To cheat; to take unfair advantage; also to maneuver for advantage.

Obviously The Jockey Club failed to look in the dictionary. Otherwise they should have seen that definition No. *1* is not for men who make rules, but rather for men who *ride* horses, such as Hartack, Shoemaker, Turcotte and the other men in the Jockeys' *Guild.* As for the historical definition, it rather strains the imagination to visualize Ogden Phipps, chairman of The Jockey Club, leaving his mansion to wander about as a "minstrel or vagabond." But the last part of the definition concerning "tricky dealing" is perhaps relevant. After all, Richard C. Whitney, a former president of the New York Stock Exchange and member of The Jockey Club, was sent to Sing Sing in 1938 for one of the biggest stock manipulations in history. So much for the name.

As for the membership, that and the governing body of stewards is listed in *The Racing Calender,* official organ of The Jockey Club, which is published in *The Thoroughbred Record.*

Bostwicks, Clarks, Guests, Klebergs, Morrises, Phippses, Vanderbilts, Whitneys, Wideners . . . here is a roster that would make a guest list for a White House banquet, although there are no relative paupers such as Richard Nixon listed there.

Exemplary among this list is Robert J. Kleberg, Jr., who traces his ancestry back to the man who married the daughter of Captain Richard King—an apt choice of name for an individual who has conquered and rules a piece of American turf larger than many royal kingdoms. King Ranch, nearly a million Texan acres spreading over seven counties, larger than the state of Rhode Island, was acquired largely by dispossessing the local Indians and Mexicans with a private army.

The Racing Calendar

THE JOCKEY CLUB

300 Park Avenue
New York, N.Y. 10022

OFFICERS

Ogden Phipps, *Chairman*
Nicholas F. Brady, *Vice-Chairman*
Louis Lee Haggin II, *Secretary-Treasurer*

STEWARDS

Nicholas F. Brady
John W. Galbreath
Louis Lee Haggin II
Francis Kernan
Paul Mellon
John A. Morris
Ogden Phipps
John M. Schiff
John Hay Whitney

Calvin S. Rainey, *Executive Secretary*
Nathaniel J. Hyland, *Assistant Secretary*
Frank Kalbac, *Assistant Treasurer*
Kenneth Noe, Jr., *Handicapper*

MEMBERS OF THE JOCKEY CLUB

Eslie Asbury
Albert C. Bostwick
George H. Bostwick
Nicholas F. Brady
Baird C. Brittingham
George M. Cheston
John C. Clark
Stephen C. Clark, Jr.
Leslie Combs II
J. Simpson Dean
Vincent De Roulet
F. Eugene Dixon, Jr.
Jack J. Dreyfus, Jr.
William S. Farish III
Anderson Fowler
Daniel M. Galbreath
Charles E. Mather II
Peter McBean
William L. McKnight
Paul Mellon
James P. Mills
John A. Morris
James B. Moseley
John M. Olin
Henry A. Parr III
Perry R. Pease
W. Haggin Perry
Ogden Phipps
Ogden Mills Phipps
George A. Pope, Jr.
Joseph M. Roebling
Donald P. Ross

Today Mr. Kleberg runs an empire that has colonies in three U. S. states and three foreign countries. Twelve hundred people live on King Ranch; thousands of quarter horses and Santa Gertrudis cattle graze its plains; wild animals—birds and beasts of great variety—inhabit its hills and streams. Six hundred and fifty wells gush gas and oil (under license to Humble Oil), and thoroughbreds of one of the world's largest racing and breeding operations—from which came Triple Crown Winner Assault—gambol in its paddocks. What the total wealth of this kingdom is (and it is privately owned) can only be guessed at. It is enough to qualify Mr. Kleberg for membership in The Jockey Club, make him an important figure in international racing and endow him with more lasting power than an American President.

If a total were made of the personal assets and credentials of all the men on this list it would add up to something like $10 to 20 billion, half the space in the Social Register and most of the key seats in the directorships of U.S. corporations, banks, foundations, museums, hospitals, and universities.

There are few Jews on the list. No blacks. Nor women, even though there are women owners and trainers. In the 1950s a Jew was admitted to The Jockey Club. After all, times were changing and it would perhaps look well to have one on the list—particularly if he is old-established money. And so Captain Harry F. Guggenheim of *the* Guggenheim family was admitted to the select circle. It is interesting to note, however, that, as with Guggenheim (who married the immensely wealthy Alicia Patterson), the two other Jews, admitted in the 1960s, also married into rich, old-line WASP families: John M. Schiff, who married the daughter of George F. Baker, Jr., and Jack L. Dreyfus, Jr., who married Joan Personnette. But Hirsch Jacobs, Jewish ex-pigeon trainer from Brooklyn, despite the fact that he married a gentile and was, additionally, the "greatest horseman in American history" (*Newsweek*, 8/24/70) never made it.

Ironically, the man who put The Jockey Club together was the son of a Jew. The family of August Belmont II, one of the organizers of The Jockey Club and its iron-fisted chairman for thirty years, was originally named Balmain (some claim it was Schoenberg). His father, who metamorphosed into August Belmont I on arrival in the United States, was born of the Jews Simon and Fredericka (Elsaas) Balmain in the Rhenish town of Alzei in 1816. Something of a mercantile prodigy, young Balmain joined the Rothschild banking house at fourteen to learn the business, sweeping floors and emptying trashbaskets at no pay; in three years he was on his way to Italy to conduct Rothschild negotiations with the Papal Court. He acquired Italian art, money, and women and soon was dispatched to Cuba on another

Left: William Woodward (with jockey J. Stout) receives a silver plate for a victory of one of his horses. Woodward, who owned the Triple Crown winners Gallant Fox and Omaha, was chairman of The Jockey Club from 1930 to 1950.

Below: William Woodward, Jr. and wife, with Nashua, jockey Eddie Arcaro up. Mrs. Woodward accidentally killed her husband with a gun during the 1960's.

August Belmont II (left), builder of Belmont Park, with trainer Sam Hildreth. Belmont was one of the founders of The Jockey Club and its second chairman. He also bred Man o' War.

Jule Fink, a racehorse owner who, in a landmark constitutional case, tested the power of The Jockey Club to exercise licensing power in New York racing, and won.

Rothschild mission. Hearing of the financial panic raging in the United States, he immediately changed course for the States in 1937, changed his name from Balmain to Belmont and set up his own financial operation on Wall Street. With Rothschild affiliation, and his own business acumen, he soon became one of the richest men in the country. He married the Quaker daughter of Commodore Matthew C. Perry and, having the advantage of Continental insouciance, became a leader of New York society, outshining even the Astors and Rhinelanders. He also dabbled in racehorses.

August Belmont II came into the picture when rugged individualism was at its zenith in America. It was the age of the Robber Barons and the Empire Builders—Goulds, Harrimans, Morgans, Whitneys, Vanderbilts, Bradys, Carnegies, Phippses and Fisks. Subways were being built so Belmont hammered out New York's IRT. Canals were being constructed; he sliced out the Cape Cod waterway. Opera houses were being erected; he became a director at the Met and married a singer who to this very day presides as its grande dame. In the horse world it was the same. Racing stables were being put together. Belmont bred no less a horse than Man o' War—originally named *My* Man o' War by Mrs. Belmont in honor of her husband's marching off to battle. Race courses were being laid out and August Belmont built the most opulent of them all: Belmont Park. And now, a perfectly legitimate first-generation WASP, he was able to obtain what his *landsmen*—the Guggenheims, the Schiffs, and the Lehmans, members of "our crowd" from across the tracks—required another half century to get: a seat in America's House of Lords, The Jockey Club.

August Belmont II presided over The Jockey Club and, by extension, the American horsey set until his death in 1926. During this period thoroughbred racing evolved into a great commercial enterprise. With public participation through betting, the sport expanded throughout the country. Giant racetracks and breeding farms spread from Florida to California. It was the era of Man o' War, Sir Barton, Morvich, Zev, and Exterminator; the time of the great international match races, the period during which the Kentucky Derby developed into the best-known horse race in the world. It was also the period which saw the entry of new blood into the sport, side by side with the old, established wealth.

Over all of this The Jockey Club was supreme. But in 1952, some fifty years after The Jockey Club's formation, the horsey set was given a severe jolt. Marshall Cassidy, Executive Secretary of The Jockey Club, refused to renew the license of Marlet Stable, the racing *nom de course* of a man named Jule Fink. The charge was "associating with gambling groups to the detriment of the best interests of racing." Presumably the action would go unchallenged, as such actions always had in the fifty-year history of the racing colony. Marshall Cassidy was the faithful servant of the horsey set. As Executive Secretary of The Jockey Club he placed his masters' interests above all else: the non-Club owners, the racing professionals and the public. He was ambitious, provincial and officious. With Jockey Club backing he rose to become undisputed czar of racing in New York and, by extension, the rest of the country. In this role he was responsible for the handling of the Fink case. Nevertheless it cannot be denied that he was a great factor in modernizing horse racing. He pioneered, among other things, the mechanical starting-gate (to facilitate and equalize the starts of races), the photo finish (to give more precise evidence of finishes), the film patrol (to provide motion picture records of the running of each race) and the method of identifying horses by "nighteyes" (growths on a horse's legs which, like fingerprints on humans, are unique to each animal).

Cassidy regularly submitted confidential reports to the Stewards of The Jockey Club (according to Toney Betts, New York *Mirror* turf writer in his book, *Across the Board,*) on "suspect" personalities in the racing business. And "associating with Jews and Italians" (evidence of which was gathered by a private force of Pinkertons) was apparently for him, and by extension for The Jockey Club, sufficient to stigmatize a man. This was a charge that, in his book, Mr. Betts, who read The Jockey Club report, said that Cassidy had placed against jockey Bobby Merritt in denying him a license.

Jule Fink, however, decided to offer challenge. After a defeat in the lower courts, which upheld the licensing powers of The Jockey Club on the basis of a 1934 New York State law delegating such prerogatives to the Club, he went on to the Court of Appeals. There, two years later, under the marshalship of Charles H. Tuttle, a former counsel to The Jockey Club, the lower court was reversed by unanimous decision. The Appeals Court held that (*The New York Times,* 3/8/51) "the licensing power given by the Legislature to a social and exclusive group of sportsmen was an unconstitutional delegation of legislative authority . . ." and constituted "the exercise of sovereign power by individuals who are neither chosen by, nor responsible to the state. . . ."

"Under its rules," continued the *Times,* "The Jockey Club laid down the principle that it had the right to deny a license to any 'undesirable.' The Club's rulings had the effect of law only in New York and Delaware, but they were accepted almost verbatim by custom in all states. This state of affairs was ended by yesterday's decision."

The Establishment had been challenged in its own courts by a flashy-suited "Speed Boy" (so named because he favored speed horses in his highly successful system for picking winners).

Of course, as the *Times* article noted, "The Jockey Club, under the decision, still retained considerable authority in American racing by its ownership of the *American Stud Book.* Without a listing in that register, no horse foaled in the United States, Cuba or Mexico can race in the U.S." Further, "If the state administration is willing, The Jockey Club could still retain influence in racing licensing. This could be effected by having representatives of The Jockey Club—not named as such—appointed to any licensing bureau set up within the State Racing Commission." The outsider's challenge had been sustained, but the inner circle was still very much in control and unto itself. Henceforth it would only need to be somewhat more imaginative and circumspect.

CHAPTER 3

Affairs of the Horse: A Preview—'03 to '31 to '68

Horse show? That's where a bunch of horses show their asses to a bunch of horses' asses showing their horses.

—Graffito on a wall of the men's room at the National Horse Show

SOMETHING IMAGINATIVE, though hardly circumspect, was afoot on a windy March evening in 1903 as a corps of New York *paparazzi* shifted impatiently about in the cold outside the gates of the city's most princely estate. They had been waiting for hours trying to take photographs of the "party of the century," the banquet with which Jockey Club member Cornelius K. G. Billings would celebrate his ascension to the presidency of The Equestrian Club.

Parties of the century, so-called, were not uncommon in this perhaps most opulent of American eras; there was a new one almost every week. Members of the topmost strata of society, with their untouched, untaxed millions, strove to outdo each other, either in the lavishness or the *bizarrerie* with which they mounted their festivities. Banquets on the order of Belshazzar's feast were near as commonplace as a workingman's bash at the corner saloon.

J. P. Morgan, for example, who disliked hotels, thought nothing of leasing a six-floor mansion in San Francisco, dismantling it from top to bottom, redecorating and refurnishing it to his own taste, and then dispatching Louis Sherry and twenty-five assistants all the way from New York to cater a dinner for just one night.

Or consider the Bradley Martin party of 1896. That was an attempt by Mrs. Bradley Martin, a kind of socialite Elsa Maxwell of the period, to upstage anything that had ever been done in the way of a costume ball, including even the spectacular Duchess of Warwick masquerade in England earlier in the century. If the number of lines captured in *The New York Times* is any criterion of success, the Martin ball was a most resounding triumph, for its coverage spread over a page-and-a-half of the main paper in addition to eight pages of the Sunday magazine supplement, as much space as might be devoted to reporting a major war or national scandal such as Watergate. The guests—which included Astors, Cushings, Delafields, Harrimans, Hitchcocks, Schermerhorns and Van Cortlandts—launched a major invasion of shops and museums to outfit themselves as authentic reproductions of historical characters, all to dance quadrilles in the ballroom of reconstructed Versailles at the Waldorf Hotel.

J. P. Morgan and Mrs. Bradley Martin were not members of the horsey set. But entertainments such as theirs, created for them by those impressarios of party-giving—the Louis Sherrys, Rectors, Delmonicos and Oscars of the Waldorf—nevertheless set standards of spectacularity which the horsey set simply could not let go unchallenged. They provoked into action that most basic of all the set's drives: the need to win, to be best. A horseman such as Jockey Club Chairman William Woodward, a man who had everything a human being conceivably could desire, including riches, power, three Kentucky Derby and two Triple Crown winners, could be so obsessed by the need to be "first" that he spent a lifetime and a small fortune trying to win the Royal Ascot Gold Cup—and never made it. Others strove with equal fanaticism to win such laurels as Horse of the Year, Best of Class, and the Futurity Cup.

It is not surprising that it would be the horsey set that would come up with the real titleholder for the party of the century. This despite the fact that Cornelius K. G. Billings, the man who staged it, disliked the very kind of publicity that makes such labels possible, and, indeed, saw to it that the press never was able to cover his party.

The son of a wealthy horse breeder, Billings was born in 1861 at Saratoga Springs, New York, the very Camelot of the society that revolves around the horse and horseracing. By the time he was twenty-six he was already running his father's Chicago Gas Light & Coke Company, the largest public utility in the west. From this base he climbed to the chairmanship of Union Carbide, presently the nation's twenty-fifth largest corporation, along the way amassing an immense fortune.

At the turn of the century he moved to the nation's *largest* city, New York. There he bought its *highest* point, Fort Tryon, the old Revolutionary War citadel on upper Riverside Drive. This he used as a site to build the *biggest* mansion in the area—the size of a medieval castle—in addition to the *finest* stables in the country, to house, among others, Lou Dillon, the *fastest* trotting mare in the world (he was also part owner of Omar Khayham, a Kentucky Derby *winner*).

With such an array of superlatives in his coat-of-arms, Billings had no trouble dominating The Equestrian Club, and on his election to its presidency he decided to celebrate this additional "mostest" with an appropriate toast: a stag party at his mansion for members of the Club.

Almost immediately a wave of gossip started. This was stimulated, no doubt, by memories of the notorious Seeley stag party some years previously, where the original "Little Egypt," imported from the St. Louis World's Fair, entertained her blue-blooded guests so effectively that venerable Louis Sherry's was raided and as a result Little Egypt was elevated to the mythic status she holds to this day.

Billings was incensed by the publicity building over his own affair. He called in Louis Sherry, who was to cater the party. A. S. Crockett described this in his book, *Peacocks on Parade,* (Sears, 1931.) "I'll be out of my wits before this affair is over!" Billings said. "I'm beset day and night by reporters and cameramen! They lie in wait at my gates! They follow my carriage through the streets! I must get rid of this notoriety!"

"Leave it to me," said Sherry reassuringly. "Give me carte blanche with this affair, and we'll fool the newspapers as they've never been fooled before. Notify your guests, as quietly as possible, that instead of going to your home on Saturday night, they meet at your apartments in town."

The night of the party, as planned, Billings' thirty-two male guests gathered at the Hotel Netherland. From there they were driven down to Sherry's. In one of the small banquet halls they had pre-dinner drinks around a table on which, as if to set the stage for the affair, stood a life-size stuffed horse, mounted over a huge bed of roses. In the midst of the preliminary festivities, however, Billings and a guest, former Mayor Richard Grant, suddenly excused themselves and left the room.

At Billings' mansion, meanwhile, the press maintained a frantic vigil, for, to keep up the illusion of a party about to take place there, preparations for the pretended festivities continued: waiters reported for work, grocers carted in provisions, florists delivered flowers.

Downtown, thirty-three blooded horses from Billings' stables had already reached Sherry's rear entrance, having been raced at top speed through the city to exhaust them so that they would stand quietly for the task they had to perform. One by one they were carried by elevator to the grand ballroom that had been transformed by a corps of gardeners and decorators into a stretch of open country. Real trees, shrubs, grass and flowers had been planted. A fresh-water brook babbled over rocks, live birds twittered and flew about, while overhead, against an azure sky, throbbed twinkling stars and a harvest moon as authentic as the magic of money could contrive.

During all this, the bewildered guests down in the small banquet hall, finally tired of toasting the stuffed horse on its bed of roses and began asking for the whereabouts of their host, Billings. A waiter suggested they might look for him, whereupon they all rose and followed him to the grand ballroom.

There, arranged in a huge circle like so many Lipizzaner stallions about to execute a choral movement from Swan Lake, were Billings' thirty-three horses. And on two of them were mounted Billings and the mayor of New York.

"Mount!" commanded the Chief Magistrate, and thirty-one members of the horsey set, in full evening attire, took their places on thirty-one blooded steeds. Thirty-one Sherry waiters, dressed as grooms in scarlet hunting coats, white breeches and yellow top boots, helped the amazed guests to the saddle.

Over each horse was slung a table, securely anchored to the animal's flanks. From its shoulders hung two saddle bags containing buckets of iced champagne; in front of each horse stood a trough of feed to divert the animated chairs from cavorting. And while the beasts munched on oats *à la Louis Sherry,* the humans took sustenance from Krug '98 through long nippled tubes that led to the saddle bags. At the sound of a dinner chime, they began putting away the following feast:

22 Name Mr. K. G. Billings 32 Persons.

House

Saturday
Date March 28/1903 Time 8 P.M.

Menu.

Caviar and Hot Toast

—

Potage Tortue Clair en Tasse

—

Truite au Bleu Sauce Vert

—

Carré d'Agneau
Legumes Place

—

Chicken Guinea Hen
Salade Coeur de Laitue à la Riche

—

Asperges Hollandaise

—

Pêches Flambé Chaud.

—

Cafe

—

Ginger ale in Bottle for Mr Billings and Mr Halstead & L.S.

Cocktails in the Room
Equipment in Horses
Flowers for decorations
King '98
Rye and Scotch
Apollinaris
Cigars in Cases
Small tables and Chairs
Byron take Photograph

Left: Menu for the "party of the century" given by C. K. G. Billings at Louis Sherry's.

Below: In 1903, Cornelius K. G. Billings, multi-millionaire horseman, staged the "party of the century" to celebrate his election to the presidency of the Equestrian Club. In the grand ballroom of Louis Sherry, thirty-three diners, seated on horseback and served by liveried grooms, consumed a royal feast and sipped champagne through rubber hoses connected to bottles placed in their saddle bags.

But that was not the end of it; it was, after all, a stag party. When cigars had been lit, the unlikely combination of Fred Stone, the foremost comedian of the day, starring on Broadway in *The Wizard of Oz*, and Kid McCoy, light-heavyweight champion of the world, headlined some entertainment that finally leaked through to the New York *Tribune* as follows:

> . . . at close of dinner, while coffee was served, Fred Stone and Kid McCoy took their places and went on with their specialty [not described] to the delight of the banqueters. . . . Then Richie Ling and his twelve showgirls in their new ermine gowns, costing $500 each and made especially for the occasion, sang and danced, after which a change of costume was made (!) for the Turkish wives' dance.

The Seeley party required the intervention of Police Commissioner Theodore Roosevelt to save the good name of its noted cavaliers. What twelve American showgirls did that could be described as a Turkish wives' dance was perhaps nothing shocking by modern standards. But it should be remembered this was the cream of New York's horsey set, the party was at fashionable Louis Sherry's, Mayor Grant was present, and the traditions of Queen Victoria still theoretically prevailed.

At any rate, each guest went home with a solid-gold matchbox, a gold-initialed leather cigar case, and one of the costly sterling silver menus that had been molded approximately in the form of a horseshoe. And even though the horses had been driven thirty miles before dinner and had stood on their feet all night, on the way out one steed still had enough energy left in his shanks to leave behind a demolished elevator as *his* memento to the occasion.

Said Mr. Fred Stone, "Never saw anything so clever, either on or off stage. Topped anything in the U.S. or Europe, even Mrs. Vanderbilt's famous monkey party. It was indeed the party of the century."

Another party, perhaps not a "party of the century," but nevertheless typical of the dramatics with which the set celebrated its role as improvers of the breed, was that tendered to Jockey Club member Joseph E. Widener in 1931 at the height of the Depression.

The grand ballroom of the Hotel Biltmore in New York was transformed into a miniature Belmont Park, complete with a turf racing course, in honor of its president, Mr. Widener, of Mainline Philadelphia.

First, among those doing honor that night to Mr. Widener's leadership, in addition to Richard Whitney, were Governor Franklin D. Roosevelt, Mayor John McKee, Tammany Leader John F. Curry, Republican Leader Samuel S. Koenig, Major General Hanson E. Ely, Admiral Cary T. Grayson, William DuPont, Jr., Walter F. Chrysler and the distinguished party-giver of some twenty-years earlier, Cornelius K. G. Billings—a fairly good cross section of that period's equivalent of the military–industrial–political complex. In addition, a cablegram was received from the Earl of Derby. Lord Derby had very kind words for Mr. Widener's unstinting devotion to the horse on both sides of the Atlantic.

To start the festivities off, the sound of horses' hooves was heard clip-clopping in a post-parade across the thinly cushioned Biltmore dance floor, as though it were a field for the Fall High Weight Handicap. Following this, there was a series of horse tableaux depicting, among other things, the life of Fred Archer, the cockney boy who rode five Epsom Derby winners, including the illustrious Ormonde. No detail was left unattended to produce an authentic work of theater. A real honest-to-goodness Englishman, Captain A. M. Marshall, was employed to play the role of Archer, and a thoroughbred named Brown Derby (not an honest-to-goodness Derby winner) was assigned the part of a Derby winner.

Next came a performance by a United States Cavalry team, consisting of a platoon of spit-and-polish sergeants. "Soon after the arrival of the army horses," states a *New York Times* account, "a smartly uniformed member of the city's mounted police, riding one of the finest specimens ever owned by the city, reached the hotel, and later in the evening gave still another impressive demonstration of horsemanship."

Perhaps the most telling symbolism of the evening—without doubt the most lavishly staged—was the presentation of a hunting scene called the "Hunt Club Fixture." This featured a chase by three thoroughbred hunters, led by the prize-winning and aptly named Over There, down a full-fashioned mock-up of Belmont Park's quarter-mile Widener Chute to the accompaniment of a pack of foxhounds in full cry. This surely had been the first time that a tally-ho wound up with its hounds barking up the legendary Biltmore Clock.

Following this event, Mr. Widener ascended the rostrum to acknowledge over NBC radio Lord Derby's cablegram, which he did both with elegance and with the two propositions then most characteristic of the public stance of the horsey set. In effect, Mr. Widener stated that the primary interest thoroughbred breeders have in horses and horseracing is the improvement of the breed. And since, as most everyone knew, it was the cavalry which, in the final analysis, defeated the Kaiser, no patriotic American would quarrel with the horsey set's devotion to the sport of racing, even in a depression. Moreover, since it is the racetrack which provides the ultimate test that eliminates those stallions least likely to improve the breed, it is therefore horseracing which produces the best horses, which helps defeat the enemy, which contributes to a strong and therefore secure America.

However, bad publicity resulting from this sort of bacchanal, particularly in a period when the poverty-stricken Okie had become a symbol of the national conscience, compelled thoughtful members of the set to call for a more restrained comportment. Parties at which racehorses ate better than most Americans were given a low profile. What eventually emerged was a horsey variation of the standard charity ball.

At the Belmont Ball of 1968, for example (the Ball is an annual affair to promote the Belmont Stakes), the accent was more on the clothes-horse than the horse. Indeed, there was not a horse in sight even though the ball was held at a racetrack—the Terrace Room of the new $30,000,000 Belmont Park—dispensing with the need to improvise costly replicas in hotel ballrooms. Accompanying it all was still the desire to propogate the notion that great public largess flowed from the sport of kings.

The old-line Whitneys were still in attendance in the person of Jock's sister, Mrs. Charles Shipman Payson, co-owner of Greentree Stable and sole owner, among her other equities, of the New York Mets—the latter being an example of the sports-conglomerate syndrome that seemed to be spreading.

A more telling change in the tone of the 1968 ball than that entertainment was no longer equine was that the music was no longer Victor Herbert. In line with suggestions from its sponsors for a new profile, the music was hard rock!

"Turn me on at Belmont!" blasted the twenty piece combo of Meyer Davis, the noted society maestro, in a piece composed especially for the party.

"It doesn't turn *me* on," declared Mrs. Payson, turned out in a Mainbocher floating orange chiffon with diamond sunbursts on her wrists. " 'Big Daddy . . . Blow your mind' . . . We can't hear a thing!" What she meant was that the loud rock compelled her to lift her transistor to her ear in order to hear the radio broadcast of the game her Mets were playing in St. Louis.

Mrs. Cortwright Wetherill, the former Ella Anne "Tootie" Widener, one of the younger set (she improves the breed both at Andover, England, and Happy Hill in Kentucky) was of a different mind. It was Tootie who had set up the annual Belmont Ball for charity instead of for self—of the more than $100,000 raised, most not surprisingly went to her Heart & Lung Foundation, which she also founded. The balance went to the National Racing Museum, the Center for Performing Arts, and Skidmore College, all admirable and all located at the horse capital, Saratoga Springs, N.Y.

Tootie couldn't remember the actual sum herself, though she had no trouble recalling the amount of the check her father—who gave the 1931 Biltmore party—had written for her Philadelphia debut party. The drapes alone had cost $40,000, and Maestro Meyer Davis had conducted an orchestra the size of Leopold Stokowski's Symphony. Now he was playing her theme song, "It's a Lovely Day Today."

When blond, six-foot-two Mrs. John A. Morris arrived at the party, her long graceful neck circled with a multi-tiered pearl choker, Maestro Davis performed a few bars of her theme song, "My Kind of Girl." Mrs. Morris' scarlet racing colors are the oldest in America and her gown was a classic pink crepe by Mainbocher. The choker was her husband's first gift to her.

"There's no use getting new jewelry, anyway," she said. "They just steal it from you."

But rock music, charity balls, and a return to old jewelry were not the only ways in which the horsey set was adapting itself to the social changes taking place around them. Attention also had to be paid to some of the new forces pressing at the gates of the old citadels and actually acquiring some of the landmark castles.

The presence at the 1968 Belmont Ball of Mrs. Donald C. LeVine was perhaps symbolic of such adaptation. Although from Philadelphia, like Tootie Widener herself, and indeed a sister of Princess Grace of Monaco, Mrs. LeVine nevertheless had a socially flawed background, only one generation removed. Her father, John Kelly, despite having sufficient resources to gain entry into thoroughbred racing by way of the presidency of the Atlantic City Racetrack and having a daughter who presided as a true princess, began as a bricklayer. Despite Kelly's physical size and financial clout, diminutive ex-dentist Dr. Leon Levy, a major shareholder in Columbia Broadcasting System and a power in the New Jersey Establishment (even if he could not make it to The Jockey Club) tended to treat the big Irishman Kelly like an office boy. But the time had come for the ruling group in the horsey set to lower the bridge over the moat. Mrs. LeVine, along with others such as John Schapiro, scion of an ex-junk dealer from Baltimore, and Jack J. Dreyfus and John M. Schiff at The Jockey Club level, were being cautiously admitted to the inner circle.

"We call ourselves Red Brick Stables," said Mrs. LeVine upon the occasion of her first attendance at a Belmont Ball—even without a theme song of her own from Maestro Davis. "It was named after my family—they're in the brick business." (Red Brick horses are still on the New Jersey circuit.) "But some day I hope we'll have a horse good enough to bring here."

The following accounts of the great families who have no problem in bringing their steeds to Belmont highlight the world Mrs. LeVine—and countless others—aspire to with such heartfelt dedication.

Left: William Collins Whitney, founder of the Whitney racing dynasty.

Below, left: John Hay Whitney leads his Belmont Stakes winner, Stage Door Johnny, to the winner's circle. His sister, Mrs. Charles S. Payson, co-owner of their Greentree Stable, follows close behind.

Below, right: Harry P. Whitney on his polo pony, Cottontail

Mary Elizabeth Altemus, of Philadelphia, was one of the best horsewomen and one of the most beautiful ladies in the country when she married John Hay Whitney in 1930. After a divorce in which she received three million dollars and the fabled horse farm and estate called Llangollen in Virginia, Liz Whitney went on to become one of the most publicized women in the U.S. She acquired hundreds of racehorses—many of them top runners—dozens of canines and other animals, and three more husbands. Today, although her legal name is Mrs. Cloyce Tippett, she is still known the world over as Liz Whitney.

Mrs. Cloyce J. Tippett has thoroughbreds racing and/or standing at stud all over the world—from Virginia to Florida to California to France to England to Ireland to Australia. Liz Whitney is one of the shrewdest horse racers, breeders and sellers of the horse world. Queen Liz's reputation for clever bargaining and negotiating, both in horses and in the King's English, has become a matter of legend. Even the Russians accorded her the red-carpet treatment when they invited her to drive a *droshky* around the Hippodrome. They then traded one of their best thoroughbred studs for three of her horses—a deal in which the Queen fared extremely well. Colonel Tippett is here seen at her left.

Left: Cornelius Vanderbilt Whitney with his wife, Mary Lou, at the Saratoga auction sales.

Below: Mr. and Mrs. Payne Whitney at the Saratoga races in the 1920's.

THE WHITNEY DYNASTY

CHAPTER 4

William Collins Whitney
(1841-1904)

After having gratified every ambition and swung the country almost at his will . . . W. C. Whitney had turned to other amusements, won every object that New York afforded, and not yet satisfied, had carried his field of activity abroad, until New York no longer knew what most to envy, his horses or his houses.

—Henry Adams

THE WHITNEYS, AS A FAMILY GROUP, have always ranked at the top in the hierarchy of the American horsey set. There have been individuals—such as Jockey Club chairmen August Belmont and William Woodward—who were just as prestigious in the inner councils, but when the Whitney Dynasty combined its total assets there was little doubt as to which family was Number One.

Even though the DuPont and Mellon clans might have overtaken the Whitney family in collective financial worth, there was a time when the Whitneys were Number One in wealth. Payne Whitney, father of John Hay "Jock" Whitney and Mrs. Joan Whitney Payson, Eisenhower's Ambassador to Great Britain and owner of the New York Mets baseball team, respectively, in 1927 left an estate worth $239,301,017, the largest recorded in the United States up to that time.

Capital of that size does not gather dust in equities such as municipal bonds. Jock and Joan, granting their own abilities to sense the nuances of the business as well as the sports world, never lacked shrewd advisors to help move their holdings upward. A modest investment in financing the production of *Gone With the Wind* may not have been responsible for making Joan one of "The Ten Richest Women," as she is headlined in women's page features, but it was sizeable enough to make Jock hasten to get rid of his share.

"*Gone With the Wind* is the biggest money-making film of all time," observed a visitor to the Whitney office. "How is it that Mr. Whitney is divesting himself of so profitable an investment?"

"Makes his tax bracket too high," replied Sam Park, one of the financial wizards the Whitneys employ to disengage themselves from the problems of making too much money.

The Whitney scion who carved out the original duchy was William Collins Whitney. Unlike his contemporary, the lumpen "Commodore" Cornelius Vanderbilt, William Collins Whitney was an educated man of rather distinguished lineage. The original American forbear, John Whitney, arrived in the colonies in 1635 aboard the *Arabella*, which placed second to the *Mayflower* in the European immigrants' race to the colonies. Members of the Whitney family had served in the English Parliament continuously since 1313 and could claim descent from William the Conqueror; in the colonies they produced businessmen, legislators and military men. Josiah Whitney was a general in the Continental Armies; Eli Whitney (who died poor) invented the cotton gin, one of the prime factors in the industrial revolution from which the succeeding generations of Whitneys were to make their millions.

It was into this modest but comfortable middle-class world that William Collins Whitney, great-great grandson of General Josiah, was born on July 5, 1841, in Conway, Massachusetts. Young William spent his college years at Yale, complaining about its unrewarding classical curriculum and the narrowness of its academic mind, while outside the Civil War raged on.

"In religion it drove us all to the bad—but no matter about that, the instruction was bad, stupid, not stimulating to the mind. It was by bad methods and we learned nothing."

These objections, however, by no means provoked him to hasten to the battlefront to join the Union Army, in the tradition of his ancestor General Josiah Whitney, who helped win independence for the colonies. Instead he suffered through his studies and, after a year's apprenticeship in a lawyer's office, was admitted to the bar just as the Civil War hostilities ceased.

He immediately entered the practice of law in New York City, wet his feet in the municipal politics of Boss Tweed's era (of whom he was to become a bitter opponent) and, in 1869, made two moves that were to have important consequences for the fortunes of the present-day Whitneys. One was his marriage to Flora Payne, sister of Yale classmate Oliver Payne, who was to become one of the largest stockholders in Standard Oil Company and a major contributor to the oil component of the dynasty's wealth. The other involved his first big venture into the stock market, where eventually he was to make his own millions.

In a few years, during which he served brilliantly as New York City Corporation Counsel, Whitney was already beginning to play a leading role in state and national politics. It led to his appointment as Grover Cleveland's Secretary of the Navy.

It was during his tenure as a Cabinet officer that Whitney laid the foundation for the great fortune that was built up and passed on to his heirs. Except for Andrew Mellon or perhaps Albert Fall, no presidential Cabinet officer ever changed his financial status so impressively during his term of office as did William Collins Whitney.

In 1884, the year of his appointment as Navy Secretary, Whitney was elected a director of New York Cable Railway Company, one of the more than thirty independent transit companies in the city, many of them consisting entirely of horse-drawn vehicles. Soon he had the controlling interest. From this base he quickly set about to form a holding company, which was then placed into the hands of Thomas Fortune Ryan.

"If he lives long enough," observed Whitney of his associate, "Thomas Fortune Ryan will eventually have all the money in the world." A good start toward that position was made with the Whitney–Ryan holding company, for it was not long before it had absorbed nearly all of New York City's transport routes.

This was done by the technique of grossly overcapitalizing the holding company through repeated increases in watered stock, so that it was thereby able to acquire valuable subsidiary companies for relatively small sums. Whitney remained respectably at his desk in Washington while Ryan operated for him in New York. Among the more spectacular deals the two of them executed were the sale for $1,000,000 of the Broadway Railroad Company that had been purchased for $25,000, and the Lexington Avenue Line, which sold for $10,000,000, having originally cost $2,500,000.

Launching of such deals resembled the dynamics of a horserace, with competitive tycoons literally using any trick in the book to beat the opposition for the prize with the investing public, not unlike the $2-bettor, paying the bill. James R. Keene, in whose house The Jockey Club was formed in 1894, was an arch competitor of Whitney's on both Wall Street and on the race course. In the financial race to gain control of the New York transportation system he bought up opposition shares, sold short, dumped securities on the market, and drove stocks lower, trying to outmaneuver Whitney and Ryan. All to no avail, since he himself was outmaneuvered by similar tactics and wound up losing $5,000,000, while the fortunes of Whitney and Ryan continued to increase.

Investigation of the affair by the New York State Public Service Commission, reminiscent of similar inquiries by The Jockey Club of its feuding members, conveniently enough came some three years after Whitney's death and yielded nothing. The books of his holding company had been sold as junk two years previously and no evidence existed to support the claims of angry stockholders that the holding company's construction bills had run as high as $600,000 a mile.

Nevertheless, with his share of the profits William Collins Whitney went on to other adventures. Along with Thomas Fortune Ryan, Whitney somehow persuaded James B. Duke of the American Tobacco Company into taking him into his increasingly profitable industry. The same techniques of optioning the opposition, cornering the market and other operations that marked this halycon period of American entrepreneurism worked again. Whitney and Ryan, without ever having turned a spade into a tobacco field, found themselves co-directors of one of the world's largest tobacco combines.

These pursuits, in addition to ventures into utilities, banking, steamships, mining and other fields—including the almost mandatory association of any successful tycoon with the Metropolitan Opera Company—made William Collins Whitney the near prototypical industrial Renaissance man of the period. With all his money, he had no further need to vanquish the Keenes and Dukes, no desire for elective office, and no place to go. He was ready to take his competitive drives to that perennial jousting field: the race course.

In 1898, as Teddy Roosevelt was leading his charge up San Juan Hill, William Collins Whitney was channeling his competitive drives into the makings of what was to be one of the most impressive racing establishments in the world. He started out by hiring Samuel C. Hildreth, the country's foremost trainer; he retained John E. Madden, the foremost turf consultant; and he appointed his brother-in-law, Sidney Paget, who already had vast experience in the field, to manage the business for him. Horseracing, like tobacco or transit or, in fact, most other businesses, was an enterprise where impressive quantities of money enabled one to start right at the top.

The Futurity Stakes of 1900, which was run at Sheepshead Bay, New York, illustrates how man's aggressive instincts may be sublimated into the need to win a horserace. Whitney's thoroughbreds, Elkhorn and Ballyhoo Bey, were entered against three horses of his old Wall Street—now his racing—rival, James R. Keene. Although Whitney's best horse, Ballyhoo Bey, was not given much of a chance, he was determined to best Keene on the racetrack as he had done on Wall Street. He imported from England the leading jockey of the day, the cocksure American expatriate Tod Sloan. On the enemy side, Keene's riders concocted a plan to box Sloan in on the rail with the three Keene horses. But one of the Keene jockeys failed to deliver at a crucial moment and Sloan broke through. For Sloan's reward, in addition to a $5,000 advance, Whitney presented a roll of bills which he pulled out of his pants pocket. "Here," he said, "it's $9,000. I've given you everything I have in my pockets." Then, as an afterthought, he reached into his vest pocket and gave Sloan his watch. "Now you have everything I have."

In 1901, Whitney also began to race a stable in England. He made a considerable record there, winning more races than he did in his homeland. The trouble was that all his conquests were made with bought horseflesh, for he had not been in the business long enough to have bred his own three-year-olds. Indeed, he went to his greatest victory in England—the Epsom Derby—with a rented horse, Volodyovski, leased from Lady Meux. After the race, in which his hired horse had beaten a horse of the Duke of Portland, Whitney identified what must be one of the most basic motivations for becoming a horseman.

"It was fine," he said, "but they tell me that I will never know what the real feeling is until I have won a big race with a horse I bred myself."

He began buying expensive stallions, imported and domestic. He became caught up in the enchantment of breeding and bloodlines. And he developed the formidable Whitney Stud, whose victories on the turf to this day no one can definitely prove were due to its expensively bought pedigrees or to its unquestionably superior training assets . . . or to simple racing luck. Nevertheless, with no more than six years in racing, and even less as a breeder of thoroughbreds, he did not hesitate to publish a volume that espoused a breeding theory which has left its mark to this day. In its introduction he wrote:

"Count Lehndorff, in his admirable book of *Recollections*, called attention in 1883 to the desirability of breeding only from race mares [those that had gone through the strain of training and survived] . . . if one wished to minimize the elements of uncertainty and increase the chances of success."

Whitney was suggesting, whether he realized it or not, that working "mothers" make the best mothers.

CHAPTER 5

Harry P. Whitney
(1872-1930)

"Assuming," said one Sunday supplement, "it has taken you ten minutes to read [the previous page] the Whitney heirs have grown $1,666.67 richer since you first glanced at the page."

—Cleveland Amory, *Who Killed Society?*, on H. P. Whitney

THE AGE-OLD CUSTOM of primogeniture—the right of the eldest son to preferential inheritance that guides noble families in the distribution of their properties—was ignored by William Collins Whitney. Leaving an estate of $25,000,000, which included his racing stables and substantial interest in Belmont Park and Saratoga, Whitney willed one-half of his property to his *youngest* son, Harry, while the eldest, Payne, received only one-tenth. Payne had committed the sin of opposing his father's hasty remarriage following the death of his mother, Flora Payne Whitney. The alienation, which grew more intense with the passing years, persisted up to the time of his father's death. Payne was not even present at that event.

It requires no special Freudian insight to conjecture which of the two Whitney scions would continue the hobby of racing thoroughbreds that so personally identified the father. Payne limited himself, most of his life, to a rather token breeding operation—and even that under the influence of his wife—while Harry, with a princely panache, immediately took up the sword of filial loyalty. He lost no time in buying up his father's horses, either privately or in flourishes of emotional overbidding at the public action of the estate in Madison

Square Garden. It was as though it were a form of sacrilege to let the dynasty horses pass into other hands.

Harry made his home in his father's townhouse at 871 Fifth Avenue, and remained there until his death in 1930. It was not a difficult thing to do since William Collins Whitney left behind a Manhattan chateau worthy of a Bourbon duke.

Among its countless trifles it contained the largest private ballroom in the city, hung with rare Boucher tapestries and panelled with gilded oak from the chateau of Baron Phoebus d'Albert, a field marshall in the armies of Louis XIV. Cathedrals, castles and museums from all over Europe contributed their sarcophagi, marble wells, stained glass, Florentine ceilings and enough Gobelins, Tintorettos, Raphaels and Van Dycks to recreate a Renaissance palace.

Although Harry P. Whitney managed to triple the considerable fortune he inherited, he did so by shrewd investment rather than by the active direction of business as had his father. As a young man at Yale, he had come dangerously close to wandering off into the literary arts. As with all Whitneys he was on the varsity crew, but he also found time to publish poetry, serve as editor of the Yale *News* and even seriously considered entering the field of journalism. But his father expressed his displeasure at the profession and Harry Payne obediently turned his attention to more conventional business. (One generation later, however, a W. C. Whitney grandson would buy the New York *Herald Tribune*).

With one notable exception—the Hudson Bay Mining & Smelting Company, one of the world's largest copper producers, which he organized himself—Harry P. Whitney let his money do the work for him. An investment with the mining Guggenheims made him a large fortune, as it had previously done for his father. In addition, he had directorships in the banks, railroads, steamships and other companies handed down to him by William Collins Whitney.

Harry P. Whitney, rather than being a businessman who occasionally attended to his horses, was a full-time horseman (even though he listed his thoroughbred activities as a hobby) who occasionally looked to his investments. Not the least of these was the merger of the Whitney and Vanderbilt dynasties, when Harry married Gertrude

Vanderbilt, great-granddaughter of the old "Commodore," Cornelius Vanderbilt. The new Mrs. Whitney, never particularly excited about horses, left her husband to his preoccupation and indulged her taste for somewhat raffish Americana. Something of an upper-class Bohemian, she embraced such disparate primitives as Buffalo Bill Cody and the denizens of Greenwich Village with both her patronage and her own sculpture, much of which now adorns cheery nooks at the Whitney Museum.

Mr. Whitney, on the other hand, indulged himself in several patrician sports, including deep-sea yachting. Each summer he sailed the Eastern maritime coast with million-dollar masted dreadnaughts that competed with those of his in-laws for various cups that generally remained within the conglomerate cupboards.

When not occupied sailing yachts, he busied himself with popularizing polo. This was a sport in which he performed with some excellence, achieving a rating of 10-goal handicap. As captain of his American team, he vanquished the British on land by defeating them in three polo matches before he retired from the sport in 1912.

But it was in thoroughbred racing and breeding that Harry P. Whitney made his mark. His silks of Eton blue and brown cap dominated the golden era of American racing from 1915 to 1925. He led the list of winning owners for a decade and helped to greatly popularize the sport of kings, American version. In the words of Kentucky "Colonel" Matt Winn, president of Churchill Downs, "It was Harry P. Whitney, not I, who put the Kentucky Derby on the map with his filly, Regret." Colonel Winn was referring to the tremendous publicity that the Kentucky Derby received in 1915 when the male-dominated race was won for the first time by Whitney's female three-year-old, Regret.

Another horse of his own breeding, Upset, was the only horse ever to beat Man o' War. Not so pleasurable, however, was the fact that, almost as an act of retribution, Man o' War later came back at another Whitney horse, John P. Grier, and in the words of his groom "broke the heart of Grier at the eighth pole."

Even as Man o' War will be remembered long after the name of the man who happened to buy him as a yearling, the name of another horse that Harry P. Whitney owned will likely be remembered long after his owner. The name was Equipoise; the horse's dam never won a stakes race and yet (contrary to William Collins Whitney's breeding theory of successful race mares producing great racehorses) gave birth to one of the greatest runners of all time. So great was Equipoise's courage that, after stumbling in the mud and losing twenty lengths at the start of the Pimlico Futurity, he came on to overtake two of the speediest horses of the day, Mate and Twenty Grand, and win by a comfortable margin.

And so it was with Harry P. Whitney, who, through his thoroughbreds, dominated the golden age of racing until the Great Depression of 1930. Then, with sure timing, he quietly and comfortably disappeared from the scene. Still, during the Depression there was only one brief period when his horses were not on display. That was the year when his brother-in-law, the first Alfred G. Vanderbilt, went down on the *Lusitania.* Chivalry called for flags at half-mast in memory of a downed rival.

CHAPTER 6

The Payne Whitneys

Helen Hay Whitney (1876-1944) Payne Whitney (1875-1927)

Quod habeo desidero. ("*I like what I got.*")
—Family motto of Mrs. Payne Whitney

PAYNE WHITNEY might have been left relatively out in the cold with respect to his father's fortune, a large portion of which came from American Tobacco Company investments, but the deficit was more than made up by his mother's brother, Oliver Payne, one of the founders of Standard Oil Company. Payne Whitney is probably the only man in the world who made nearly $50,000,000 by virtue of having been *dis*inherited by his father. It was chiefly because Payne Whitney had opposed his father's remarriage that Uncle Oliver Payne bequeathed that vast fortune to him.

Payne Whitney may not have followed in his father's footsteps as far as horseracing was concerned, but he was certainly his father's son in financial affairs. By shrewd investment, he managed to increase his fortune by some $125,000,000; a rather staggering sum considering the value of a dollar forty-five years ago. In 1924 he paid an income tax of $1,041,951, an amount surpassed only by John D. Rockefeller, Jr., and Henry Ford. This quite possibly made the Whitney family one of the three or four wealthiest families in the country.

Payne Whitney lived on a 500-acre estate on Long Island, known as Greentree, and indulged his taste for the physical by creating a private sports complex in which an Olympiad might comfortably have been staged. At one time or another his back yard contained a polo field, a baseball diamond, indoor and outdoor swimming pools, squash courts, court tennis and ordinary tennis courts complete with sufficient Turkish baths to steam out an entire Roman legion. And in the event any of his guests might have come unprepared, there was a field house equipped with every type of sports clothes, in every size: Peele boots and spurs, Wetzel breeches, Norfolk jackets, white flannels, shirts, lounging robes, beach pajamas, swim trunks, fresh linen and dinner clothes, plus a lavish assortment of cosmetics.

As though such a wealth of matériel were not enough, Payne Whitney was also fortunate in his choice of a mate to share it with. Helen Hay, whom he met through a roommate at Yale, had enough connections to have a U.S. president and his entire Cabinet as guests at her wedding. Her father, John Hay, had been McKinley's Secretary of State and was, at the time of her wedding to Payne, also doing the same job for Teddy Roosevelt. In addition, on her bridegroom's side, his father had been Secretary of Navy for President Cleveland. As a promising poet, she enjoyed friendships with luminaries such as Rudyard Kipling, who occasionally composed poems to be hung on the walls of her house.

Despite her certified social background, Helen Hay Whitney was more interested in the society of horses than that of men. Her husband, at least at the start of their marriage, did not quite share this interest, still smarting with feeling against his father, although he eventually subscribed to The Jockey Club membership. But Mrs. Payne Whitney was smitten by the thoroughbred from the start. At first her interest was centered on steeplechasing, that equine competition that is more closely allied to the hunt than flat-course racing. Besides, racing (that is, betting on racing) in New York State in 1911 to 1913, the time that Mrs. Payne Whitney became seriously interested in it, was prohibited by statute under the so-called Charles Evans Hughes law, a sort of law-and-order reaction to previous racing excesses. So, along with the rest of the New York racing set, Mrs. Whitney had to go slow for a while. Many, however, went underground for the duration. At Piping Rock on Long Island it was something like an elegant page out of bootlegging operations a couple of decades later. Instead of speakeasies there were illegal bookies, instead of rum-runners there were clandestine horse-runners, instead of gaudy stick pins there were fashionable shooting sticks.

After repeal of the Hughes law, Mrs. Payne Whitney went on to create or, more precisely, to sponsor the creating of a racing stable named Greentree, which was to become one of the most important in the racing world.

Red Bank, New Jersey, at the time a favored enclave, was designated the home of Greentree; an advisory council of crack turfmen was appointed under the direction of the turf's Cardinal Richelieu, Major Louie Beard—with the result that Mrs. Whitney was soon crowned "Queen of the American Turf."

Red Bank became inadequate as the court of so expanding a monarchy just as Kentucky was emerging as the fashionable place for thoroughbred breeding. In 1927, the Queen of the American Turf established her own Versailles on five hundred acres of prime Kentucky bluegrass (coincidentally, not far from a Kentucky town also named Versailles). The Whitneys would assemble each summer solstice amid the regal splendor of Derby Week at nearby Louisville to name its new yearlings, such as the legendary Twenty Grand, and to visit with his equally legendary sire, St. German's, who had been imported from England to serve the resident mares.

Payne Whitney played a kind of prince consort role to his wife when it came to actually racing the thoroughbred. He indulged himself mainly in the area of pedigree and breeding. The birth of Twenty Grand from a mating of imported St. German's with one of Greentree's homebred mares was realized only after Payne's death in 1929. It was enough of an achievement in the horsey world to have warranted the lowering of the flags of Churchill Downs and Belmont Park to half-mast on his demise.

Besides leaving behind the magnificent Twenty Grand, Payne Whitney made other notable bequests. His personal fortune found its way into the Payne Whitney Psychiatric Clinic of New York Hospital, a colossal medical center which the Whitneys financed practically to the point of ownership and of which Payne's son, John Hay, became a director at the mature age of eighteen. And, as if to balance the Payne Whitney charities between the mental and the physical, the Whitney family underwrote the Payne Whitney Gymnasium at Yale, one of the most well-appointed drill fields in the academic world.

Mrs. Payne Whitney died in 1944. She had, in the course of her thirty-four-year reign as Queen of the Turf, won one Kentucky Derby, and one Belmont Stake in addition to other stake races.

Helen Hay Whitney was the compleat sportswoman. Her favorite dogs were buried in a special canine cemetery on the Whitney grounds, her favorite horses were entombed, embalmed, and emblazoned. And one of her last requests was a petition (usually treated as a decree) to William Woodward, Jockey Club chairman, that her favorite jockey, Eddie Arcaro, be reinstated from suspension. She died in New York Hospital, which the family had financed almost singlehandedly.

CHAPTER 7

John Hay "Jock" Whitney (1904-)

I don't think that my sister would mind my boasting that my Herald-Tribune, *as of the moment, must be considered several lengths ahead of her Mets.*

—John Hay Whitney, in a speech at the Thoroughbred Club, 1963

TWENTY GRAND, one of the outstanding thoroughbreds of his time, was a horse of heroic bloodlines. Out of a Whitney mare by St. German's, an English stallion which Payne Whitney had imported after much study, Twenty Grand was the pride of the entire Whitney family.

"The most magnificent thoroughbred I had ever seen," said Mr. Whitney's son, John Hay, in a *Blood-Horse* article of April 26, 1969. "It was very gratifying to all of us when, after breaking the track record in the Kentucky Derby, he went on to win us our first Belmont. Because, you see, it was the vindication of my father's breeding theories. But," he added sadly, "little did we know at the time what was in store for him at stud."

John Hay Whitney was referring to the fact that Twenty Grand was to prove sterile despite the costly efforts of fertility experts imported from the four corners of the globe. Moreover, although Payne Whitney's breeding theories may have seemed to his son to have been vindicated, they did not appear to hold much weight for his brother. Harry P. Whitney simply would not accept St. German's when Payne willed the stallion to him, sire of a Belmont winner or no. And it must have been an irony for John Hay Whitney, who was himself an outstanding athlete—Groton heavyweight boxing champion, Yale varsity oar, gentleman jockey, 6-goal poloist—but in two marriages a childless man.

How much a part this childlessness played in his determination to win at everything he undertook is up to question, but it by no means afflicted him with that self-doubt and unease sometimes seen in individuals with exalted position but less exalted family background.

Indeed the difference between an eager-beaver, what-makes-Johnny-run scion of a nouveau riche and one coming from the secure old horsey set might well be illustrated by how they sometimes react to the informal use of their name. John Hay Whitney, for instance, has been addressed as "Jock" by people in every walk of life with no apparent effort on his part to discourage it. John Fitzgerald Kennedy, on the other hand, despite the fact that he made it to the Presidency (a job, incidentally that most of his social class would not even bother with) always preferred not to be called "Jack," even though his wife, well-born as she is, smilingly responds to the name "Jackie."

"Your President's reaction seems rather an odd one," remarked Lord Birchett, chairman of the English-speaking Union at Ambassador Jock Whitney's farewell dinner, "particularly since his father, your predecessor here, had no such reaction to being called Joe. At any rate, the name Jock has certainly always been good enough for us."

Doubtless a boost to Jock's self-confidence, in the social area at least, was the fact that Whitney's grandfather not only had held the most prestigious post in the American diplomatic service—Ambassador to the Court of St. James—but also had been a Secretary of State. Indeed, Jock Whitney holds a pedigree unlikely to be matched (unless one considers the potential offspring of David and Julie Eisenhower, who will be able to boast Presidential ancestors on both sides): both Whitney grandfathers were top Cabinet members; William Collins Whitney for Cleveland and John Hay for McKinley and Roosevelt.

As a child, being heir to the largest private fortune in the United States, he was already on the front pages, pictured in the little white gloves and straw hat that were *de rigueur* for public appearances. The Sunday supplements reported his every move all through his growth from a lisping, stuttering, nearsighted twelve-year-old at Groton to a two-hundred-pound, six-foot-one, eighteen-year-old with specially designed contact lenses astride a polo pony. Today, at sixty-eight, the stuttering has long since disappeared, the polo ponies been put away, and Jock Whitney, dressed with expensive tailoring that often piles up on him, can look back on one of the most protean lives that social position and money can make possible.

Like many of the scions of wealthy families, young Whitney started his professional life the "hard" way, getting his hands calloused in the mines of Wall Street. When he was twenty-five, he went to work as a $15-a-week buzzer boy in the investment firm of Lee Higginson & Co., one of whose partners had stroked on his father's Yale crew. In less than a year he was in the peculiar position of running errands for men with whom he would soon be directing the affairs of an industrial giant. Lee Higginson had been waging a proxy fight for control of Freeport Sulphur Co., and the messenger boy obligingly offered $500,000 to help out. (The stock has since risen in value many times over, Jock has been board chairman for years, and his former boss now works at J. H. Whitney & Co.)

During the time Whitney was running errands on Wall Street, "sweating for his supper, eating hot dogs and coffee for lunch," according to editorialists of the day, he was also running racehorses. At twenty-two, on his birthday, Payne Whitney made his son a gift of two thoroughbred yearlings (Jock's first horse had actually been the polo pony Plumita, acquired at age seventeen). A year later, on his father's death, Jock set up his own racing stable, Llangollen. In a home so dedicated to horses, his mother being the "First Lady of the American Turf," it is not surprising that Jock would share the enthusiasm. In 1929 the messenger-boy-turned-corporate-director decided to take up racing seriously from the 500-acre estate in Manhasset.

A young man who can dip into his pocket for $500,000 proxy money has no serious problem in taking up most any calling. He simply commissions an emissary, like those who collect art or companies, to undertake the mission. Jock Whitney, at twenty-five, commissioned Jack Anthony, a famous British trainer and winner of three Grand Nationals (a relatively obscure horse race that Elizabeth Taylor popularized in the film *National Velvet*) to develop a stable of steeplechasers. On his own first try at the Grand National, using a bought horse, Easter Hero, Whitney got an unlucky second. His horse, after leading a field of sixty-six, twisted a shoe and limped in behind the winner. The next year, Easter Hero went home lame just before the race and Whitney got a third with a second stringer, Sir Lindsay. In 1931 a cousin, Dorothy Paget, nosed out Whitney's Thurmond II with her Golden Miller. To this day, Jock Whitney, like a man determined to master Mt. Everest, has been trying to win the race that Elizabeth Taylor made famous. Asked jestingly, "How're things at Gloccamora?", at Belmont Park after one of his numerous trips to England for the Grand National, the former $15-a-week buzzer boy, now owner of a reported half-billion dollars, shook his head sadly and said, "Just can't seem to break my luck."

Jock Whitney had no such complaints with his other endeavors. During the 1930s, when most people were in the throes of the Great Depression, Whitney was hitting the jackpot as America's number one "angel." Absorbing a loss or two such as the $100,000 he put up for a Broadway musical by his friend Peter Arno, the cartoonist, almost everything else he touched turned to considerable gold. *Life with Father*, one of the more than thirty theatrical productions he financed, made so much money with its movie rights and other subsidiary revenues that, after years of profit-taking, he eventually turned the profits over to one of the family foundations.

Like most people, Whitney has the normal desire to make money. But on the whole, the profit motive appears secondary, particularly if it gets in the way of enjoyment.

"Jock would rather earn a few thousand in some lousy play than a million in stocks and bonds," said one of his associates.

Apparently the fever for having fun seized the entire family after the financial reports were in on some of Jock's theatrical ventures. His sister Joan and his cousin "Sonny," together with some friendly Lehman brothers, and David O. Selznick, a top Hollywood producer, formed a company that turned out the most profitable motion picture of all time. *Gone With the Wind*, over a third of a century later, long after Clark Gable and Vivien Leigh have departed, is still making a profit. But not for Jock Whitney. When more stringent income tax laws were passed and put into effect, Whitney decided that movies were no longer fun. He had his people work out a capital gains deal for future profits with Selznick and turned for his pleasure to other less tax-oppressed games.

Not that he abandoned films altogether. Whitney was indeed a true film buff, and the habit of using the public treasury as a kind of tithe-paying vehicle for sport died hard. A documentary movie called *Greentree Thoroughbred*, depicting the story of Whitney's (and his sister's) racing and breeding operations, was commissioned by Whitney in 1950. It became choice personal publicity, winning film prizes and being recommended for use in schools by *Scholastic Teacher Magazine*. Even though the budget for the film was minuscule compared to that of *Gone With the Wind*, its cost was charged not to the Whitney private purse but to Greentree Stud, Inc., where it could be written off as a business expense.

America's number one angel also functioned as one of America's most lordly hosts during this decade of the Depression. At the country seat in Manhasset over which his mother presided but where Jock had functioned as head of the clan since his father's death in 1927, a steady stream of distinguished guests were treated with a grandeur appropriate to visiting heads of state. A full-sized polo field was cut out of the side of a hill to provide entertainment and servants in full livery provided cooling drinks in silver tankards; there were handymen, gardeners and grooms to cheer the master's team. There were game rooms, billiard rooms, movie rooms, gymnasium rooms, wine rooms—each one enhanced by the world's largest private collection of Impressionist and Post-Impressionist art—which provided divertissements in a house the size of the Louvre.

From this, which was one of at least a half-dozen similarly appointed establishments throughout the United States and England, Jock and his guests ventured forth to the Piedmont Hunt, the Belmont Stakes, and to the grouse shoots at Balmoral. There were some twenty-eight cars of every design, including four Rolls Royces.

On the polo field Whitney was an average performer with a 6-goal handicap. Captain of his own team, a group that boasted such outstanding poloists as Tommy Hitchcock, Pete Bostwick and Gerald Balding, Whitney was nevertheless always assigned to the defensive back position, which he disliked. It called for a passive role that did not sit well with his own strong aggressive drive and pervasive need to win. Unfortunately, he was nearsighted and, though one reasonably suspects he picked up the tab for the team, the back position was where his peers decided he should be. One day the back position became too much for him to tolerate. He galloped away from his goal and into the action, scoring seven goals while Tommy Hitchcock, who was one of the two or three greatest poloists in the world, made only six.

"I guess I out-goaled Tommy because I was mounted on a superior pony," apologized Whitney, apparently unaware of his own fierce competitive drive.

Whitney had also tested his spurs on the racetrack in the role of a gentleman jockey in a steeplechase race in England. The experience was so depressing that it not only was his maiden effort as a rider but his swansong as well. During the course of the race he led his horse, a rather capable performer with a good record, up to a fence to take the jump. But with Whitney in the saddle for the first time the horse, instead of going over the fence, went through it. It was a case of the nearsighted leading the blind, for later investigation revealed that the horse had gone blind just before the race. Jock Whitney promptly retired as a gentleman jockey.

During this period Jock Whitney also became involved in what many considered America's preeminent social event up to that time. As a young blade-about-town, he had sent trays of Cartier jewelry to Tallulah Bankhead's apartment, just as they did in the movies, with the invitation to "select what you like;" he had escorted dozens of beautiful, talented, rich and desirable young women to the very best places. But when it came to marriage he selected what *he* liked.

Mary Elizabeth Altemus, of Philadelphia Mainline society, was perhaps the most expert horsewoman of her day. She was also one of the most beautiful of women, on or off a horse, and a lady of antic (some might say raunchy) and often irrepressible spirits. For those who believe there's something in a name, even close similarities in the sound and morphology of a name, note the closeness of Altemus and Artemis, the Greek goddess of the hunt. Indeed, Cleveland Amory in his *Who Killed Society?*, in an interesting (perhaps intentional?) typographical error, refers to Liz Altemus as Liz Artemus, which isn't quite the right spelling for the goddess but at least is pronounced like her name.

The wedding took place in the fall of 1930 at the peak of the Depression, to the delight of Sunday supplements throughout the world. The following from New York's *Daily News* is typical:

John Hay "Jock" Whitney

MILLION $$, WHITNEY'$ GIFT TO HI$ LI$

Falls-of-the-Schuylkill, Pa., Sept. 25—Shortly after John Hay (Jock) Whitney was married in splendor today to Mary Elizabeth Altemus, he reached into the pocket of his immaculate cutaway and presented the new Mrs. Whitney with a check for $1,000,000.

The bride of Manhattan's richest bachelor and sportsman can spend it for anything her fancy dictates.

A demonstration such as an American community ordinarily reserves for its channel swimmers and trans-Atlantic fliers greeted the bride this afternoon when she arrived at the Church of St. James the Less for the marriage.

Ten thousand inhabitants of this suburban village gathered and overran the ancient churchyard burial ground for a glimpse of the hometown girl who was about to wed the heir to a $200,000,000 fortune. . . .

Not since the marriage of Estelle Manville to Count Folke Bernadotte, nephew of the king of Sweden, in Pleasantville, N.Y., two years ago has there been anything comparable to today's public outpouring of curious bystanders at a private social event.

The ceremony was performed by the Rev. Endicott Peabody of Groton, Mass., where Jock attended prep school. The Rev. Dr. Charles Jarvis Harriman, rector of the church, assisted Dr. Peabody.

Jock allowed himself one small gesture of vanity on his wedding day. The Whitney heir is never seen without glasses. Even on the polo field he wears spectacles of non-shatterable glass. But yesterday he discarded specs long enough to take his vows at the altar.

Except for the $225,000 diamond necklace gift of Jock's mother, Liz's costume might have been that of any society bride, so closely did it conform to the snowy simplicity tradition has declared fitting.

Chiffon Over Metal: Her tall, slender figure was sheathed in metal cloth over which white chiffon was draped in Grecian style with a long train. Her veil was of white tulle, held by a spray of orange blossoms and the bridal bouquet was of orange blossoms. Her only jewelry was her square-cut diamond engagement ring and her fabulous necklace.

The little church was filled with old-fashioned white jasmins and lilies against a background of fern, and all the bride's attendants were in white.

Mrs. Robert S. McKim of New York, matron of honor, wore a

white velvet frock, trimmed with deep circular ruffles forming a cape on the shoulders. Her white velvet hat had an off-the-face brim, and she carried a bouquet of lilies.

The bridesmaids fluttered down the aisle in white chiffon gowns made in the Empire style with long skirts and high waistlines, coquettish low square necklines and long, pointed sleeves embroidered with rhinestones and pearls.

Adele Astaire, musical comedy star, managed to walk down the bridal trail sedately enough and her bridesmaid partner was Lisa Norris, Liz's cousin. Mrs. L. Wister Randolph, another cousin; Loulie Thomson, Mrs. Henry W. Sage, Jr., Mrs. Charles S. Payson, Jock's sister; Mrs. Richard Meyers and Mrs. Persifor Frazer 3d filled out the coterie of bridesmaids.

Robert Benchley, the humorist, wearing a very pleasant smile, served Jock as best man. Ushers were Adele's brother Fred, Tommy Hitchcock, Jr., Charles Shipman Payson, Richard S. Scott, J. Wendell Smith, Donald Ogden Stewart, another famous humorist; Gardner D. Stout, W. Stuart Symington, James J. Wadsworth and Cornelius Vanderbilt Whitney.

The couple are to honeymoon at Jock's Virginia estate, that boasts the oldest and finest mansion in Fauquier county in the Blue Ridge range, a swimming pool, polo fields, modern stables and a private airplane landing field. Later they will divide their time between a Manhattan apartment at 972 5th Avenue, and the Whitney estate at Manhasset, L.I. August, of course, will be spent on the Whitney estate at Saratoga.

Both Jock and his bride have distinguished themselves in the world of sport. With his mother, Jock has raced the Greentree stable since the death of his father in 1927. Jock plays an excellent game of polo and has one of the finest strings of ponies in the country.

His bride is one of the best known sportswomen in the east and has won countless trophies in the horse show ring here and abroad. Mary Elizabeth made her debut here in 1923 and has been identified with New York society as much as with that of Philadelphia.

Shortly after 8 P.M., a New York contingent of the wedding party was deposited in a twenty passenger airplane of the Curtiss-Wright flying service and flew safely to Curtiss airport, L. I., where their motors waited to take them home.

Jock and Liz, however, boarded a special train over the Pennsylvania railroad, consisting of one Pullman, the Adios, and a baggage car, and headed for Washington, D.C. Only a maid and a butler accompanied them.

They will honeymoon on his new estate at Upperville, Va., a

> magnificent country place where they will make their home for the greater part of the year.

This was not the golden age of America's princely racing families. That period, spanning the epoch of Man o' War and Exterminator, of Harry P. Whitney and August Belmont, had come a decade or so earlier. Now haggard men were roaming the streets vainly looking for work, breadlines were the staple of every American city, and Douglas MacArthur, on horseback, was firing on veterans who were demanding their war bonus. Nevertheless, John Hay Whitney and his bride ranged the far corners of the thoroughbred world, from Tattersall's in London to Fasig-Tipton in Saratoga, prospecting the bloodstock sales. They soon acquired the largest string of racehorses in the country. And, understandably, considering the personalities, the horses raced in Liz's name. Being a woman of strong will, Liz was also able to put on a first-class show wielding a talented mallet on a women's polo team.

At Llangollen, near Upperville, Virginia, heart of the Old South's fox hunt country, among the neat, white-pillared antebellum mansions, the couple presided over a 2,000-acre enclave. In 1931 they laid out a private steeplechase course modelled after Aintree's Grand National (a running of which Jock was never to win) and played host to 20,000 people to watch the first running of the Llangollen Cup. It was a three-mile chase over brush with $5,000 added, the richest prize ever offered at a private meeting. The uninhibited hostess of these spectacular meets would transport herself about in her specially designed coach of fuchsia and purple (dressed in slacks of the same colors to suggest her racing silks), flailing at her tandem of four pure-white mules. On the occasion of the first running of the Llangollen Cup, according to the *Loudoun-Fauquier Magazine*, the Lady of Llangollen "made a dashing entry, driving a high-wheeled jaunty cart with General Billy Mitchell on horseback acting as a sort of outrider."

Life at Llangollen continued in a way that was the very model of the carefree, the relaxed and the uninhibited. If guests could avoid the dogs that Mrs. Whitney permitted to wander unrestrained through dining room, living room, and even bedroom, then all they had to do to get to the ballroom, which generally displayed more notables than a state banquet, was to step around the occasional pig or goat that lingered in the doorway, or duck the inebriate pet bear that decided to come in and join the fun. Liz Whitney, in fact, so loved animals that she once preserved a dead pet in her frigidaire for weeks before she could be induced to part with it.

Before long the conservative Jock Whitney had apparently had enough of the theatrics of his real-life Scarlett O'Hara, opting at least temporarily for her fictitious celluloid counterpart. The excitements of shepherding the production of *Gone With the Wind* and other movies in his Hollywood portfolio were perhaps no match for the bright lights generated by a turned-on Liz Whitney, but nonetheless Jock Whitney decided to separate himself from his tempestuous real-life Liz. The cost: $3,000,000 in cash and the deed to those Hanging Gardens of the Babylon of Virginia known as Llangollen.

World War II had broken out, and in 1940 Jock decided to add the military arts to his repertory of skills. He went up to Plattsburgh, New York, for army training and from there became in 1943 a public relations officer for the 8th Air Force in London.

Following a year's tour in England, he moved up to Colonel on the staff. One afternoon in the fall of 1944, while howitzers were thundering in the fields of southern France, a somber voice disturbed the quiet of an afternoon at Belmont Park in New York.

"Ladies and gentlemen, your attention please," announced Belmont's race caller. "Mr. John Hay Whitney, a member of The Jockey Club, has fallen into enemy hands. I repeat, ladies and gentlemen, Colonel John Hay Whitney, owner of Greentree Stud, has been taken prisoner by the German army in France."

The story behind the announcement was that Whitney and two OSS men had wandered behind German lines while inspecting a forward operation of Allied troops in France. The three were taken prisoner and, together with some forty other captives, locked in a box car and shipped to the east. One of the prisoners succeeded in picking the lock on the door, and a number of them, including Whitney, leaped out. They broke up into small groups and Whitney, together with two comrades, hid in the woods until they were rescued by a band of French guerrillas.

About his experience as a prisoner of war, Whitney is reported to have said, "German interrogators would ask me why we were fighting. I'd reply, 'For freedom,' and the Germans would say, 'Oh, you know perfectly well you don't have any more of it than we have.' And then these American kids would corroborate the Germans. I never heard one of our soldiers say he was fighting because of anything Hitler had done or for any moral reason."

As a result Whitney decided there was "a fundamental block in our educational system," and he decided to do something about it.

"Doing something about it" manifested itself in the John Hay Whitney Foundation, with a capital of $10,000,000 to help handicapped minorities acquire educational opportunities otherwise unavailable to them. The Foundation has also been made beneficiary of the $10,000,000 capital of J. H. Whitney & Co., Jock's risk-venture investment firm that backs "handicapped" new businesses and which, despite the risks, has done well enough to make millionaires of its partners. This, together with the fact that Whitney, to express his antipathy toward racial discrimination, has insisted that J. S. Whitney & Co. hire, for example, black office employees as well as white, has placed the firm in the forefront of those businesses that can label their mail with the slogan, "*We Are an Equal Opportunity Employer.*"

In the long history of Greentree Stable, however, including the period since Jock Whitney and his sister took it over from their mother in 1944, neither the tax-deductible "business" incorporated as the Stud nor the tax-free Foundation has managed to endow an American black with the opportunity of becoming a jockey in the Whitney thoroughbred operations. Black grooms, stall-muckers, exercise boys—but no blacks wearing Greentree colors in races. This is, of course, true not only of Greentree Stable. It is endemic to the Establishment in control of the sport. Many reasons are offered by apologists for this situation, notably in the case of jockeys, including an astonishing one that the Negro slave was so well-fed during bondage—because his master had a stake in keeping him strong and healthy—that he outgrew his white contemporaries and now is too large to be a jockey. This argument fails to dispose of the fact that, with very few exceptions, one cannot find a black *trainer* around the tracks even in the supposedly progressive New York area.

It cannot be said that Jock Whitney is a rigid conservative or traditionalist. He has often done things that have caused raised eyebrows in old guard circles.

His second marriage, for instance. After he had divorced Liz, he did an about-face in the matter of the selection of his new partner. The apparent antithesis of the tempestuous Mary Elizabeth Altemus, Betsey Cushing was a quiet, elegant lady, one of three sisters who cornered the marriage market in billionaires; one marrying Vincent Astor, a second William Paley, and the third Jock Whitney. Betsey Cushing had previously been married to James Roosevelt, which made no difference to the traditionally Republican Whitney, who also immediately adopted the two Roosevelt daughters she brought to him. Betsey Cushing was not particularly enthusiastic about racehorses, and had a rather liberal outlook on numerous social issues.

There was, for example, the matter of the Social Register. In 1945, after his marriage to Betsey Cushing, a rather quiet affair when compared to the wedding with Liz, Whitney decided to scratch himself from the Social Register. This was rather an unprecedented step: one might be struck from the roles, but one never resigned from the Social Register.

"Some people would consider our action snobbism in reverse," stated Whitney. "The truth was that Betsey and I and the kids felt that the Social Register was a travesty on democracy and anti-the-American-stream. It is absurd to think that a compilation of names and addresses can dictate who is and who is not socially acceptable."

To what extent Betsey influenced her husband in shifting to the Democratic ticket in 1964 is uncertain, but the fact is that Jock Whitney personally and through his New York *Herald Tribune* actively supported Lyndon Johnson in the presidential contest with Barry Goldwater.

Something else happened that seemed incredible at the time: the marriage of Whitney's adopted daughter, Sara Delano Roosevelt, on the Lower East Side of New York. Sara was an independent-minded Roosevelt, but nevertheless, while the world looked on at what might well have seemed the happy ending to an old-fashioned soap opera, Jock Whitney, tall, aristocratic and Episcopalian, gave his heiress daughter away to Anthony di Buonaventura, son of an immigrant Italian who owned a three-chair barber shop on East 17th Street. The spectacle managed to co-opt the complete front page of the New

York *Daily News* with a banner headline: EAST SIDE YELLS AS SARA WEDS. Inside, a centerfold pictured thousands of local citizens leaning out of tenement windows and pressing against police barriers while a Deputy Chief Inspector and a platoon of policemen threw a protective cordon around the arriving relatives of the bride, including the three Cushing sisters, Mrs. Vincent Astor, Mrs. William Paley and Mrs. Jock Whitney. This socially impressive entourage was not able to gain the bride admittance into the Church of Saint Mary, Helper of Christians. The Reverend Anthony Bregolato was compelled by a tradition greater than himself, and he quietly married the non-Catholic Sara Delano Roosevelt on the *far* side of the communion rail. A few years later, the second Roosevelt daughter, Kate, married the son of a Jewish immigrant, William Haddad, a crusading reporter from the *New York Post.* Whitney democracy? Roosevelt independence? Perhaps a combination of both.

In 1956 John Hay Whitney was appointed by President Eisenhower as Ambassador to Great Britain. Until that time he had been actively involved in government only in areas having to do with his sports, his hobbies or philanthropic interests, such as the New York State Racing Commission, and Federal committees concerned with the promotional use of film to promulgate the economic concepts of big business enterprise. Running for elective political office was a rarity among the set, although Sonny Whitney, a cousin, and Stuart Symington, the husband of a cousin, and Averill Harriman, the second husband of a cousin's first wife, had all run for political office. But that did not seem Jock's style. Indeed, he was reported not to have been especially keen on the idea of his ambassadorial post. "It would be looked upon as another case of rewarding a big party contributor with a juicy diplomatic post," he said. He had, of course, been just such a contributor, in addition to having been chairman of the New York United Republican Finance Committee, which raised large sums for Eisenhower.

This post was also to provide a valuable exemption from a 1954 New York State law that prohibited politicians from racing horses in the state. Three Republican party officials had their stables' licenses placed in doubt—Jockey Club member John Hay Whitney, who had been chairman of the United Republican Finance Committee, Mrs. Ogden Phipps, wife of the then Jockey Club vice-chairman and long a member of the same finance committee, and Frederic H. Bontecue, chairman of the Dutchess County Republican Committee. Ashley T. Cole, chairman of the New York Racing Commission, who had previously ruled for The Jockey Club against Jule Fink, now held that although the law barred from racing such individuals as chairmen of political party committees, it did not do so for chairman of political party *finance* committees, or, for that matter, any member of the finance committee. Mr. Bontecue resigned in protest against the law; Mr. Whitney and Mrs. Phipps got their licenses and continued racing.

Jock Whitney, in any case, was eminently qualified to represent America at the Court of St. James. He had the money that such an assignment requires. He already had enough of his own private housing so as not to create a native housing crisis on arriving with his personal staff. He was also able to bring with him a private art collection large enough to make Sir John Rothenstein of the Tate Gallery comment: "beyond comparison . . . the most splendid collection of Impressionist and Post-Impressionist painting in private hands in Great Britain." And there were his horses, although there was still no luck with the English Grand National. Today, the $15-a-week buzzer boy who started with $40 million is still trying to win the English Grand National.

"Why," asked Whitney in an address delivered at a New York *Herald Tribune* Forum and reprinted by *The Readers' Digest* of May 1952, "is there such a widespread disposition to view with shame and doubt an economic system that has brought so many benefits to all of us?" He was referring to the two American soldiers with whom he was taken prisoner and their image of a capitalist as any icy-eyed individual who wears a silk hat to bed. The only thing wrong with that attitude, he said, "is that it bears no slightest resemblance to the true image of modern capitalism. Social responsibility is a 'must' for every American corporation in its relations both with its employees and with the public. And we have not confined these material gains to our own shores but have shared them with all free peoples of the earth on a basis which assures them the same freedom to build a prosperous society."

These words were spoken only ten years before a U.S. Senate subcommittee indicated that it might call on John Hay Whitney to testify as to what part, if any, he played in negotiating a $248 million "windfall" contract with the U.S. Government. Freeport Sulphur, the little company that Whitney had picked up as a buzzer boy, and of which he was then chairman of the board, had a contract to provide raw nickel from the very government for which he was ambassador. A Government Accounting Office report stated that the contract favored the company and that documents were missing from its files. However, the nickel was to be extracted from the mines by Freeport's subsidiary in Cuba, and Fidel Castro put a permanent lien on the material gains to which Whitney referred. As a result the contract, though still in force, was never implemented; Whitney's cousin-in-law, Senator Stuart Symington, the committee chairman, indicated that if it was found he had participated he would be called. Whitney never testified.

Thus, except for his paternal grandfather, William Collins Whitney, who died before an investigation of his transit manipulations could be undertaken and who, John Hay Whitney would more than likely agree, almost fitted the image of the "icy-eyed capitalist who wears a silk hat to bed," there never has been a touch of scandal in the family from which he is descended. For the most part, the family has strictly adhered to the motto of its ancestor John Hay: *Quod Habeo Desidero* ("I Desire What I Have"), which his daughter, Helen Hay Whitney impishly translated as: "I Like What I Got."

CHAPTER 8

Cornelius Vanderbilt "Sonny" Whitney (1899-)

The horse . . . has been respected throughout the ages and by all races as an animal of great courage and stamina.

—Cornelius V. Whitney, to the *Morning Telegraph*

I retired from racing because I had little time for sport . . . besides, at that time, my stable had had a couple of bad seasons and had just about hit bottom.

—Cornelius V. Whitney, in an interview with *Sports Illustrated*

Cornelius Vanderbilt Whitney, who at the age of seventy-three is still called "Sonny," is a man in perpetual nervous motion. Appropriately enough, he descends on both sides from men who handed down a family fortune based on things in motion: "Commodore" Cornelius Vanderbilt with his New York Central Railroad and William Collins Whitney with his New York transit systems.

Since he is uniquely the scion of not one but *two* of the oldest and most prestigious American dynasties, perhaps Whitney's high tension derives from an especially potent mix of blue blood—something equivalent to a draft of vintage champagne topped off with a rare brandy. On the physical side, he seems to favor the long, lean Vanderbilt conformation, with an elegant frame that moves gracefully about like one of his thoroughbreds, whereas his cousins Jock and Joan, for all their aristocratic Whitney bloodlines, are put together on the order of one of Greentree Stable's sturdier workhorses.

Psychologically, Sonny Whitney's family identification is perhaps more blurred. "My father wanted me to be a great athlete," he has said, "and my mother a concert pianist. I never became either a great athlete or a concert pianist, although I think that, in a way, I have satisfied both of their desires."

Whitney was referring to carrying on his Vanderbilt mother's artistic devotions with his seat on the board of the Metropolitan Opera and the various Whitney museums, East and West; and to continuing his Whitney father's traditions (as had Harry P. his own father's) as a Yale oarsman, poloist, foxhunter and racehorse owner. And he seems to have been faithful to this balance of Vanderbilt and Whitney *personae* even in his four marriages. In the first two, Sonny took Marie Norton and Gwladys Hopkins, Eastern society ladies of the horsey set that his father could easily bless; with the second two, Eleanor Searle and Mary Lou Hanford, middle-class Midwestern "artistes," who, though they were not born to the saddle, could at least sing a song or read a line in a manner that might have pleased his mother.

The problem of the Vanderbilt–Whitney nexus did not, however, always lend itself to so neat a solution. Sonny, even more than Cousin Jock, was an exception to the practice of staying out of the active direction of business. He also sought elective political office. This intense drive to make good on his own, which has kept him in whirling motion all his life, may or may not derive from the fact that he was never close to his father, but he did try to win an election to Congress right in the heart of the horsey enclave of Long Island, home base of both his parents' families.

Nineteen thirty-two was the peak of the Depression and working-class Americans had a less than worshipful approach to the more fortunate. Cornelius Vanderbilt Whitney sensed that a thirty-three-year-old millionaire-playboy called Sonny might draw jeers from those members of the unemployed, and the combination of Vanderbilt *and* Whitney might even precipitate violence. During the campaign he dropped both Vanderbilt and "Sonny" and became plain old Cornelius Whitney—a name with a hint of the Yankee industrial revolutionist who invented the cotton gin and who died as poor as the constituents he would be addressing. He and Mrs. Whitney barnstormed with an entourage in an open Packard touring car from the halls of Old Westbury to the shores of Montauk Point. The newspapers helped to insulate him from violence by obligingly referring to him as Cornelius Whitney—all except the *Herald Tribune* (which Cousin Jock later acquired for Republican liberalism), which reported his political activities on the *society* pages. The result that although Sonny carried his home base of Old Westbury, he lost the election and once again returned to being Cornelius Vanderbilt "Sonny" Whitney.

Like Cousin Jock, Sonny Whitney, after a "playboy" existence here and abroad, started his business career at the bottom of the ladder. However, unlike Jock, it was not in the gold mines of Wall Street but at the bottom of a very real ladder—one that led to the mines of his father in Virginia City, Nevada. In the morning, Whitney, heir to $50,000,000, trudged underground with a pick and a bag, collecting samples of ore for testing by the assay office. When the whistle blew in the afternoon, Sonny climbed out of his father's mine, washed off the soot, and after getting into the riding habit which his valet had laid out for him, rode off to the hunt with the current Mrs. Whitney.

This is not to imply that Sonny Whitney did not seriously involve himself in the businesses with which he was associated. He did indeed—almost to the point of vengeance. It was as though, as a reformed playboy, he had to prove something both to himself, to the world and to his father, for he declared with some fervor that he had decided to "recoup for his father the $14,000,000 he had put into a series of mining ventures."

When Sonny was still a young man, Roscoe Channing, the head man of Harry P. Whitney's Nevada mines, sent him to Toronto to secure an option on another company's unprofitable operation, the Flin Flon mine in Manitoba, a division of his father's Hudson Bay Mining and Smelting Company. As soon as the deal was closed, more of father's millions was poured into the investment to work the mine with a new ore-reclaiming process that Channing had developed. It turned out to be a very profitable investment and in a few years a substantial part of Harry P.'s initial capital had been recouped. On his father's death Sonny inherited the controlling interest is what is now one of the largest silver, copper and zinc producers in the world. Today Cornelius Vanderbilt Whitney is chairman of the board of the Hudson Bay Mining and Smelting Company.

The other big enterprise that Whitney got into as a young man—and a not surprising one, considering his overwhelming need to be in motion—was Pan American World Airways, of which he was a founder. Already a pilot at the age of eighteen, it was inevitable that he would actively get into aviation. It was nothing at all for him to take part in expeditionary flights that mapped the routes and selected the landing fields of the new airline. It is here that Whitney most passionately claims he "did it on his own." His initial investment in Pan American, he likes to point out, "was made with money I myself had made between 1924 and 1926."

He doesn't say that he bought 150,000 acres of his father's Mexican farmland that had been put up for auction, and then sold it back to the Mexican government for a profit of $500,000. It was not until after his father's death that Sonny was able to do anything that was not, in some way or another, connected with his father, his father's money, or money he had inherited from his father. Even his great racing stable and particularly Equipoise, the greatest horse he ever owned, was handed down to him by his father.

Whitney also had other enterprises upon which he expended those energies that were left over from polo, horseracing, hunting and other outdoor activities that kept him in constant movement. One of these was the 100,000 acres of prime forest land in the Adirondacks left to him by his father. There, while lumber and other products flow out to market, Sonny and his current companion, periodically relax surrounded by deer, bear, wolf, and mountain lion. It is some ten or eleven miles from the outer gate to the main house, but there is always a selection of fine horses at hand not only for transportation but also to hunt the deer and wolf, the bear and mountain lion. There are also stewards, guides and various other residents. At night, it is Sonny himself who leads the entertainment. Taught to play the piano by virtuoso Joseph Hoffman, Sonny Whitney is quite capable of putting together a respectable jam session with himself at the piano and a combo of instrumentalists comprised of relatives and some talented sons of his staff.

Then there is the Marine Studios, a kind of piscatory Disneyland that Sonny built near St. Augustine, Florida, and which attracts droves of tourists each year who come to look at the deep-sea animals that stock the watery zoo.

In addition, an agricultural operation known as C. V. Whitney Farms functions as part of the empire. This is a farming project that is an entity apart, but which is nevertheless inextricably involved with that other agricultural operation, the C. V. Whitney racehorse business/sport. The 500 head of Black Angus cattle, besides appearing at shows, also fertilize the pasture for the benefit of the thoroughbreds (droppings from cattle being considerably better as fertilizer than synthetics).

With all these holdings, it is something of a question for the Internal Revenue Service computers or a researcher of apochryphal data as to where Sonny stands with reference to Jock in the peerage of the Whitney Dynasty. In terms of wealth, *Fortune* Magazine (1968) rates Jock in the $200–300 million category. While Sonny, for some unknown reason, is not listed in that report, independent sources estimate that he is in the same league or at least fairly close to it. But that is not necessarily the last word on the matter of how much wealth either of them has accumulated over the years. Perhaps Sonny's bureau of the budget was less skillful than Jock's in finding the tax loopholes that Congress has graciously incorporated into every tax law. Or perhaps the gross tithes that he levies never amounted to as much as did Jock's. At any rate, Sonny's inherited capital of $20,000,000 had little trouble in expanding itself to at least many times its original value. This despite the usual spate of foundations, charities and tax-loss write-offs, which have been developed ever since publicist Ivy Low counseled John D. Rockefeller to give away dimes.

The upward flight of Sonny's capital was achieved, to large extent, in concert with Jock and others of his peers and relatives such as William K. Vanderbilt, Jr., in such enterprises, for instance, as the movie business and Pan American Airways. The result is that C. V. Whitney has ruled over as many businesses as has the British Empire colonies, and his sun is still far from setting. As one time or another he has been in mining, motion pictures, commercial aviation, marine zoology, agronomy, banking, agriculture, lumber and racing.

This has led to his acquiring appropriate accommodations to house himself, his retinue and staff throughout the world. He has a summer place in Saratoga, stables at Belmont Park, baronial lodges in the

Adirondacks and South America, a hacienda in Mexico, Marineland quarters in Florida, a mansion on the horse farm in Kentucky, the Flin Flon house in Canada, and an apartment in the exclusive River House in New York City. He might fish in a cold stream on his Adirondack vastness in the morning, for lunch fly down to Saratoga to see a new two-year-old off to the races, move on to his Park Avenue offices for an afternoon meeting and end the day in Manhattan at River House after a Serge Obolensky soirée at the Plaza.

While Sonny was still an undergraduate at Yale, he was sued for $3,000,000 by Evans Burrows Fontaine, a Ziegfeld Follies girl whom he met at a party given by Mrs. William K. Vanderbilt, Jr. Mrs. Fontaine not only claimed that Sonny had promised to marry her but that he was also the father of her son. The suits dragged on for years, defended by a battery of Whitney family lawyers, headed by 1924 Democratic presidential candidate John W. Davis. The result was that the showgirl wound up the loser, paid a $131 bill for costs and listened as the judge wagged a warning finger and warned her about ever again bothering Sonny with litigation.

Evans Burrows Fontaine may, in the long run, have done Cornelius Vanderbilt Whitney a good turn. In a newspaper interview at the time she stated, "Sonny's a kindly, amiable young chap and he means well, but he really doesn't know what it's all about . . . He has no initiative, no ambition. He doesn't know what it means to do a day's work to earn a dollar for himself." It was after this, following his return from a Paris marriage to an Old Westbury neighbor, Marie Norton (who kept publicly protesting throughout their engagement: "Why should our splendid friendship be marred by such an incident? We are in love and Miss Fontaine does not interest me at all") that Sonny went underground into his father's mines "to try and earn a dollar for himself." But the "splendid friendship" with Miss Norton soured in marriage. After the birth of a son and a daughter, Marie went to Reno and eventually became the wife of W. Averill Harriman.

Sonny soon married again, this time Gwladys Hopkins, a gentlewoman who fancied society steeplechase races. That union also foundered despite its common dedication to the thoroughbred horse.

This marriage produced a daughter, Gail, who lightened the nation's ennui in the 1950s with her antics as page one debutante of her day.

Sonny Whitney now began to turn away from the upper-class horsey set to the middle-class entertainment world. There he met Eleanor Searle, his third wife. A long, lean, willowy woman, Eleanor came from a long line of improvers of the souls of men. Her great-grandfather had founded the First Lutheran Church in Plymouth, Ohio, and it was to this middle-class church in the "wrong" Plymouth that the family whose ancestors had landed at the "right" Plymouth congregated for the wedding.

Before she married Sonny Whitney, Eleanor had sung in concert and opera and in radio and churches, her specialty being religious music. But she went to Reno in a blaze of publicity over a battle for Whitney money. She finally settled for $3,000,000, the same amount Cousin Jock had given his Liz, establishing, it would seem, a kind of a standard going rate for letting go of a Whitney.

Since then, Eleanor has had a resurgence of religious inspiration, and now lends her talents to the Reverend Billy Graham and the International Christian Leadership Movement. Before she met Graham, she told Enid Nemy of *The New York Times,* ". . . I had always called myself a Christian, but I had been a pew warmer. I used to think good Christians were kooky, far out, intellectually retarded and socially inhibited." Now she is convinced that materialistic philosophy flourishes when Christian leadership fails. How is it then that the famous Mrs. C. V. Whitney is still on the Ten Best Dressed Women's list? "I think," she told Ms. Nemy, "everyone enjoys looking at something attractive. We should all be as attractively dressed as we can be."

Sonny, now fifty-nine, finally met Mary Lou Hosford, a fragile, five-foot-three ash-blonde drama student from Kansas City. Mary Lou became a film star overnight in one of Sonny's movies, after he found her in a Phoenix restaurant. With smart dispatch, Sonny obtained his Reno divorce from Eleanor in 1958, the day before he married Mary Lou. It was twenty-four hours before his daughter Gail, America's most publicized society belle, was "eloping" at New York's St. Regis Hotel with Richard Cowell in a picture story that managed to make the deadline for a two-page spread in *Life*.

On a 530-acre wooded estate in Old Westbury, Long Island, Harry P. Whitney, Sonny's father, had built a country home that included a colonial manor house of nineteen rooms and eleven baths; a French château of thirty rooms with supplementary facilities; two stables with stalls for sixty-five racehorses and dormitories for grooms above; a horse training track; six cow barns to house the cattle to fertilize the horses' pasture; seven cottages for one hundred fifty resident help; an indoor clay tennis court and swimming pool, two squash courts, a bowling alley and boxing ring with steam rooms, Turkish baths and other miscellaneous health aids. When he became captain of his polo team, Harry P. Whitney added a polo training field and a full-sized gymnasium in order that he and his teammates could stay in shape during the off season.

When Harry P. Whitney died in 1930, Sonny acquired, as had his own father, the paternal home. He also bought, again as had his father, the paternal horses and stables, but said, in an interview with Alfred Wright of *Sports Illustrated,* "I never would have gone into racing in the first place if it weren't for the family tradition."

This seems quite plausible, for, apart from racing and breeding thoroughbreds, Sonny had plenty of diversion in which to satisfy his fierce competitive instinct. There was his polo, which, being less a spectator sport than racing, captured his interest more than owning a racing stable. As did Cousin Jock, Sonny captained his own team, the Old Westbury, composed of himself, Michael Phipps, Cecil Smith and Stewart Iglehart. It won the national championship in both 1937 and 1938. The two cousins often engaged in spirited contests with each other and on one occasion Jock split Sonny's head with a polo mallet.

There was also his array of businesses. But there *was* this great racing stable, perhaps the world's best, at hand. And in 1930, on his father's death, Sonny took over the H. P. Whitney Stud. Along with it came Equipoise.

The opportunity to own an animal such as Equipoise would be enough to transform most anyone into an ardent racing fan. Sonny Whitney, despite having all the world's goods, services, and delights at his fingertips, was smitten. Equipoise was one of nature's greatest handiworks, and, like Man o' War, one of a company of gods among horses; he was the very symbol of the word courage, a characteristic which most men exalt in their heroes.

Equipoise was the first horse to carry Whitney's blue-and-brown colors to victory. That was in the Pimlico Futurity of 1930, a race in which, even as an infant two-year-old, Equipoise already demonstrated the great heart that was to set him apart from other horses. Running against Mrs. Payne Whitney's crack Twenty Grand and another great horse, Mate, Equipoise stumbled in the mud at the start and as a result fell back some twenty lengths. He came crashing on through the mud like a warhorse and defeated Twenty Grand by a half-length with Mate a close third. This victory immediately put young Sonny Whitney at the top of the list among his peers by making him the nation's leading money-winner for the year.

Equipoise also demonstrated in other ways that fierce aggressive drive with which the owners of racehorses strongly identify. When asked by Bob Considine of the *World Journal Tribune* to name the one horse which above all others could fulfill everything an owner could ask for–speed, endurance, courage, strength–Whitney replied:

"I happen to have owned the horse. His name was Equipoise. Equipoise had that ineffable something that no computer will ever be able to discern: the competitive spirit. Horses have it just as humans do. Equipoise couldn't bear the thought of another horse passing him in a race. He was disqualified on several occasions for biting the neck of a horse that tried to pass him."

Not only did Equipoise do on the racetrack what his owner may often have felt like doing to his own competition, but he was also the source of much other ego gratification, something that the very rich, especially the aristocratic very rich, are sometimes alleged to find lacking in their lives. During a World War II career of not inconsiderable excitement and performance, Colonel C. V. Whitney recalled as one of his most memorable experiences the following incident with a war correspondent who stumbled into his tent out of a sand storm during the campaign in Africa. He told Oscar Otis of the *Morning Telegraph:*

"He was from Kentucky and a horse writer," said Whitney. "He proceeded to tell me that he thought Equipoise was the greatest horse he'd ever known, except for one thing–his owner had ruined him. I didn't tell him that I was the owner, so he just kept on and on. It wasn't until the man got back to headquarters that he found out that I was the Whitney who owned Equipoise!"

Equipoise also brought Sonny into contact with people his own social position might otherwise have precluded. In a talk at a racing writers' dinner, Sonny said:

"In 1932, I was sitting in my office when a Mr. Capone called. It was Al's brother. He wanted me to send Equipoise west to meet a horse named Gallant Sir and offered to put up $25,000, a huge purse for those days. I agreed. I went and won it, despite there being a horse put in to provide interference for mine. I thought no more about it until years later when I was in the Bahamas making a few wagers in a casino, and a man tapped me on the shoulder and said the boss wanted to see me. The boss turned out to be Mr. Capone. He apologized all over the place, for his conscience must have bothered him for trying to stop a good horse like Equipoise. He poured champagne and we drank a toast—to Equipoise." The graciousness of Godfathers is not to be underestimated, especially with the right people.

This great animal, and others in his stable, went on helping to make Cornelius Vanderbilt Whitney's life a thing of profit and pleasure. He topped the owners money-winning list four years in a row. But in 1935 when Equipoise, after making an unsuccessful attempt to win the $100,000 Santa Anita Handicap, was retired to stud only $38,000 short of the world's record money winner, Sonny began to think of quitting. This finally became a fact in 1937, after his two entries in the Belmont Futurity finished fifth and seventh. He sold most of his racing stable and his yearlings and held only his breeding stock and his farm.

"I was too busy with other interests," said the now thirty-eight-year-old Sonny. "I had very little time for sport. Besides, at that time my racing stable had had a couple of bad seasons and had just about hit bottom. So I decided to sell all the horses I had in training."

During the years 1937 and 1938 Sonny Whitney did, though, manage to find time for the sport of polo, where he was on a winning streak: two national championships with the fillip of beating Cousin Jock's Greentree team.

It was not long, however, before tradition and, according to his own story, rather poignant reminiscences of youthful times passed managed to bring him back into racing.

"In 1927," he relates, "I went down to the Kentucky farm with my father and some of his cronies to see his three-year-old Whiskery run in the Derby. At that time I had no particular interest in racing.

"Whiskery won and that night, when I returned to the farm, my father and his friends were playing poker in his private railroad car. I went out for some air. I saw a fire burning in the distance so I walked over to see what it was.

"Dozens of men who worked on the place—they were all colored men in those days—were grouped around the fire singing strange, weird chants I had never heard before. It was almost like some pagan rite.

"A few yards away from the fire I saw a horse tethered, so I went up to one of the men, who didn't have the faintest notion who I was, and asked him about the horse.

" 'That's Regret,' he said. To celebrate that day's victory the men had gone down to the barn and brought the only other Whitney horse to win the Derby up to the hill as part of the ceremony.

"I sat around there until two in the morning listening to that wonderful singing, and for the first time I had some appreciation of the real emotions that go with horseracing."

Some might carp unkindly that it is somewhat surprising that a man who has been unable to find a black jockey or a black trainer for his horses—though an ancestor of one of his better thoroughbreds was developed by the outstanding black trainer of the nineteenth century—could find sufficient enough inspiration in a group of blacks singing spirituals around a bluegrass bonfire to reinvest himself and his millions in racing. Nonetheless that is how C. V. Whitney has reported it in talks to thoroughbred clubs and breeders associations.

And, of course, there was the legitimate and ineffable lure of fine horseflesh. Addressing the National Press Club on the occasion of his winning the 1954 Washington, D.C. International with a never-say-die horse named Fisherman, Mr. Whitney said: "He [the horse] has always been a figure of great imagination and commanded great respect throughout the ages and by all races. Now why is that?

"Because the horse as developed is an animal of great courage and stamina. These are characteristics that all people like—courage, bravery and stamina."

In 1939, coincidentally the dawn of the age of the tax loophole, Cornelius Vanderbilt Whitney, duke of Old Westbury, holder of the Legion of Merit, the Distinguished Flying Cross and the International Polo Cup, had rejoined the sport of kings. A few years later, a little brown horse named Fisherman, which never knew how to quit (like another thoroughbred named Equipoise) rewarded his master with one of his most memorable experiences in racing, by winning the Laurel International. "This only shows," said Whitney, "that if you take a sporting chance, it often as not turns out wonderfully."

Sonny Whitney had reinvested in his old hobby, and it indeed turned out quite wonderfully. He placed Ivor Balding, a relative of one of his old polo friends, in charge of his thoroughbred operations, and sent him to Cornell to learn agronomy. He bought Mahmoud, the Aga Khan's Epsom Derby winner, to stand on his farm as the senior stallion and he otherwise streamlined the new business. He even found capital in the bluegrass earth, by selling one half of the farm's acreage. Sonny also acquired a herd of Black Angus cattle that would grow to some five hundred, headed by Ankonian 3263, a $35,000 international prize bull. This was not the herd's only purpose. The Black Angus cattle had the assignment of fertilizing the grass on which his thoroughbreds dined, a sort of organic health food theory which Ivor Balding brought back from Cornell.

At the age of sixty-one, in 1960, Sonny Whitney was the leading money winner of the year, with the added honor of being the only owner, other than Calumet Farm, to win more than a million dollars in a racing season. He never had the pleasure of having a Kentucky Derby winner, but actually he was not especially fond of Derbies. Whitney's ideal was the great and telling Belmont Stakes, run over the crushing distance of a mile and a half, where the thoroughbred must show his courage and, above all, his stamina. Whitney has had his goodly share of Belmont winners, and other memorable winners, such as Mameluke, whose great stretch run defeated Jockey Club chairman George D. Widener's grand old Battlefield by a half-length in a running of the Metropolitan Handicap.

At Belmont Park's Turf & Field Club a few days after the race, a gentleman paused in front of George D. Widener's box and spoke with every sincerity:

"I'm so sorry. I wish it hadn't happened."

"That's all right," replied Widener. "You should have been here, you'd have had a real thrill."

"No," the gentleman said. "I told my wife that in the first place I didn't want to beat George Widener and, in the second place, I didn't want to beat that grand little horse. You know, I love him. It's fine to beat other horses, but I just don't like beating Battlefield."

The gentleman, of course, was Cornelius Vanderbilt Whitney, owner of Mameluke. Perhaps Sonny Whitney indeed disliked the idea of beating George D. Widener in the Metropolitan Handicap. Or perhaps it occurred after his victory in that Metropolitan that, after all, it was George D. Widener's grandfather who had helped his own grandfather win another Metropolitan, the very Metropolitan that was the source of his great wealth: the Metropolitan Transit Company of New York.

CHAPTER 9

Mrs. Charles Shipman Payson (Joan Whitney) (1903-)

"I don't know what in the world you would ever write about me. [Mrs. Payson is the owner of the New York Mets, Greentree Stable, eight homes, several art galleries, a book store, and a varied assortment of the world's artifacts.] I don't do anything interesting."

—Taken from an interview in *Sports Illustrated*

NATURE, AS THOUGH to demonstrate its indifference to man-made distinctions, occasionally produces startling look-alikes in opposing classes, a caprice that throughout history has been useful, disturbing and amusing to numerous distinguished personages. Howard Hughes, for instance, is reported to use a paid look-alike decoy to divert pursuers: J. P. Morgan was often "seen" at lower-class grog shops by startled witnesses; Louis XI walked the Paris streets in the guise of a knave.

Two ladies of the present decade are unlikely yet rather convincing candidates for the lists. One, possessor of $300,000,000, Mrs. Charles Shipman Payson (Joan Whitney); the other, Ms. Bella Abzug, New York City's volatile Congressperson.

Both ladies have a passion for large, floppy hats that drop about round full faces; both adorn their ample figures with flowery prints of somewhat boisterous design; and both occasionally erupt, in large voice, at noble efforts of their favorite baseball team, the New York Mets.

The resemblance, however, there ends. Bella must stand in line for a ticket to an afternoon of baseball at Shea Stadium unless, in her role of politician, she can manage a free ticket, whereas Joan, the owner of the Mets, has no problem at all getting in free. Mrs. Payson also owns one of the world's largest racing stables, while Ms. Abzug's only apparent connection with the horsey set is her friendship with Howard Samuels, the New York Off-Track Betting czar.

Joan Whitney Payson shares the largest individual fortune ever probated in the United States, which, along with her brother Jock, she inherited from her father. Not to be overlooked, however, are the enormous accretions to her wealth that have resulted from joint investments with Jock. The two have functioned as one of the world's most successful brother-and-sister team in enterprises ranging all the way from picking blueberries during school vacations on their father's New Hampshire estate (a penny for 100 berries picked, presumably to learn the value of a dollar) to backing *Life with Father* and *Gone With the Wind.* The colossal profits from these, two of the biggest money-makers in their field, prove that they learned their lesson well.

This close relationship has persisted throughout the lives of these two Whitneys (they jointly own Greentree Stable, they co-direct the destiny of major museums and hospitals, even their private art collections complement each other); wherever Jock's Midas hand has moved, Joan's has not been far behind.

Where Jock has had his J. H. Whitney & Company to prospect the investment terrain for risk ventures which could net an appropriate profit, Joan Payson has had her own enterprise, known as Payson & Trask, an investment firm operated by her husband and a man named Trask, distinguished for his financial abilities. But even the area where Joan Payson placed her tax-exempt dollars was largely determined by this close bond to her brother. Her Helen Hay Whitney Foundation, for instance, was designed primarily to aid research in rheumatic fever, most especially—and not unreasonably—because Jock Whitney had once come down with that disease.

However, Joan Payson seems to have a preference for owning rather than performing. She owns Greentree Stable, she owns Tom Fool, onetime Horse of the Year, she owns the Mets, she owns much of the

Museum of Modern Art and New York Hospital, she owns Rembrandts, El Grecos, Corots, and Matisses.

While Mrs. Payson has owned racehorses all her adult life, and, as such, been hunting winners, for her baseball has also been a kind of hunting. Out in the open air, vicariously stalking the "prey" from a "shooting" box, the delicious disappointment of its escape, the ecstasy of the kill—in other words, a total commitment to the search for a trophy, to catch a winner.

In baseball, as in most other arenas, the Whitneys usually are victorious—even when they lose. The Mets cost Mrs. Payson some $4,-500,000—a dubious pleasure, as someone has said, "for the privilege of growling at Casey Stengel." Despite all the hullaballoo about the poor ineffectual Mets, the team actually operates at a profit. Once again, when it is balanced out, the Whitney fortune is in no way nicked by "losing" indulgences that the family calls sport.

Joan's ability to come out on the plus side of the ledger can in part be attributed to the unusual way in which she completed her education. After finishing the relatively exclusive Miss Chapin's classes and going on to Barnard College, she attended Brown's Business College, which taught her something more than secretarial shorthand. Despite the fact that she tends to wince at the mention of Brown's Business College, claiming that it makes her sound more businesslike than she deserves, her own profit-and-loss ledgers prove she benefitted from her experience there.

Joan Payson would of course never flaunt her immense wealth. Money itself always remains in the background for the horsey set, underplayed, although it seems to multiply as the lilies of the field. As one of her stockbrokers has mournfully observed, "Mrs. Payson would rather win fifty cents on some baseball game than realize $5,000 on a stock transaction."

Conversely, Mrs. Payson delights in flaunting her position on the totems of the sports hierarchy. Her number one automobile, generally a Bentley, disports a license plate bearing the legend METS 1. Car number two, usually a more modest compact, is there to back it up with METS 2. In her private Pullman coach, Adios II, every blanket, footstool and pillow is emblazoned with the Mets insignia.

Joan Whitney Payson may indeed be the compleat spectator insofar as sports are concerned. In horseracing she leaves the active and of the operation to Jock, that is, those peripheral breeding and training activities in which an owner with a large professional staff such as Greentree's must engage himself. But she is completely identified with her horses, particularly as regards the running of the race. Direct action is what she is interested in; she is there for the race totally involved in the effort to win. Her body language during the running of a race is a barometer of the intensity of her emotional investment in an animal that she often hardly knows and frequently has not seen before. As one of her stable boys put it, "Right before a race, Mrs. Payson is full of life. She laughs and jokes with her friends. But if you look close at her face you get a feeling she's just hiding her nervousness. It's like she's dying till the race goes off. And when it does, she just stops talking and goes tense and pale all over. She never gets up and hollers the way we do." He might have added that if the horse, particularly one in a major race, lets her down, she drops her binoculars into her lap like a two-dollar bettor who has just lost the rent money.

For this "good woman gone right, the universal wealthy aunt basking in the glint of a crystal ball that always told a good fortune," as David Dempsey describes her in *The New York Times* Magazine of June 23, 1968, the symbols of victory at times seem even more important than victory itself. For just as she has utilized the insignia of her Mets, so has she appropriated the symbols of conquest in that race of all American races, the Belmont, two of which were won by horses she co-owned with her brother.

"For many years," said Jock (as reported by William H. Rudy in *The Blood-Horse* of April 26, 1969), "my sister and I had a method of tossing a coin when a mare was sent to breed to see who would take the trophies from her produce.

"Now what we're doing, if we're lucky enough to win trophies, is we each take every other one."

Who got the trophy of Stage Door Johnny (their last Belmont winner)? he was asked.

"My sister has that one," he said.

And who got Capot's [the previous winner]? he was asked.

He thought for a moment and replied: "Why, she's got that one, too."

On the day of the Mets' first pennant victory, a lady with $300,000,000 in stock, tax-free bonds, eight homes, a stable of horses, baseball players and old masters, had herself a ball at her personal ballpark. She rode to her "royal box" at the stadium in an orange-colored cart generally used to haul pitchers from the bullpen to the diamond. She climbed the short flight of stairs with an arthritic limp, took her place in the front row of the box and, dressed in a plain suit, spooned ice cream out of a cardboard cup while from the attending multitude a great cheer arose that was carried on national television. Said one of her millions of admirers, "It comforts people to know that someone with all her money can lose and still go on trying. It makes them feel good. They like Mrs. Payson. A team that she owns can't be all that bad."

As befits her status, Joan Whitney Payson has, in addition to her royal box at Shea Stadium, the proper number of residences to accommodate her passage through the annual parade of sports. And to lend a touch of hearth and home to her faraway places, her gallery of art masterpieces—Goyas, Corots, El Grecos, Matisses, Cézannes, Toulouse-Lautrecs—in addition to her zoo of pets, follow her on the seasonal journeys. Home is the large colonial house that she built in Manhasset on a piece of Greentree next to Jock's place; in May at Kentucky Derby time, she moves her court to the antebellum brick mansion on the 1000-acre breeding farm in the bluegrass country outside Lexington; in early summer it's the seashore, in a big New Englander at Falmouth Foreside along the southern coast of Maine; August finds her back with her thoroughbreds in a great Victorian structure at Saratoga; comes winter, she checks in close to the Hialeah races at her place at Hobe Sound, a fashionable resort island off Palm Beach (the Whitneys would never be found in a place as conventionally social as Palm Beach); and in between, the Paysons can be found at their penthouse *pied-à-terre* on upper Fifth Avenue, New York City.

Charles Shipman Payson, a rugged six-foot redhaired entrepreneur, shares very little of his wife's sporting interests and is rarely seen with her at the races or at a ball game. However, like all of his Whitney in-laws, he was at least a Yale oar. He has also made his presence felt as the father of five children and eleven grandchildren.

Of these, daughter Sandra, Lady Weidenfeld, lives in London; Payne, Mrs. Henry Middleton, in Rome; and John, with his wife, in Portland, Maine, his father's hometown. Daniel Carroll Payson, the first son, died as an infantryman in the Battle of the Bulge.

Only daughter Lorinda, wife of Vincent de Toulet, former ambassador to Jamaica, seems interested in carrying on the Whitney horsey tradition. Perhaps she was that Payson child who one day at Saratoga, on noticing the many Whitney horses prancing about, was reported in *Sports Illustrated* of August 14, 1962, to have exclaimed, "Look, Mummy, everyone in the family's got a prize. Grandma's horse won, Uncle Jock was second, you were third—and Cousin Sonny won the booby prize."

THE WIDENER DYNASTY

CHAPTER 10

Peter A. B. Widener I

(1834-1915)

"Let us discuss the matter first," a stockholder urged. "No," declared Peter A. B. Widener I with quiet ruthlessness. "Vote first and discuss afterwards."

—From a meeting of Metropolitan Securities Company stockholders meeting

PETER A. B. WIDENER II, one of the latter-day Wideners, once observed that although he had had a private schooling befitting a crown prince—with tutors and masters summoned to the family's 110-room palace—it nevertheless took a war to provide his real education.

"I hate war," he said, speaking of his experiences in World War I in his book, *Without Drums* (G. P. Putnam's Sons, 1940.) "I shall always work against it. I pray my children shall never know it as I have known it. And still I owe much to the World War; *much of the best I have learned is a consequence of it.*"

In a sense the same could be said for Peter A. B. Widener I, the young man's grandfather and founder of the dynasty. Although Grandfather Widener did not actually attend that "university" of his own time—the Civil War—he did receive what might be called an extra-curricular education from it. It was this experience that enabled him to build a fortune for himself and his heirs. The son of a Philadelphia brickmaker, not overly burdened with goods of this world,

Peter A. B. Widener I quickly learned that supplying a warring army could be more profitable than marketing peacetime commodities. He chose butchering instead of bricks, the occupation of his father, and he wound up with a government contract to provision Union troops in his area with meat. How much of this meat came from the four-legged animal with which his heirs later fell so in love is uncertain, but undoubtedly there was some butchering of horses, for in the Civil War, as in all wars, an army marched on its stomach and the most available animal meat at this time when cavalry was still king was, of course, the horse.

The Philadelphia butcher boy learned enough from the war about marketing meat so that he was able successfully to launch one of the first chains of meat stores in the United States. This yielded dividends over and above immediate dollar profits. Butcher shops in those days were places where politicians congregated, much like country folk around the cracker barrel, and he was able to make some powerful connections. These he used to gain entry to another public sector once again involving the horse—the horse-powered transportation system of Philadelphia. At this point Widener's story begins to sound much like that of the founder of another great dynasty, William Collins Whitney. Indeed, as both men operated during the formative epoch of the nation, Peter A. B. Widener's career in many ways does parallel that of his contemporary. Not only did Widener vastly increase his fortune in transit speculation, as did Whitney, but he was also Whitney's associate in the capture of both the Metropolitan Traction Company and the American Tobacco Company.

But unlike William Collins Whitney, Peter Arrel Brown Widener, despite his four-part name, came from the wrong side of the tracks. The first American Widener, Johann Christoph Widener, of hardy German stock, had come to Philadelphia as early as 1752; another had been a captain on George Washington's staff. But whereas Whitney had been born into wealth sufficient to get him to Harvard and a profession, Peter A. B. Widener was a poor man without formal education who had started his work life as a butcher's apprentice.

This affected Widener's outlook on life considerably less than it did that of his son and heir, Joseph, who through his ardent cultivation of "society" and his intense devotion to the racehorse, revealed how greatly it pained him to have come from the other side of the tracks. What Peter A. B. Widener did was simply to set himself the task of making enough money to buy the tracks. He did this by becoming not only one of the originators of United States Steel, which forged the tracks, but also became a large stockholder in the Pennsylvania Railroad, which owned them. The Stotesburys and Drexels and Biddles and other Philadelphia Mainliners could stay nestled behind their moats in Rittenhouse Square, but, by God, if they wanted to move about the land, they'd damn well have to move on tracks that were owned by Peter A. B. Widener.

Not long after he had hung up the sign, *Peter A. B. Widener, Butcher,* over the meat stall in Spring Garden Market, establishing a center for political gossip as well as for the purchase of pork butts, he was well on his way to being recognized as the Republican Party leader of Philadelphia's Twentieth Ward. It was at this time that the newly arrived municipal politican got his first big opportunity in the world of free enterprise; namely, the Federal Government contract to "supply the mutton to all the Union troops within a ten-mile radius of Philadelphia." It was as though Boss Tweedy were supplying the whiskey to all taverns within a ten-mile radius of New York's Tammany Hall, and as his grandson and biographer, Peter A. B. Widener II, concedes, there "must have been a slight political tinge to this happy stroke of fate."

By the end of the Civil War the man without education had made himself a member of the city's Board of Education. In 1873 the City of Philadelphia (in effect its Republican Party), having jailed its treasurer for conspiring with a banker named Charles Yerkes to pilfer the municipal coffers, looked around for an honest man to fill the job. Peter A. B. Widener I was, by his own admission, not anything if not an honest man. "I got ahead in the meat business because I was honest," Peter II reports his grandfather as having frequently reminded him as a young man.

This news reached the ears of the party bigwigs and, as young Peter later wrote, "the Republicans found their honest man. In 1873, the one-time son of a German bricklayer was appointed City Treasurer to fill out the jailed predecessor's unexpired term. The next year the people of the city expressed their trust in Grandfather by electing him to the office."

In a rather open-faced addendum, however, young Peter pointed out that "The City Treasurership was the most lucrative political office of the day. To the City Treasurer accrued all the interest on city deposits as perfectly legitimate spoils of office—legitimate, that is, from a politician's point of view."

Now, with his bank account growing from his string of butcher shops and his City Treasurership, Peter I moved rapidly up the political ladder. Presently he was operating on the top level: with the boss of bosses of the whole state of Pennsylvania, William H. Kemble. In 1875, with Kemble pulling the necessary political strings and W. L. Elkins and Widener supplying the capital, the team organized the Philadelphia Traction Company, which eventually embraced a large part of the public transit of the state. Shortly thereafter, Widener joined the Whitney-Ryan combine in New York that took over most of that city's public railways. Then on to Chicago to take over the North Side Lines, having pooled resources with the repentant banker Charles Yerkes, now released from jail after embezzling the City Treasury that Widener represented. Later, the team moved into Pittsburgh and Baltimore traction. In the end they controlled over 500 miles of transit track in over a half dozen major American cities.

Before he had turned forty, Peter A. B. Widener, erstwhile butcher, had acquired immense transit holdings in addition to his stake in United States Steel, American Tobacco, Standard Oil, International Mercantile Marine and the Baltimore and Ohio Railroad. He had long since put aside his meat cleaver and his butcher's apron for the cigar and topper; he had changed roles from ward healer to national benefactor; he had even had his portrait painted by John Singer Sargent. Nevertheless the sign, *Peter A. B. Widener, Butcher,* remained, at least as far as the old guard in Rittenhouse Square was concerned, indelibly stamped on his public image.

Widener's financial state of affairs was now one that often has led its fortunate principal to the thoroughbred horse, its racing and breeding. The sport of kings is characterized by a history of commoners who came across the tracks with new millions. August Belmont I had done it in his time; others such as John Kelly (Princess

Grace's bricklaying father), Jack Dreyfus, John Schapiro and Sigmund Sommer would do it later. But not Peter A. B. Widener I. Perhaps he had had enough traffic with Civil War horsemeat ever to be really enamored of the horse. Or perhaps the stubborn German provincial who had made his way from a stack of pork butts in Spring Garden Market to a top position on the political pork barrel was just too proud to make his way across the tracks on the back of a horse, even if it was a thoroughbred. Widener always delighted in making a point in public of his less-than-thoroughbred beginnings, often to the distress of his younger, more socially ambitious relatives. Once, when on an inspection tour of a frontier town with a group of business colleagues, Widener, discovering that the stock of food in his private Pullman had run out, went foraging with his friends for new provisions. He found a local butcher who awkwardly began carving away at a side of lamb. *Without Drums,* by Peter A. B. Widener II, reports the dialogue as follows:

"You haven't been at the trade very long, I'd guess," said Widener.

"Maybe you'd like to try it yourself," the butcher said.

Off came Widener's hat and coat, up went his sleeves and, with his audience of financiers looking on, he skillfully carved away at the side of lamb.

"You're a better man than I am at this," conceded the butcher. "That's the damn finest piece of carving I ever saw."

It was a characteristic incident—instead of draping his humble background in the silks of some fashionable racing stable, Widener deliberately thrust his plebian past into the noses of his peers, and his avoidance of the in-bred world of horse racing did not diminish. His son Joseph was compelled, even in his adult years, to conduct his own horseracing activities on the sly. An ironic state of affairs for the founder of one of the horsiest dynasties in the land.

Peter A. B. Widener chose to associate himself with men rather than with horses. The men that Widener cultivated, however, lived in the past centuries: Rembrandt, Van Dyck, Rubens, Raphael, and Benvenuto Cellini. He assembled their works into what is considered by many to be the greatest private art collection in the world. To house this vast treasure, a gallery on the order of a wing of the Metropolitan Museum was built into Lynnewood Hall, the Widener family home in the suburbs of Philadelphia. The home itself was nearly as impressive as the masterworks that hung on its walls. A Georgian palace of 110 rooms set on 300 acres, it was one of the last of the American-edition Versailles types that the nineteenth century rags-to-riches barons constructed in their own self-image. Its gardens were, in fact, a replica of those at Versailles and were laid out by Jacques Greber, who redesigned the outskirts of Paris. The vast limestone pile with its priceless treasures of old masters soon became a rendezvous for art lovers of all lands, not only kings, queens, princes and heads of state, but also old-liners from Rittenhouse Square and Chestnut Hill. Peter Arrel Brown Widener was now on the right side of the tracks.

He had also raised a family and put his stamp upon the nation. In 1858, while still a butcher, Widener married Josephine Dunton, a woman of considerable intellectual ability but from a family of no social standing. They had two sons. One of them, George D. Widener Sr., along with his son, Harry Elkins Widener, one of the world's great book collectors, went down on the *Titanic*. The other son, Joseph E. Widener, creator of the family's racing stable, became manager of the vast Widener estate at the death of his father. The Widener family had the largest fortune in Philadelphia, indeed, one of the largest in the country. The Widener home was among the most magnificent in the world, valued at $8,000,000. The Widener art collection was the most important in America, valued at $50,000,000. The Wideners erected and endowed the Josephine Widener Branch of the Free Library of Philadelphia; it cost them $1,000,000. They endowed the Widener Home for Crippled Children for $2,000,000. They founded the Harry Elkins Widener Memorial Library at Harvard University for another $1,000,000. They invested $11,000,000 in various other memorials. In spite of all this, it would take the Widener family at least another generation to feel wanted in Rittenhouse Square, although they were the proprietors of one of its most prominent landmarks, the Philadelphia Ritz Carlton Hotel.

Peter A. B. Widener died in 1915. His life had spanned four wars: from the Mexican War in 1846 through the Civil and Spanish-American wars to World War I in 1914. Butcher apprentice in the first of these wars, entrepreneur in the second, industrial magnate

Left: Peter A. B. Widener, the "butcher boy" who built one of the world's great fortunes and amassed one of its finest art collections.

Below: Joseph E. Widener with a group of Seminole Indians at Hialeah. The Florida racetrack, built on ancestral Indian land, for years arranged for the Seminoles to appear before post time in connection with the track's promotional programs.

Above, left: George D. Widener, a chairman of The Jockey Club, waited a lifetime to get a Belmont Stakes winner. Jaipur won the Stakes for him in 1962, with Willie Shoemaker up.

Above, right: Educated in isolation like a prince, a young man whose life was "set to music," as he put it, Peter A. B. Widener II at first disliked horses. The sight of the golden stallion Fair Play, Man o' War's sire, changed his mind.

Right: Peter A. B. Widener III (center), fourth generation scion of the Widener dynasty, with his wife, the former Patricia Massie and trainer F. J. Wright at Aqueduct. Mrs. Widener died in 1963 in a crash of the family's private plane.

in the third, bourgeois potentate in the last, he finished up creating his own dynasty with all appropriate marks and privileges.

But finally war, from which he had profited early in his career, became a threat. The Kaiser's legions disturbed the leisurely sunning of his grandchildren on the Côte d'Azur. His family's yachts no longer enjoyed the freedom of the seas. "Something must be done against the damn Huns," he announced. And it was all his associates and friends could do to prevent him from sailing his yacht, the *Josephine,* through the German submarine nests to execute a personal Dunkirk and bring his family home. Peter Widener II's *Without Drums* provides more details:

"They may never get home," the old man, now eighty-one, complained over and over again. "They're blowing up ships over there."

But before the torpedoing of the *Lusitania,* on May 7, 1915, had given the old man the chance to say, "You see, I told you so," his family had been safely repatriated. Six months later Peter A. B. Widener was dead.

In the Van Dyke Room at Lynnewood Hall, on the night of November 7, 1915, his body lay in state. It rested in a solid bronze coffin, guarded by four of his oldest retainers and surrounded by a group of the world's most precious paintings, all of which, except for one, was covered with black crepe. That exception was the massive John Singer Sargent portrait of the old man himself, directly above his coffin, which reposed on four pillars. Twenty thousand dollars worth of flowers, gifts of such men as John D. Rockefeller, Andrew Carnegie, J. P. Morgan, Charles Schwab, Jacob H. Schiff, E. T. Stotesbury and E. H. Gary, sent a heavy fragrance throughout the vast establishment. Only family members were permitted within the Van Dyke Room during the short Episcopal service. Some two hundred of the nation's mighty remained in another room. The next day the body was moved to Laurel Hill Cemetery and there laid in a crypt of the Widener mausoleum. There was no pomp, no ceremony, no show of ritual. This was Peter Widener's last and most personal act, and its simplicity was appropriate to the man.

CHAPTER 11

Second Generation: The Racing Wideners Joseph E. Widener (1872-1943)

"Don't send me any bills. There is a sum to your credit in the bank. Run the stable and don't tell me how much it costs. I don't want to know."
—Joseph E. Widener, to the manager of the French Division of his racing stables

CAPTAIN EDWARD J. SMITH'S White Star Liner, *Titanic,* which sank in the North Atlantic on April 14, 1912, dispatched to their graves more aristocrats in a given period of time than any single instrument since the guillotine of the French Revolution. The world's greatest disaster also rearranged the roster of more exclusive clubs, the ownership of more blue chip stocks, and the assignment of more racing silks than any event in history. Alfred Gwynne Vanderbilt, Sr., passed the reins to Alfred Gwynne, Jr., future Jockey Club steward and president of both Belmont Park and Pimlico Race Course—the only man to have presided over both the Preakness and the Belmont Stakes, two of the three legs of racing's Triple Crown. George D. Widener, Sr. (who went down with his book-loving son, Harry Elkins Widener), opened the way for his other son, George D. Widener, Jr., to become a Jockey Club chairman as well as Belmont president when young Alfred Gwynne Vanderbilt went off to his war; for sixty years he was to be a racer and breeder of some of the world's best thoroughbreds.

With his brother George Sr.'s death on the *Titanic,* Joseph E. Widener, youngest son of the first Peter, was left with the lion's share of the vast Widener estate and the power to create from its resources a first-line racing dynasty. He proceeded vigorously in this endeavor as have other wealthy second-generation scions.

He began by racing a stable of thoroughbreds when he was eighteen, although he did it in secret by registering the horses in a trainer's name. Because of his father's disapproval of racing, he also went in for driving teams of spirited horses four-in-hand from the seat of a surrey, or coaching, as it is called. It was a sport that endowed him with a prematurely bald head, a result of an injury to his pate in a horse show at Madison Square Garden. Thoroughbred sports also eventually led to a vice-chairmanship of The Jockey Club and the presidency of both Belmont Park and Hialeah Race Course, whose plant he considerably improved and expanded, characteristic of his willingness to commit both his own money and his energy into the modernization of the sport.

As if to redress—perhaps erase—the social stigma of his father's beginnings, Joseph Widener was determined to be invited through the front doors of those inaccessible mansions on Rittenhouse Square through whose service entrances his father had once delivered mutton chops. He finally managed it through his marriage to Ella H. Pancoast, one of the belles of Philadelphia's Mainline society. Yet despite this union and his attention to such stylish matters as having Tautz of London send over a man twice a year to measure him for a wardrobe that filled several rooms, he never was considered by Mainline Philadelphia to measure up fully to *its* standards.

He received cruelest evidence of his lack when his daughter Fifi was ready to make her debut. An organization known as the Assembly, a group that regarded itself as the nonpareil arbiter of society, declared Fifi Widener inelegible for its list. At the same time her father was asked to serve on a civic committee that was *sponsored* by members of the Assembly.

"It seems I have the good taste to be asked to join this civic project," Joe Widener protested, perhaps missing the point, "but somehow my daughter still lacks the credentials of eligibility for the Assembly. I refuse."

When the governing group reversed itself and decided to invite Fifi because her father's cooperation was vital to their civic committee, Widener managed to swallow his stubborn pride. He was, in fact, overjoyed by this belated and tortuous acceptance into the Mainline fold. Fifi was invited to the Assembly Ball as an "out of town" guest, even though her home was only a stone's throw across the city line and her father and grandfather had underwritten millions in philanthropies to the city. Her mother was still left off the guest list, an act that defied the Assembly's inflexible tradition of inviting mothers as chaperones.

Undoubtedly his father's origins played a role in all this. He was still considered the son of a first-generation interloper and it would take another generation before thoroughly assimilated WASP Wideners such as his nephew George and his son Peter II would be accepted. Despite his generational taint he did make it to the vice-chairmanship of The Jockey Club (a full chairmanship of that august body was to come to a later Widener in the person of his nephew George).

Joseph Widener may have tried hard to live down the socially unacceptable bourgeois within, but something of the commercial entrepreneur always remained. In a review of the contemporary racing scene, *The New York Times* said: "In 1931 and 1932 a great expansion of horseracing took place in various sections of the country all traceable to the pioneering efforts of Mr. Widener in Florida."

The article referred to Widener's achievement—after having made Belmont Park, as England's Lord Derby said, "more beautiful than anything we have in my own country"—in creating at Hialeah what he called "the Belmont of the South." Many conservative lovers of the thoroughbred, particularly the English, maintain that racehorses should be rested from late fall to early spring to keep from burning them out. America however, is a nation of consumers, and the racehorse is not exempted, not even by many of those who claim to love the thoroughbred.

Palm Beach throughout the long winter months was felt to need the excitement of the thoroughbred, despite the golf and the tennis and the surf. So Widener money and connections and energy pushed through a scheme at Hialeah for a "Belmont of the South" where the top thoroughbreds could compete during the winter months. This was achieved by the legalization of racing in Florida, evicting the bookies from the "outlaw" tracks and instituting the pari-mutuel system of betting that changed the sport into one of the most commercial of businesses. The state of Florida shared the take, and the sport became a year-round operation that followed the set in its pursuit of the sun, with rest and relaxation for the owners but little for the horses. Hialeah was transformed, screened off by two miles of pines imported from Australia. Seminole Indians, who had been removed from their lands, were retained to lend a note of color and pageant at post time as droves of pink flamingoes fanned the summer air with the flapping of their wings.

"I was sure," said Widener, "that the solid citizens of the state of Florida could see the advantages of racing in their community, and would support the efforts of their legislature."

After he had rid Hialeah Race Course of bookies (bookies still legally operate on the racetracks of England, even at Royal Ascot, the Crown's own race course, giving them a rather pleasant country-fair quality), Joseph Widener came north and made Belmont a "Hialeah of the North." A betting transaction now took on the impersonal character of a visit to a supermarket. But the pari-mutuel system was in the interest of the public, Widener argued, as he pushed the bill for the legalization of the betting machines at New York racetracks. If there was any question about the sport of racing becoming commercialized, the new method settled that. Since the introduction in 1933 of the pari-mutuel in New York, attendance and betting volume has risen astronomically in those states where racing is legal. In addition, since 1933 the purse distribution in the country has increased from $8,516,325 to $198,500,380 and the aggregate of racing days from 1,746 to 6,624. The sport of kings has in fact become the nation's number one spectator sport.

"In the long years in which father was associated with racing," said Joseph Widener's son, Peter A. B. Widener II, "he engineered many reforms and improvements. He did everything possible to keep racing clean and attractive for the public." Young Peter was not exaggerating. Joseph Widener was indeed a pioneer in the drive to eliminate the practice of drugging horses to effect the results of a race. Not only does the skillful and undetected injection of a needle into a racehorse permit betting coups to be made, it also does violence to the horse. Withdrawal of horses from the drug habit is as painful and as difficult as it is for humans. Sometimes it takes a year or more to get a young mare which has been consistently doped to breed; frequently it causes sterilization in a stallion. When one considers what could happen to expensive stallions such as Dancer's Image, which after winning the Kentucky Derby of 1970 was disqualified for having been drugged, one sees that it is the owners of such horses, such as Widener, and not only the public whose interests are seriously affected by drugging. Widener also successfully fought sponging, a practice that caused one of his horses, named Mister Sponge, to lose a race he should have won because of the insertion of a small sponge in his nostrils to impede his breathing. Camouflaging, or "ringing," is another vice which Widener helped eliminate. This involves sneaking a superior horse into a race camouflaged with the name, color and markings of an inferior horse so that no one will expect the impostor to win, thereby providing the perpetrators with a betting coup at a big payoff.

Elimination of these evils was, as Widener's son claimed, done to "make racing attractive for the public." And no doubt they did. But there was also the matter of the Widener Chute at Belmont Park. This creation of Joseph Widener was a 5½ furlong straightaway that was intended to give green young horses the kind of a straight short sprinting course that two-year-olds require in order to develop. It was wide enough to give a large field of nervous young horses room to bear in and out, and it had no dangerous curves, qualities that made it very attractive to owners who wanted a course on which to test a new two-year-old without risking the horse's safety. But for years the Widener Chute drew ridicule from the ordinary patron and the racing press. The course was laid out in the center of the infield at a distance of what seemed a hundred miles away. In addition to being obscured from view by tote board, it was screened off by haze and miscellaneous horticultural embellishments. This meant that although Widener and his friends in the private viewing areas were in a position to surmount these obstacles with their high-powered binoculars, the two-dollar bettors on the ground had either to bring along a periscope or be twenty feet tall to see what the horses were doing. Finally, the danger of riot growing more real year after year, this example of making racing "attractive for the public" had to be abandoned.

Joseph Widener, like most of the major Eastern racing personalities in the period just after World War I, had a stable in New York. He also had a small breeding operation in Pennsylvania. In addition he raced a string of horses in England and had a stud at Chantilly, France, which he had bought from Prince Murat. But Kentucky and its bluegrass was the promised land for anyone seeking the pinnacle of the thoroughbred world.

With his father dead, Joseph Widener was now his own man, heir to a fortune estimated at $200,000,000, with nothing more pressing to do than manage the Widener estate and its $50,000,000 art collection. And so the butcher's son bought the Elmendorf Stud in Lexington, Kentucky, one of the most prestigious breeding farms in the bluegrass. One of the first things he did with his new acquisition was to scrap a $1,000,000 marble palace built there by James Ali Haggin, leaving only the great Doric columns which formed part of the façade, and the broad marble steps which led to it. This was done to provide an appropriate setting for a horse cemetery that he planned to design. Then, as though to be in a position eventually to furnish the cemetery with occupants of commensurate stature, he bought three stallions, sixty-four mares and thirty-six weanlings from the fashionable stable of August Belmont II, including Fair Play, the sire of Man o' War. In one stride Joe Widener, suspect in his credentials to Philadelphia society, had qualified to be the American host of thoroughbred racing's first lord from across the sea, the Earl of Derby himself.

Edward George Villiers Stanley, the seventeenth Earl of Derby, spoke like Rudyard Kipling, looked like John Bull and bestrode a horse like a son of Victoria and Albert. The earls of Derby traced back to 1483. In 1782 one of the earls established what was to be the world's most important horserace, the Derby at Epsom, named after what was then the Empire's most distinguished racing family. From that time forward all the Derbies in the world—from roller skate to Kentucky—were to be beholden to the earl for their name. Further, one of the most telling arguments against the theory that the best bloodlines make the best racehorses is that, for all their having the foremost stud and the best pedigrees in the world, the Lords Derby couldn't win one of their own Derbies in a period stretching from 1787 to 1924, when the seventeenth earl finally won it with Sansovino.

When Lord Derby came in 1930 to see the Kentucky race that was named after his family, it was Joseph E. Widener who was assigned his host. Mr. Widener showed the Earl his possessions, his private railroad car, his incredible art collection (many paintings of which had been bought from strapped British nobility) and, of course, his Elmendorf Farm.

During his visit, the Earl, impeccably well-mannered, also demonstrated a very British sense of humor: "About this kind of hat I'm wearing," said the earl to Colonel Matt Winn, the P. T. Barnum of the horseracing world. "It's not the same as with your race here at Churchill Downs. My family was, of course, responsible for the name of the race . . . but not the hat. Besides, I wasn't aware that you called it 'darby', that is, we would call it 'darby' if it were named after us. But it's a billycock, really, named after Billy Cooke, the first gentleman to wear a derby."

The earl saw Gallant Fox, one of America's Triple Crown winners, triumph in the Kentucky Derby; lunched with President Hoover in the White House; and climaxed his trip by addressing the Pilgrim Society in Boston at the approximate moment that Mahatma Gandhi was being jailed by the British government. Bostonians, whose colonial ancestors were driven out of England in 1620 by Lord Derby's compatriots, applauded his speech on world peace, even though the Colonial Office had just imprisoned the world's most dedicated advocate of non-violence. Reaction among Lord Derby's American friends was strong, however, against the commoners in Parliament who had the temenity after his long service in public affairs—such as helping consolidate the Empire in Africa—to levy taxes on inherited wealth. This moved *The New York Times* to editorialize:

> Those who met Lord Derby when in this country will feel special regret that he has been compelled to sell a good part of his famous stable. The reason is that same heavy pressure of taxation which has compelled so many rich men in England either to economize severely or part with some of their treasures. None of these things will, of course, move Chancellor Snowden, who will take them as a satisfactory proof that his scheme to make those pay who have is working well.

Another famous English horseman also once gave up his stud, not because he too was taxed beyond endurance but because public affairs took all his time. Lord George Bentinck had sold all his racehorses when he entered politics. Not long afterward he had word that Surplice, one of the horses he had disposed of, had just won the Epsom Derby. On hearing the news, Lord Bentinck, as Disraeli recorded in the biography of his friend, gave a "sort of superb groan" and immediately returned to his desk. In England, where the first families not only raced but governed, the duties of empire tended to take much of the pleasure out of the sport of kings.

"That's the way things are at home these days," complained the earl to Joseph Widener as he boarded the *Aquitania* for the trip home. "We'd like to have them the way you have them here. But at Epsom Downs, for instance, there are 260 commoners who must now be consulted and made to agree before we can move a brick."

As an art collector Joseph Widener displayed the same acumen for developing (exploiting) the product as he had with horses. The purchase of a major segment of August Belmont's stable had given him a formidable racing and breeding stock (some of which he immediately resold at sizeable profit); the death of his father had placed in his hands a major part of the output of the world's master artists.

Artistic creations of the world's great minds and talents tended to become, in the Widener view, "products," something on which to set a price. Two Turners, for instance, which he had seen on one of his European art hunts, became the subject of cablegrams back and forth across the Atlantic like so many buy-and-sell offers on the soybean futures market. Joe liked them at the price; his father back in Philadelphia thought that no Turner on earth was worth the asking money. Joe insisted that they were a bargain not to be passed up; father finally yielded with permission to close the deal, adding two more fine trophies for the showroom at Lynnewood Hall—two, in fact, of Turner's most valuable—"Keelman Heaving in Coals by Moonlight" and "Venice," subjects that called to mind respectively the product from which Wideners culled a fortune and the place where they vacationed on its fruit.

It was with Rembrandts, however, that the Wideners had their biggest success. Peter managed to buy up at least a dozen of the Dutchman's best creations, including his most famous, "The Mill." Hearing that its owner, the Marquis of Landsdowne, was in sufficient economic straits to think about selling the painting, the founder Widener decided that he wanted to cap his Rembrandt collection with the master's finest. In 1911, he made an offer. But, in what provided one of the most sensational art news stories in history, the British people rose to protest the treasure leaving the country. Counter-offers were solicited from the National Gallery in London, public subscriptions were suggested to raise the necessary funds. Time and money, however, were on the Widener side. The cash was not available by deadline time. To give even more notoriety to the whole business, the great masterpiece had hardly been set in place at Lynnewood Hall when, from among a group of visitors to the gallery, a woman ("who must have been a little mad") suddenly emerged and began slashing at the painting with a hatpin. The reason for her outrageous act was a mystery, though some felt it an act of protest against Widener presumption.

The race for "The Mill," however, was by no means the end of the Wideners' forays into the international Rembrandt market. There was the equally sensational Prince Youssopoff case, in which Joe Widener procured two Rembrandts in a manner that would have made his father proud.

Joseph Widener had for a long time been on the trail of two marvelour Rembrandts—"A Gentleman with a High Hat, Gloves in His Left Hand" and "A Lady with an Ostrich Feather in Her Right Hand." The paintings had been owned by the Youssopoffs for a hundred years. When the Russian Revolution broke out, Prince Felix Youssopoff fled to Paris with the Rembrandts, leaving behnd his $305,000,000 fortune, his castles and his Cossacks. In no time Joe Widener quickly made him an offer for the Rembrandts. He induced the pressed émigré to part with the paintings with the promise that he could redeem them by repaying the purchase price with eight percent interest "if he found himself able again to keep and personally enjoy these wonderful works of art"—a shrewd gamble on a man waiting for a counter-revolution to return his estates.

Prince Youssopoff somehow got enough money to redeem his paintings, but Widener contended in court that since the prince had borrowed the money he was not "able to keep and personally enjoy" the paintings. And besides, he insisted, the prince well knew what he was signing, that he'd gotten a bargain by then current market prices and that a contract was a contract. The prince rejoined that under the laws of England, where the contract was consummated, or even under the laws of Widener's home state of Pennsylvania, where negotiations began, the financial ability of the prince to keep the paintings for his own use would not be sufficient reason for foreclosure. Mr. Widener replied that the prince had "borrowed the money from one C. S. Gulbenkian . . . and if he regained the Rembrandts he intended to turn them over to Mr. Gulbenkian. . . ."

The contest for the works of art continued until finally New York's Court of Appeals sustained the lower tribunal decision in Joseph Widener's favor. The prince's lone satisfaction would have to rest with his compatriots' snubbing of Widener heirs who might seek entrée to aristocratic émigré circles in Paris.

In 1940, the entire Widener Collection, the greatest private art hoard in the world, among it the two Youssopoff Rembrandts, was given to The National Gallery of Art in Washington, an institution endowed by Andrew Mellon, a onetime partner of the founder of the Widener dynasty. The Widener family felt that "such a gift to the nation is one small step in the direction of disarming those individuals and ideologies that are foreign to the American way. Every true American," said Joseph E. Widener's son, Peter II, "wants to stamp out the 'isms' here as a builder would a nest of termites. The meaning of the gift goes beyond any generosity implied in it. It is in practical compliance with the trend of the day. It is another evidence that democracy, in its fullest scope, is working to preserve the fine arts and culture."

Others would take note that the Widener dynasty has always, like most Americans, been keenly aware of another fact of democratic life, namely, the Internal Revenue Service in Washington, D.C. Unlike most Americans, the Wideners were in a position to do something about it, and not only in the art field. In 1927, Joseph E. Widener, who "always wanted to share the enjoyment of his treasures with as many people as possible," went to the courts to be reimbursed for several hundred thousand tax dollars on the grounds that he had incurred at least equivalent losses in his effort to improve the breed of horses. On another occasion he was fined several hundred dollars for not declaring a watch that he had brought in from Europe. One wonders about the extent of tax savings involved in the estimated $50,000,000 of European art that was "given" to the American people.

CHAPTER 12

Third Generation: George D. Widener, Jr. (1889-1971)

"I think this sort of thing gives a very wrong impression of racing," stated George D. Widener, as he refused to have his horse isolated in a receiving barn and placed under guard prior to a race. "It tends to mislead the public into wondering if everyone connected with racing is not dishonest."

—From *The Thoroughbred Record*

José Ortega y Gasset, in his *Meditations on Hunting*, has written: "The life we are given has its minutes numbered and, in addition, it is given to us empty. Whether we like it or not we have to fill it on our own; that is, we have to occupy it one way or another. Thus the essence of each life lies in its occupations." The animal, he goes on to point out, is given not only life, but also an unchanging repertory of conduct. His instincts have already decided what he is going to do and what he is going to avoid. He is therefore completely programmed for life, with none of the problems of emptiness and so cannot be said to occupy himself with one thing or another. "But man," Ortega continues, "is an animal that has lost his system of instincts, retaining only instinctual stumps and residual elements incapable of imposing on him a plan of behavior. Thus it is said that when man becomes aware of existence, he also becomes aware of terrifying emptiness. He does not know what to do; he must invent his own occupations."

For the first and second generations of the Widener dynasty this need to invent an activity presented no problem. Peter I had an empire to build and he occupied a lifetime building and preserving it. Second generation Joseph Widener busied himself developing the popularity of racing, hunting Rembrandts, Fair Plays and acceptance by the elusive society of Mainline Philadelphia; the founding Peter's other son, George, and his son the rare-book hunter, Harry Elkins Widener, went down on the *Titanic,* which concluded their life problems.

But the third generation Wideners—George, Jr., and Peter II—were vulnerable to that emptiness of which Ortega spoke. Both were tall, blue-eyed, handsome facsimiles of the American Anglo-Saxon aristocrat, bred from their fathers' intermarriage with Pancoasts and Duntons. They had two generations of immense wealth behind them. They had been raised by a corps of French nannies in an American Versailles adorned with Rembrandts and Van Dykes. The family had the first Daimler in the Philadelphia area (as early as 1898) and George himself drove his own electric surrey to school at the age of eleven; Peter's broken toys were, in his words, "quickly replaced with the latest, most expensive new gadgets."

Each, however, had a diametrically opposite orientation toward that objet d'art that has succored and occupied so many lives not motivated by conventional needs of getting and surviving. Peter, whose father, Joseph, was one of the leading horsemen in the world —vice-chairman of The Jockey Club, president of Belmont and Hialeah, confidant of Lord Derby himself—could not abide horses. "I never went near our racing stables nor the racetrack," he said. "I talked art with Father but kept silent when horses were the topic. It was a sore point between us for many years. It hurt him very much."

George, on the other hand, whose father had shown little interest in horses, seemed to live for nothing but the thoroughbred. George D. Widener was the compleat career man in racing, one whose activities as owner, breeder, leader and curator spanned over six decades. If any man should have been entombed with his horses it was George D. Widener. He was the perfect embodiment of a knight of the horsey set—an "exemplar" of racing, as he is memorialized in the National Museum of Racing in Saratoga Springs.

George D. Widener looked like a thoroughbred. He was tall, fair, blue-eyed, with a John Barrymore profile and the lean figure of the Swedish tennis-playing king. His clothes and his manner always eminently suited his image of courtly cavalier: elegant fedora cocked at just the right angle, ready to be tipped gently and gracefully at the ladies; the suit, furnishings and shoes the quietest and best from the most exclusive London shops. George slipped effortlessly into the milieu of a future Jockey Club chairman.

With only his uncle Joe providing any kind of racing tradition in the Widener family, twenty-three-year-old George enthusiastically entered the sport in 1912—the year his father went down on the *Titanic*—with the purchase of a stallion and some broodmares from Kentucky. He registered his light and dark blue hoop silks in 1913 and was elected to The Jockey Club in 1916. That was the year that members of the Widener family having their annual fling in Europe had to be rescued from the threat of the Germans along with their stable of expatriate thoroughbreds. It was also the year that George purchased an historic old stud farm near Philadelphia with the German-sounding name of Erdenheim, which had been the home of the great stallion, Leamington, and the birthplace of Iriquois, the first American winner of the Epsom Derby. He immediately set about to make it a proper showplace. He brought his broodmares up from Kentucky, imported a fashionable French stallion and remodelled the house so that from his veranda he could "command a view of the entire property, with the barns and track well within the range of vision."

Meantime, he drew his weekly paycheck from the Widener Estate, a self-perpetuating conglomerate of American equities which is said to have yielded the Widener heirs some $70,000,000 in income alone. Some of this went into the purchase of a nameless but pedigreed yearling thoroughbred at the Saratoga Sales. A year later, the yearling, now named St. James, put George Widener into the first rank of American racing as a winner of the Belmont Futurity. A few years later, now in Kentucky with a piece of his uncle Joe's famous old Elmendorf Farm, he was now a serious breeder, and the trade press reported, "Mlle. Dazie, a daughter of Fair Play, dropped a foal to St. James' service which strongly resembled his sire and which appeared to have inherited his speed." Jamestown, the son, was even faster than the sire and also won the Futurity. This made St. James one of a select list of three Futurity winners, alongside Scapa Flow and Man o' War, to sire a Futurity winner. From 1923, when St. James won the Futurity, until 1970, horses owned by George Widener earned nearly $10,000,000 and won practically every great race except the Kentucky Derby.

Widener's blank record in the Kentucky Derby resulted from a peculiar sentiment. He was a lifelong crusader against over-exploitation of the horse. Accordingly, since he felt that spring, the season when the Derby is run, is too early in the year to expect a three-year-old to run a distance of one-and-a-quarter miles, he never entered a horse in the nation's most famous classic. He was stubborn, some thought to the point of sentimentality, in his complaints about the abuse of horses.

"How long has it been since you saw horses walked and grazed in the quiet of the stable-yards afternoons," he would complain to trainers who kept their horses in the claustrophobic confines of a stall except for an hour or two of exercise. "How long since you saw trainers line up a set of horses on the track, to be saddled for their gallops and work there, and be rubbed out before returning to their stables?"

George D. Widener, even more than his family predecessor in racing, Joseph Widener, was totally committed to the horses both as an administrator and as an owner. His uncle had, as his biography in the National Museum of Racing states, "two all-consuming hobbies: art and racing." George Widener had only one consuming interest, the horse.

The question was to arise as to whether George Widener's racing activities were in fact totally a hobby, or whether they were a business—an occupation engaged in for profit. This was an issue that shy, gentle George Widener himself, who so loved horses, pressed into the courts of the land. He was joined by his uncle, who suddenly reversed the claim of his biographer that he raced as an all-consuming hobby. A *New York Times* dispatch from Washington, October 12, 1927, reported:

WIDENERS TO DEDUCT $800,000 IN TAXES

The United States Board of Tax Appeals, in a decision made public today, ruled that Joseph E. Widener and George D. Widener of Pennsylvania could deduct from taxable income for the years 1919 to 1922 about $403,000 as a result of losses which they suffered in the conduct of racing stables, and also charge off necessary expenses which may swell the total to double that amount.

They had contended that these were business losses, properly deductible, and the Commissioner of Internal Revenue had refused their plea.

Joseph E. Widener, whose residence is given as Elkins Park, Montgomery County, Pa., according to the decision, owned and operated horseracing and breeding stables which he had started about twenty years ago. His breeding stables were in Kentucky and his horses-in-training were quartered at Belmont Park and Elkins Park. Mr. Widener stated that he took an active part in the management and devoted a large portion of his time to that work. He did not bet on the races, the decision added.

The claim of George D. Widener for tax relief had to do only with the year 1919. His breeding stables, started in 1916, were at Chestnut Hill, outside Philadelphia, and his horses-in-training were quartered at Belmont Park. He stated that he devoted more time to his racing stables than to his other interests.

It was stated also in the decision that while Mr. Widener had hoped to make a profit he had, in fact, sustained a loss during every year of operation, ranging from $30,000 to $79,000.

The ruling, written by Commissioner Sternhagen and accepted by a majority of the board, held that the conduct of a racing and breeding stable in the circumstances involved in this case constituted a business and that the expenses and losses were deductible from taxable income in computing the tax.

Six members of the Board of Tax Appeals dissented from part of the majority decision which made the losses and expenses of the racing stables deductible.

The ruling was later sustained by the Federal Court of Appeals in Philadelphia in June 1929, a landmark decision that became the foundation upon which the modern sport of kings rests. Henceforth spokesmen had a right, under the free enterprise system, to deduct the costs of a sporting activity which they might claim to be a hobby —except when addressing the Internal Revenue Service.

From that day in 1927, signalling the epoch of the "tax shelter," billions of dollars have been written off in the breeding and racing of horses as a business. George D. Widener, attempting to reconcile and make everything perfectly clear, went on for nearly forty-five more years referring to his occupation as "the sport of the business of racing."

"My activities are racing," he declared in an interview in *The Blood-Horse*. "It has always been that way because I was fortunate enough to be in a position to make it so. I did not seek it, but once that was the fact, it seemed to be a useful and creditable way of life. I have devoted most of my adult life to just that. Although I am on the board of several corporations, my chief interest has been the turf and its improvement. I am hopeful that this will be considered of value."

Surely his life was not without satisfaction. He was president of Belmont Park and the National Museum of Racing. He was an "exemplar" of racing, and was honored by jockeys, turf writers and ordinary horsemen in addition to his peers in the Thoroughbred Club and the Turf & Field Club. He was also chairman of The Jockey Club.

Perhaps most impressive of all he (with his wife) won over 1,200 races and had bred 100 stakes winners in his lifetime. One of these was Jaipur, the most spectacular horse he had ever bred, which won for him his first and only Belmont Stakes in 1962. Another was Crewman, who raced as a three-year-old the following year.

"Crewman is a magnificent-looking colt—stands nearly 16-2, I would guess," said Mr. Widener, with the pride of a parent, in the *Blood-Horse* interview. "He's in marvelous condition for this time of year. He has such beautiful action, you know."

"Does Crewman have the kind of temperament that Jaipur exhibited last year when he refused to be led onto the track and had to be sent to the farm for a rest?"

"No such temperament, no temperament at all," Mr. Widener said with a laugh. "There's no Nasrullah in him, you know."

Crewman was a son of Sailor; two other Sailor colts were ranked along with Crewman as among the ten top colts in the country.

This was a matter in which Mr. Widener took great pride. "Sailor—that's my own breeding, you know." Then recalling that Sailor was by Eight Thirty—another of his own stallions—and that his dam, Flota, was a Jack High mare, he added with an even greater note of pride: "I guess Sailor is the best that Eight Thirty ever got."

George Widener died in 1971, at the age of eighty-two, in his mansion next to Henry Frick's museum on Fifth Avenue in New York. He had spent most of his adult life raising his "family" according to the strictest standards.

"Mr. Widener had a thing about family," said Sylvester Veitch, one of his trainers. "He never bugged or badgered you about his horses. But he'd come over to the stables in the morning and you'd bring out the new ones for him to look at. He was a very dignified man, you know—if he didn't like the looks of any particular one, he'd never raise a row. All he'd do was turn his head away and say 'skunk.' That meant the horse didn't have the family resemblances that he held so dear. He wouldn't say so, but you knew you'd have to get rid of that horse. Made no difference if you thought he had racing potential or not—he had this thing about family."

George D. Widener himself was a childless man.

CHAPTER 13

Peter A. B. Widener II

(1896-1948)

"The real aristocrat is never a snob. This is a lesson I have well learned through the years, a lesson mother first taught me."
—Peter A. B. Widener II

For cousin George, who came from exactly the same background, the horsey life was a great joy, but for Peter A. B. Widener II it was, as mentioned, a chore from which he spent more than half his life trying to disassociate himself. Perhaps if his father, Joseph, had not been so fascinated by horses young Peter might not have found it necessary to rebel against his tradition. But Joseph Widener had little time for his family and particularly for his son. French governesses attended his upbringing so that by the time he was ten he was that rarity: a Philadelphia boy that spoke French like a Frenchman. Until he was thirteen, he had never set foot in a school either public or private. And when he finally did he was sorry.

"I wasn't happy at school," he said, speaking of his days at the exclusive Chestnut Hill Academy. "I was homesick and lonely. I did not get on well with other boys. I was shy and ill at ease with boys my own age. All my life had been spent with grownups."

Even after he entered Chestnut Hill his life was one of constant trips back and forth to Europe with his mother, who required special fittings from her French couturiers. As a result Peter was almost always in the company of his mother, and his education, as his father futilely protested, was dependent on his mother's fancies in fashion. "I just won't go without him, and I'm going," she declared to her husband on the eve of each trip. When he went on to St. Marks, a favorite preparatory school of socially prominent American families, Peter, to protect his delicate health, was chauffeur-driven to classes on the order of his grandfather.

It is hardly surprising that Peter's youth would be spent in rebelling against his father—and in making a special point of disliking that which his father held so dear: the thoroughbred horse. (Payne Whitney had had something of the same reaction against his own father a generation earlier.) Young Peter took to hiding out in the barns of Lynnewood Farm, part of the acreage of the Widener Estate that was devoted to supplying delicacies for the family table. Lynnewood Hall had its own agricultural division, its own power plants, upholstery shops, and other services. In the poultry barns Peter learned to raise and handle game cocks; often he would enter his chickens in local cockfights.

"I and George [the chicken foreman] moved among the crowds with our birds in our baskets or under our arms," he said. "I felt as exhilarated as the prince who used to walk the streets at night incognito. I was as dirty as the other boys there, and my clothes were as patched."

He also became expert at killing and plucking chickens. Occasionally one of his broilers would be served up to the family at dinner.

"That's one of my chickens," Peter would exclaim proudly on such occasions.

"Disgusting!" his father would respond, having little sympathy with his son's agricultural devotions. "Almost takes your appetite away!"

Young Peter saw nothing Oedipal in his dislike of horses. Rather, he attributed his antipathy to falling on his head in a spill from a horse, while taking riding lessons prescribed by his father.

"I never forgot that spill," he said, "and neither did mother. She was very much in charge where her son was concerned, so I never took another riding lesson."

Peter was at Harvard at the time of the outbreak of the "war to save democracy." And it was there, he later said, that he learned his first lessons in democracy. This came about when he discovered that some students at Harvard actually worked at odd jobs to pay their way through college. It made him ashamed when, during a trip home, his father suggested he have his own car at Harvard.

"No, dad, it looks too, well, it looks—oh, pshaw, it doesn't look right for a freshman to have a car when some fellows don't even have enough to eat up there."

In any event Peter volunteered for military service, perhaps as a means of escaping from paternal dominance. He tried to enlist in an ambulance unit that was going to France, and was turned down because of flat feet, his first experience in being denied something he wanted. Nonetheless, he was determined to go to war. After a visit of the senior Widener to the office of the Surgeon-General in Washington, Peter had a physical waiver and was on his way as a buck private in a sanitary unit headed for France.

Despite his no doubt genuine yearning to carry a rifle in the midst of action, Peter's tour of duty remained only, as he put it, "a matter of carrying out slops from a base hospital and marketing in French villages for food for the unit mess." He tried his best to get to the front but, after twenty months of service, his only experience of it was as a tourist in a reconnoitering flight over the Vosges district on a morning near the end of the war. The closest he came to being under fire was in a bombardment of the working-class section of Paris by the Germans while he was on furlough at the Ritz. Nevertheless, he at least managed to move forward in the war. He was promoted to the rank of sergeant by virtue of his proficiency in French. And before his discharge he had been commissioned a first lieutenant in the Sanitary Corps.

"I was as elated as a kid with the promotion," he said. "I wrote home at once, requesting immediate shipment of six sterling silver bars, insignia of my new rank. War or not, the old habits were still strong upon me. French silver was of poor quality and bent easily. 'Always the best,' was father's motto. So I wrote the family to get the best they could buy."

Back home at Lynnewood Hall at age twenty-four, Peter A. B. Widener II told his mother, "There are no trees left to climb, nothing to do but watch the golden waves lapping about me. Muzzie, I can't take it, I am going mad."

To save himself Peter escaped from Lynnewood Hall—which for his grandfather was a home, for his father a palace, and for him a mausoleum. This time Peter progressed in his concerns from two-legged to four-legged creatures (could the horse be far behind!) as he commenced to breed and show German shepherd dogs.

Dog breeding and showing has been an occupation second only to horseracing among those socially and financially well fixed. A kennel of dogs keeps one busy and provides a family of sorts, an extension of one's identity. Ego gratification comes from blue ribbons, cups and trophies; glory from the approbation of one's peers. Social life takes on meaning not to be found in the relatively aimless routine of parties, charity bazaars and global excursions. One hurries back and forth to competitions all over the country, even the world, with one's friends in the "dog show crowd," even if not on so grand a scale nor perhaps with as much publicity as with the horsey set (though the two are by no means mutually exclusive).

During the course of Peter's moving about the world, breeding, showing and judging his specialty, German police dogs, he met a fellow dog-show enthusiast, Gertrude Peabody, of New York and Albany. Gertrude not only had the type of social background that would please father Joseph Widener, but she also loved horses and horseracing. In addition she had the kind of independence that would stand up to his father's arrogance. It was as though Peter had instantly purged his parental problem through Gertrude Peabody. He fell very much in love with this woman, who also loved horses. "It was as if," he said, "I had met my second self that day."

They were married at Lynnewood Hall, which Peter had previously so often tried to escape. Joe Widener wanted the ceremony to take place under the Sargent portrait of his father in the Van Dyke Room, but Peter insisted it be performed in the Rembrandt Room, right between the two Youssopoffs.

With Gertrude at his side, Peter Widener did an abrupt turnabout. No longer did he wince at the statement that horses were more important than dogs, or that his own hobby ran a pale second to his father's. He simply and finally made his father's passion his own. It came relatively late in his life—he was twenty-eight—but now, in more ways than one, he had come home.

What triggered Peter's entrance into his father's world was a visit to his father's stud farm in Kentucky in 1925. Up to that point he had always used the bluegrass showplace as an occasional hideaway from the café society life he led. On this particular visit his father prevailed upon him to attend a thoroughbred auction. August Belmont's stud was being dispersed to settle his estate, and Joe Widener bought one of the stallions. It was Fair Play, sire of Man o' War.

"The course of our lives," said Peter Widener in recalling that afternoon, "had been changed by a golden horse. I'll never forget him as he stood in the sales ring. The bright Kentucky sun streamed down upon him, burnishing his chestnut sides as if with gilt. He looked like a king, and he acted more autocratically than any dictator. The energy of the twenty-year-old horse, his royal impatience, got me. Then, too, it was a touching thing to see how well loved he was. Members of the many families that had had a hand in the raising and training of Fair Play wept openly as the great horse was auctioned off. Tears streamed down the faces of old men and boys who had tended Fair Play in the twenty years of his life."

Peter Widener was now hooked for life. He entered into a partnership with his father for the racing and breeding of thoroughbreds. He pondered pedigree, studied farm managment, acquainted himself with training details. In two years he had, with his father, his first entry in the Kentucky Derby, Osmond, who, although he won many other important races, was beaten in a hairbreadth finish by Whiskery, the horse that had changed Sonny Whitney's life.

It was on the racetrack that Peter A. B. Widener II decided he had found the fulfillment of his democratic instincts awakened at Harvard and in World War I.

"At Belmont Park and Hialeah and Saratoga and Churchill Downs I get 'Pete' from nearly everybody," he said. "I love the track because it is the most democratic place on earth. Racing has been called the sport of kings. It used to be called a rich man's game. But that's not the slant I take on it. The fraternity of the racing crowd includes every fellow, rich and poor alike. . . ."

Describing this new democratic life, Peter noted that it required his following the "luck of our thoroughbreds from one January to the next, up and down America and across the Atlantic Ocean. Your life pounds along a hard-beaten path that starts with Hialeah Park in January, with February and March ticking their days away on the famous Miami track. In April, or earlier, you head for Kentucky. If you have a stud farm there, you spend long contented days watching your young hopefuls getting their workouts for the Kentucky Derby, which is the first big spring stake. The end of May you pack up again. Off to Belmont Park this time, with a couple of freight cars for the horses and tack and feed you have to take along as luggage. Belmont over, you sail for Europe—or you did before the war. You decided whether it was to be France or England. Unfortunately, big racing events in both countries have always been at the same time. So one summer you made it to France with stops at Chantilly, Maisons-LaFitte, Longchamps, and Deauville, the French Saratoga. Next summer you switched to England with a trek to Ascot, Epsom Downs, and Newmarket. You hurried back to America in August. You wouldn't miss Saratoga for anything. And, of course, the big fall season of Belmont comes in September."

During the course of his nearly quarter century in the world of the thoroughbred, Peter Widener conducted himself like a prodigal son returned home. He succeeded his father as president of Hialeah Park on Joseph's retirement in 1939, purchased Elmendorf Farm when Joseph died in 1943. The equine cemetery that his father had laid out there was now filled with heroes of the racing wars. Mahupah, Man o' War's dam, had been bought by Joseph Widener chiefly for the purpose of interring her beside Fair Play, his sire. The perennial collector had been trying to effect coups to the very last. And there the parents of the world's most famous horse now rested without, however, their renowned son, whom Joe Widener had hoped to acquire but could not. Most of the other noteworthy occupants, however, were those of his father, not Peter's, for, although the son devoted himself wholeheartedly to racing, his record was not particularly outstanding. One exception was in the case of Hurry Off, who won the Belmont Stakes for him—a signal achievement for Peter, since his father had from the beginning denigrated the horse's chances.

Another success was Polynesian. The horse, who as a yearling Peter had presented to Gertrude on their wedding anniversary in 1943, seemed an unlikely prospect, for all of his breeding. He had to be weaned on cow's milk when his dam died shortly after giving birth. He also contracted a mysterious toxic blood condition that partly paralyzed his hindquarters and halted his two-year racing campaign after three starts. In addition, he became so listless that he took to leaning motionless against the sides of his stall or even a tree. As if all this were not affliction enough, only two weeks after his arrival at his stable he was attacked by a nest of hornets that sent him on a frantic twenty-minute sprint. But he always came back to deliver brilliantly. Returning to the race course as a two-year-old, he won the Sagamore Stakes. The following year he defeated the previously unbeaten Pavot in the Withers Stakes and won the Preakness over Kentucky Derby winner, Hoop, Jr. At four Polynesian had equaled the world record of 1.09⅕ seconds for six furlongs and at five he was voted champion sprinter.

Peter Widener was not to enjoy the honor of Polynesian's greatest achievement—the siring of contemporary America's most popular horse (until Secretariat), Native Dancer, Alfred G. Vanderbilt's gray flash which swept across the front pages and television screens of the 1950s. Still a young man at fifty-two, he died of heart disease in 1948 at Lankenau Hospital in Philadelphia.

CHAPTER 14

Peter A. B. Widener III (1926-)

"No, I haven't a college education, and it's nobody's fault but my own."
—Peter A. B. Widener III to Hugh McGuire of the *Morning Telegraph*

Peter A. B. Widener III is furthest removed of the major Widener scions in "point of time" from the founding father, and yet in his fashion is perhaps most like him. Seated on a sofa in his home on Lake Worth in Palm Beach, Florida, the county sheriff rolled up his shirt sleeves, shifted the gun in his hip holster to a more comfortable position, and said, "Okay, fire away." The bespectacled round-faced young man was being interviewed by the New York *Sunday News* on his appointment as chief lawman of Palm Beach County. The sheriff's jailhouse office was no doubt adequate for the occasion, but the sitting room at his Lake Worth estate was considerably more commodious than the county lockup. The Doberman pinschers could lope about without toppling the police files, the estate manager could muddy the household Persian rug with his boots instead of soiling the county's freshly waxed linoleum, and his wife could could wander in with the house guests down from Newport, bringing tea and talk and hints of the still-wet painting in her adjoining studio.

Pistol Packin' Pete, Richest Gun in the East, as Peter A. B. Widener III was called in Palm Beach during his tenure as county sheriff, is the son and heir of Peter A. B. Widener II. The fourth-generation scion of the Philadelphia dynasty might be expected to carry on the thoroughbred traditions of his family, and in his fashion he does.

At forty-seven he is the only Widener in The Jockey Club, although there are also a number of family in-laws on the roster. He still has a racing and breeding establishment—modest in comparison with the great days of his grandfather's Elmendorf Farm, most of which young Peter disposed of. Alternately over the last twenty or so years, since he took over his father's farm and stable, Peter III has returned to racing after temporarily leaving it for pursuits such as cattle raising in Florida and Montana. Elmendorf, which he inherited at twenty-three as "Little Pete," made its way down from the old American adventurer, James Ben Ali Haggin, to Joe Widener to Peter II, and then from him to Peter III and on to a combination of Tinkham Veale II and Sam Costello. It finally wound up in the hands of mercantile tycoon Max Gluck, an Ambassador to Ceylon (who, on taking office, had difficulty in recalling the prime minister's name).

Even though Peter III has and still does run a racing and breeding operation, the way he permitted a traditional, revered thoroughbred institution such as Elmendorf to slip from family hands is indication that this particular Widener is something different.

His father pointed out in the story of the "blue plate" dinner that the maverick started at an early age.

"Pete . . . and Ella . . . have not been brought up as I was," wrote the elder Widener in his autobiography. "They have been raised to value democracy more than all the money in the world. . . . I was proud of Pete on one occasion when he was twelve years old, and we allowed him to take a train from Newark to Philadelphia by himself. We gave him money for the trip, and when he got in I asked him for an accounting. He poured the money left over into my hands. It was much more than I expected.

" 'How come you have so much, Peter?' I asked him.

" 'I came down on the day coach, Dad.'

" 'What?'

" 'Yes, it's a lot more fun than that stuffy old Pullman. You ought to try it some time.'

" 'But what about dinner?'

" 'Oh, I took the blue-plate. Saves ordering.' "

Ella, on the other hand, apparently did value certain non-egalitarian rites despite her lessons in democracy; her coming-out party at the Bellevue-Stratford Hotel in Philadelphia was tabled at $100,000. She also is a leading figure in that annual select celebration, the Belmont Ball, and operates a stable both in Kentucky and in Ireland.

Like his father, young Peter did not have a formal education. He went into the army at eighteen, and later, when his father died, dropped out of the University of Kentucky to manage the Widener estate.

Whitney Stone (for more on him, please see a subsequent chapter on Saratoga), a member of The Jockey Club and one of the nation's richest men, can hardly wait to get to Saratoga each August to display his uniform as deputy sheriff of Albemarle County, Virginia. Over in Maryland, Samuel F. DuPont takes time out from overseeing his 1000-acre horse farm to patrol as Cecil County Sheriff. But few have hankered more after the policeman's uniform or been so committed as Peter A. B. Widener III.

"I had trouble with coon hunters running over the property," he told Theo Wilson of the New York *Sunday News,* referring to his farm in Kentucky. "So I was made a deputy constable and that was when I first became interested in law enforcement."

After he was appointed Sheriff of Palm Beach County, Widener was appointed chief of the Fayette Country patrol, to command a force of twenty. The question of bonding the new chief presented no problem, it was the first time in history that a company that was bonding a policeman had less money than its client.

Meanwhile Widener took time out to marry Louise Brownell van Meter of Lexington, Kentucky; another Peter Widener was born, Peter IV, in addition to a new George Widener. Also, his thoroughbred activities were not being totally neglected; he still had a breeding and racing operation worthy of the Widener name, in addition to owning a share in Leslie Comb's syndication of the great Woodward horse, Nashua.

Still, Peter A. B. Widener II remained something of an oddity. In 1956, when he was only thirty, he was appointed Kentucky State Police Commissioner by Governor A. B. ("Happy") Chandler, and now he commanded 143 troopers. Later, with Chandler, he created Kentucky's Department of Public Safety to coordinate all state police agencies.

When Louise divorced him in 1958, Peter quit policing temporarily and acquired a 70,000-acre ranch in Montana to raise cattle.

"My police job had nothing to do with the divorce. I resigned while I was having domestic difficulties because I think a law enforcement officer cannot work efficiently if he does not have a happy home life. There is too much pressure in the work." . . .

Peter A. B. Widener III moves around quite a bit, not so much in the manner of other Wideners who generally go straight toward some well-defined goal, but rather in the zig-zag fashion of a man pursuing a will-o-the-wisp. He returned to Florida with a new wife, the former Patricia Massie, and acquired a 1200-acre horse farm at Ocala, the newest of the country's breeding centers. But more than ever, there was his police work. He was now the sheriff of Palm Beach County.

"Don't get me wrong, I don't dislike the money part of it." What worried him was that he did not want people to think a millionaire sheriff was anything like a playboy sheriff.

Peter A. B. Widener III may be considered by some complete maverick—a Democrat instead of a Republican; a sheriff instead of full-time society *maven;* and, heresy of heresies, a horseman who believes that fast horses are made not born, that environment is more important than breeding.

Considering that the founding Peter was a butcher looking in from the outside at the Rittenhouse Square long noses, who is to say that familial history doesn't perhaps confirm his theory?

Above, left: Henry Phipps, founder of the powerful Phipps horse dynasty. He also built an $800 investment into a $50,000,000 steel fortune.

Above, right: Bold Ruler, owned by Mrs. Henry Carnegie Phipps, is the sire of Secretariat. He is shown here with Eddie Arcaro up.

Below: Mrs. Henry Carnegie Phipps and her brother Ogden Livingston Mills, Herbert Hoover's Secretary of the Treasury.

Above, right: Mrs. Winston F. C. ("Cee Zee") Guest, presenting a plate to owner George Lewis (far right) with trainer Eugene Jacobs and jockey Conn McCreary looking on. She is the daughter-in-law of Phipps doyenne, Amy Phipps Guest. A nude painting of Cee Zee by the famed muralist Diego Rivera was found hanging in a Mexican bar.

Above, left: Ogden Phipps, present chairman of The Jockey Club and current head of the Phipps dynasty.

Right: Mrs. Marian DuPont Scott, "Dowager Queen of the American Turf," (center) at the Washington, D.C. International. Mrs. Scott, once married to actor Randolph Scott, is the last surviving member of the once-powerful DuPont racing dynasty that is still active in the sport on a large scale. Liz Whitney Tippett is at far right.

Above, right: James E. ("Sunny Jim") Fitzsimmons, who died at the age of 91 on March 11, 1966, was one of racing's best-known and most-loved figures—a sentiment which can be seen expressed in the eyes of America's best-known jockey, Eddie Arcaro, seated beside him. He started his career mucking out stables and rubbing horses at age eleven. He was a jockey from 1890 (age fifteen) to 1901 and then switched to training. In 1923 he received his big opportunity—as trainer for William Woodward's Belair Stud, and later, for the Wheatley Stable of Mrs. H. C. Phipps. Sunny Jim, during his fifty-six-year career, trained some of the world's best horses, including Triple Crown winners Gallant Fox and Omaha, in addition to Nashua, Bold Ruler and many others. "Nobody can make a bad horse good," was his philosophy. "The main object is to avoid making a good horse bad, and a lot of it is just a matter of luck."

Two Phippses who currently carry on the traditions of the dynasty are Ogden Mills ("Dinny") Phipps (*top left*) and Cynthia Phipps (*bottom left*), son and daughter of The Jockey Club chairman. Thirty-two-year-old Dinny is already a power in the sport. He was admitted to membership in The Jockey Club at twenty-four and is presently a trustee (the youngest) of the New York Racing Association. When he isn't winning sail-fishing tournaments or national court tennis doubles championships, or driving fast cars and boats, young Phipps races a modest stable. "Just think," he recalls, "Sunny Jim (Fitzsimmons) saddled the first winner for my grandmother, the first winner for my father, and my own first winner." Cynthia Phipps, now twenty-eight, has been riding some of the world's greatest racehorses since childhood. She has used two of her mother's best steeplechasers, Neji and Mako, as hunters. Her own first racehorse was a gift from her father—a filly named Tasteful who was prepared for her racing debut in 1970 but never made it. Miss Phipps made her own debut in 1963. *The New York Times* called it the "most lavish in decades."

THE PHIPPS DYNASTY

CHAPTER 15

Henry Phipps
(1839-1930)

"I'm afraid I don't recall you," said Henry Phipps to a portly man who extended his hand in greeting. The portly gentleman was William Howard Taft, President of the United States.

WHETHER SHE IS IN HER BOX at the Metropolitan Opera or at Aqueduct Racetrack, Mrs. Ogden Phipps, wife of the Jockey Club chairman, born Lillian Bostwick of the polo-playing clan, always has continuity. So says Eugenia Sheppard, a newsperson who reports to America on the comings and goings of its princely dynasties.

"Mrs. Phipps always looks fresh and outdoorsey, as if there were horses and dogs in the distance," observes Eugenia Sheppard. "She has English skin, clear blue eyes and constant enthusiasm. She is as close as you can come to an English duchess in this country."

What Ms. Sheppard might have added is that, not only is Lillian Bostwick Phipps an American duchess, but the Phipps clan itself is as close as any group can come in a republic to being a royal dynasty. In truth, no American family, at least in terms of lifestyle—not even the Whitneys, the Wideners, or the Vanderbilts—can lay greater claim to the American title of Royal Family than the horse-loving, free-swinging, hard-playing Phippses, now in their fifth generation.

Younger Phippses laid down polo fields in Old Westbury and Yale, older Phippses threw up palaces in New York, Virginia and Florida.

Some cruised the world over in private planes, others did it in auxiliary schooners. One Phipps had already made five Atlantic crossings complete with the Grand Tour before he was a year old; another while still in his teens swung polo mallets with a Prince of Wales. Together, Phippses chased, shot and fished for big and little game—and the hunters sometimes included Phippses whose age would normally have qualified them only for toy guns—all the way from the rain jungles of central Africa to the salmon streams of Saskatchewan. For one of these safaris the Phippses' baggage alone commandeered half of all the first-class baggage space on a transatlantic liner. They built up the power of their clan by marriage to other powerful families such as the Grace, Mills, Guest, Martin and Bostwick clans. Appropriately enough, the current head of the dynasty, Ogden Phipps, is also head of the institution closest to qualifying as an American House of Lords, The Jockey Club, where, with his son, Ogden Mills—the only father and son membership in the club—he controls a nucleus of Phipps-connected votes.

If the splendorous lifestyle and the collective power of their clan is not enough to qualify them for the royal mantle, the Phippses can point to their territorial dominions. The dynasty owns more of the eastern land mass of the United States than any other private holder. Their holdings extend all the way down the Atlantic seaboard from Long Island to Florida. There are Phippses out west too: One of them, Lawrence C. Phipps, went to Colorado as a young man, became active in politics and wound up as the nation's richest senator of his time. His son, Lawrence C. Phipps, Jr., carried on the Phipps tradition of doing things in their own way by setting himself up as master of foxhounds of the most unusual hunt in the world—the Arapahoe, which over the Phipps Colorado estates hunts not fox but coyote.

The story of the Phipps dynasty and the origin of its fortune is perhaps the most exquisite example of the nineteenth-century American industrial fairy tale. In the 1840s in the town of Alleghany (now Pittsburgh), Pennsylvania, a poor Scottish cobbler named Phipps lived on a street named Barefoot Square. Next door lived another Scottish family, that of a weaver named Carnegie. Every day Phipps' son,

Henry, would knock on the Carnegie door and hand over to young Andrew a batch of shoes that Andrew's mother would bind for her neighbor for $4 a week. A friendship began that would last throughout the long lives of the two young men.

In the meantime young Henry trudged daily to a silversmith, where he labored as apprentice for $1.25 a week, while young Andrew went his way to become a superintendent for the Pennsylvania Railroad, which serviced the fast-growing steel industry. Young Andrew, now in his twenties, began dabbling in steel as a sideline to his purchasing chores, while Henry meanwhile had abandoned silver for keeping the accounts and ledgers in a gunpowder firm. When fortune smiled on Andrew with an opportunity to buy an interest in the Kloman forge on Girty's Run, he remembered his good friend Henry. Andrew gave him a half-interest in the investment in return for $800 and accepting the responsibility of keeping the Kloman books. A few years later, in the 1860s fortune, smiling once again—this time in the guise of strife among the Kloman Company owners—Andrew Carnegie was asked to bring peace among the disputants. He did so, and the result was that the Kloman Company first was turned into the Carnegie Steel Company and, thirty-eight years later, into United States Steel, when J. P. Morgan handed over a check for $250,000,000.

What enabled Henry Phipps to get on so well in the fledgling steel company he helped to found and which eventually yielded him $50,000,000 from his $800 investment, was his Scottish frugality and ingenious way with a dollar. He was a shy man, more at ease in the background where he could turn his attention to figures, payrolls and the unglamorous details of balancing books. Since cash was hard to come by in Carnegie Steel's early days, Henry was often required to use his wizardry to skip payrolls and persuade local merchants to extend credit to his workers. He also had a knack for convincing banks that it was wise to waive payments on loans. His wise old mare had delivered Phipps to so many Pittsburgh banks for the purpose of asking for waivers that she would automatically stop at the sight of a bank. And whenever Henry did get his hands on cash, he managed to stall payment in a fashion that impressed even his own creditors.

"What we used to admire about young Phipps," observed an old

Pittsburgh banker to *Fortune* magazine interviewer Richard A. Smith (in an October–November 1960 two-part article), "was the way he could keep a check dangling in the air for two or three days."

In 1905, at the age of sixty-six, after he had parlayed his millions in "little hells of steel" where men sweated through a twelve-hour workday six days a week, Henry Phipps announced that he would spend the rest of his life "improving American social conditions." One of the first things he did was to improve the social conditions of his own heirs. He provided each of his five children with approximately $4,000,000, and then set up a trust that continues, even to this day, to accumulate more millions for his family. The *Fortune* magazine interviewer, commenting on Henry's desire to improve social conditions, observed: "It was quite natural that, as a generous and loving parent he would do everything possible to make life comfortable for his children. The Phipps trust went to extraordinary lengths in this regard, even sparing the beneficiaries the discomfort of having to write their own checks. Everything was paid for by the trust: farms, racing stables, yachts. Tradesmen, servants and charities got their checks from the 'Office.' Some young members of the family even had to come into the 'Office' (which was how they described the trust) and sign a petty cash slip to get pocket money."

Phippses to this day have no need to carry cash, checks or even credit cards. One need only drop in at Abercrombie & Fitch, order a $100,000 camper or a five-dollar key ring and send the bill to the "Office." Some seventy-odd Phippses go through life in this remarkable fashion.

Undoubtedly Henry Phipps was moved by a desire to make life comfortable for the beneficiaries of his millions and, perhaps with a precognition of the appetites of his progeny, was also moved by a desire to save them from themselves. But one reasonably assumes that Henry also intended not only once again to apply his ability to "keep a check in the air," but also to convert his giving into getting. The Phipps trust (now known as Bessemer Securities) mushroomed from its initial capitalization of under $20,000,000 to its present value of some $400,000,000, despite the immense payout over the years to generations of Phippses. Some thirty-seven trust arrangements form the nucleus for seventy-six or more subsidiary enterprises organized specifically for tax or other money-realizing purposes. In essence, Bessemer Securities operates as the Phipps family money-making machine.

Later, Henry, in what was to become the classic manner of the so-called robber baron alleviating the social conditions that he himself created in the first place, gave away some $7,000,000 "to lighten the workingman's lot both at home and abroad." One million dollars was allocated for the erection of Phipps House, a model tenement in New York City, and $350,000 for the relief of Boer War victims. He also contributed $1,500,000 to establish the Phipps Psychiatric Clinic at Johns Hopkins Hospital. This came as a result of his consulting a psychiatrist there, not unlike Diamond Jim Brady's endowing the Brady Clinic at the same hospital after having been given relief by a Johns Hopkins surgeon from the ravages of one of his legendary overindulgences.

Henry Phipps, whose descendants would cavort across the Twenties and Thirties with their exploits in polo, tennis, racing, sailing and hunting, remained an introvert—a man immersed in books and ledgers and ticker tape. On one occasion in his later years, when walking through a hotel lobby, he encountered a large smiling man who extended a friendly hand. Phipps hesitated, frowned and finally said: "I'm afraid I don't know you." The man then had to re-introduce himself. He was the President of the United States, William Howard Taft.

Phipps lived on to the age of nearly ninety-one, his life spanning the tenure of twenty-five presidencies, from Martin Van Buren's to Herbert Hoover's. During that long period Henry Phipps never indulged himself in thoroughbred racing, as did his contemporary dynasty-founder, William C. Whitney. Nor did he attempt to acquire the world's art treasures, in the manner of his rags-to-riches peer, Peter A. B. Widener. But he did "unleash his heart," as one of his contemporaries said, by continuing to dole out grants, pensions, and stipends to the "workingman." For the starving masses of India he made a gift of $100,000 to an agricultural college. He even made a grant to keep the Carnegie Libraries open on Sundays, when the workingman, after his six twelve-hour days in the "little hells of steel" could come in for intellectual refreshment.

Carnegie, however, thought very little of his partner's unleashed heart. "You just can't make Henry see what an unwise old sinner he is," Carnegie once remarked. "I've many a year tried to be his guardian, but he won't be reasonable on this one special weakness that keeps him spilling largesse around—not bettering but spoiling humanity. His pockets are forever wide open as lures to the pensioners. Once I thought he was only careless, but I have learned better. Being a 'helper' as he calls it—being a 'hurter' as he ought to call it—paying out a fortune every year to those who don't earn it, is strangely what he continually regards as one of his luxuries."

CHAPTER 16

Mr. and Mrs. Henry Carnegie Phipps

Mrs. Henry Carnegie Phipps (1884-1971)

Henry Carnegie Phipps (1879-1953)

"If you should chance to see, in the paddock, a smartly but casually dressed old lady, with a waist any of her fourteen grandchildren might envy . . . hovering about Bold Ruler, that would be Mrs. Henry Carnegie Phipps."

—Charles Hatton, *Morning Telegraph,* on Mrs. Henry Carnegie Phipps

IF OLD HENRY PHIPPS did not himself quite put a royal stamp on his dynasty, that deficiency was more than made up when a member of the Mills family joined the clan. When Gladys Livingston Mills, of Newport, Rhode Island, married Henry's son, Henry Carnegie Phipps, she not only conferred on the family a fortune that had its origin in a royal grant from the British Crown, she also created the dynasty's racing stable. Interestingly enough, both the fortune that Gladys Livingston Mills brought and the Wheatley Stable that she created had their origins in debts that had been settled by a payment in kind.

On her mother's side Gladys Mills was a Livingston, a member of one of the oldest and most aristocratic families in the country. Livingstons were involved in displacing the Indians from their hereditary lands, acted as Indian Affairs agents for the British crown, signed the Declaration of Independence, and helped run city, state and federal governments. They also were pleased to name streets, towns and counties after themselves throughout New Jersey and New York—particularly in Duchess County, New York, home of the Roosevelts and Van Rensselaers. In addition, they seemed to have a faculty for putting the British Crown in their debt. Robert Livingston, who came from Holland to the colonies in 1673, wound up with 160,000 choice acres of Duchess and Columbia counties as payment or a debt owed him by King George I. From this royal patent was formed Livingston Manor. From the Revolution, in which the Livingstons were active militants against the Crown, the family emerged more affluent than ever.

Robert R. Livingston, grandson of the first American Livingston, now held a monopoly on steamboating on the Hudson River, a waterway that was practically the family's private moat. It was there that the Clermont—the first commercially successful American steamboat—was launched with Livingston backing. He also displayed the same Livingston expertise with real estate in his handling of the Louisiana Purchase negotiations for the U.S. Government. All through the eighteenth and the nineteenth centuries, assorted Livingstons were everywhere on the political, social and financial scene, the accumulated result of which made the family one of the largest and wealthiest landholders in the east.

The dowry that Gladys Livingston Mills brought to Henry Carnegie Phipps can be traced to that original royal debt. But that was not all that she brought. On the Mills side of her family was another large holding of the country's real and personal wealth, this time in the west. Darius Ogden Mills, Gladys' father, accumulated one of the largest fortunes in the west as a banker and merchant prince just after the Gold Rush of 1849. Like the Livingstons, he delighted in having towns named after him—for example, Ogden, Utah, and Ogdensburg, New York. Later he came east with his millions to contribute a Secretary of the Treasury for Herbert Hoover (his son, Ogden Livingston Mills) and the chain of Mills Hotels, one of which, still bearing the family name until a few years ago, was one of Greenwich Village's better-known flophouses. He also built, among other things, Manhattan's Tudor City. When Gladys Livingston Mills' landholdings were added to those which the Phipps clan already held, it made the Phipps dynasty one of America's largest landlords.

All this added luster to the Phipps name and enhanced its financial standing, but it remained for a second debt to provide the family with the nucleus of what was to become its greatest renown: the world-famous Phipps racing stable. In the 1920s young Gladys Mills, now Mrs. Henry Carnegie Phipps, had acquired a small insignificant stable of her own. Her husband, apparently more intrigued by Wall Street and high-stakes poker, showed little interest in racing thoroughbreds. One night, according to a story still heard today, Harry Whitney lost a small fortune to Phipps and, as was Whitney's sometime-style, offered to pay off in racehorses. He gave Phipps his choice of his new yearling crop—not an unshrewd gesture since Phipps was not experienced with horseflesh and could easily have selected second-raters. Early the next morning, before Harry Whitney had had the time to shake the sleep out of his eyes, Phipps's limousine showed up at the Whitney thoroughbred farm at Red Bank, New Jersey, to collect the debt. Coming to the front door of the manor house, still in pajamas, Whitney saw Phipps seated in front of the car and waved him on down to the stables to take his pick from James Rowe, the trainer. What Whitney did not see was tiny Gladys Mills Phipps, who knew a thing or two about horses, crouched out of sight in the back of the car. Whether it was Mrs. Phipps's horse sense or sheer luck that is such an essential if unpublicized part of the racing business, or perhaps even the fact that the five or so horses that she selected were turned over to the master trainer "Sunny" Jim Fitzsimmons, the horses she selected became some of the best runners of their generation. Dice was unbeaten until its death in its second year, Distraction broke a track record and Diavolo won The Jockey Club Gold Cup of 1929. If ever a woman could be said to have had an eye for a horse it was the slender, soft-eyed equestrienne who selected a group of untried thoroughbreds that not only more than settled the original gambling debt but came back to beat Whitney horses an embarrassing number of times.

In a sense it was Gladys Livingston Mills who founded what was to become America's premier racing empire. For this she was considerably better equipped than her husband. Neither H. C. Phipps nor his father had ever been seriously involved with thoroughbreds, but Gladys Mills had always been around horses. As a girl she had competed in horse shows. As a young woman she was part of the horsey Long Island set that patronized the horse "speakeasy" at Piping Rock during the years of the racing ban in New York State. Her father, Darius Ogden Mills, had raced in the United States and abroad, and her sister, the Countess of Granard, owned horses in partnership with Lord Derby, one of the countess' thoroughbreds becoming the champion two-year-old of the British Isles. Gladys Phipps started her Wheatley Stable with a triple-barrelled partnership. It comprised one of the most astute operators on Wall Street—her husband; her brother, a Secretary of the Treasury; and, of course, those superlative Whitney horses.

Not to be overlooked was another member of the association, not as an actual partner, to be sure, but perhaps more important to its success than any combination of bloodlines, wealth and even luck—"Sunny" Jim Fitzsimmons. Sunny Jim trained Mrs. Phipps's horses for thirty-eight years until his retirement at age eighty-eight in 1963—a man so bent by arthritis in his later years that he could hardly raise his head to see the horses he regularly sent off to win the world's great prizes. It was his enormous ability at moulding and developing the thoroughbred racehorse that helped to create the empire that has made three generations of Phippses rulers of the racing world. It also produced their greatest claim to fame: the most successful thoroughbred stallion of the past two decades—the appropriately named Bold Ruler.

Gladys Mills Phipps, who died in 1970 at the age of eighty-seven, was for the last three decades of her life the *grande dame* of the American horsey set. It is the prerogative of the rich and secure to go about without the expected trappings of position, and Mrs. Phipps used the prerogative. She made her public appearances in her simple gingham dresses, looking more like the owner of a general store than the mistress of regal establishments in Newport, Rhode Island, and Palm Beach, Florida, in addition to a good portion of the coastline in between. She appeared at Belmont Park in brown Indian-style mocassins which, in manifold variety, seem to be standard footgear for the set on a racing afternoon. That would be her lone concession to uniform or other prosaics.

"It isn't winning the race," she told an interviewer in 1939. "That isn't the reason for entering a horse in a race. I do not care much about winning the race. I almost never bet on my horses. It's just that I want them to perform like the thoroughbreds they are. That's the important thing."

Although a tiny woman and seemingly fragile, Mrs. Phipps was a mini-dynamo. She would show up at her stable in the mornings to confer with her trainer, having driven herself there in her Bentley with her two poodles at her side. As soon as she entered the barn a chorus of neighing would rise, for her thoroughbreds recognized her voice and knew her to be an easy touch. She would pass down the lines of stalls handing out sugar, often as not to horses which would run that afternoon and had no business being fed anything until after the race. But Mrs. Phipps made her own rules. Bold Ruler, in particular—her favorite—would put on an act when she arrived, for he was something of a moocher and knew how to hustle her for sugar.

But Mrs. Phipps did more than pass out sugar to her racehorses. Although she rarely interfered with the racing decisions by her trainers, she did, up to her last years, take an active role in breeding strategy. She compiled an annual list, specifying which mare was to be chosen to carry on which line, and which stallion was commissioned to do the job. She would also show up anywhere, anytime when a Phipps horse was running. Just before her death she had her helicopter settle down in the backstretch at Belmont Park in order to have a final look at one of her racers. She was the fountainhead of energy which the present generation of Phippses display in the racing world.

Unlike that other female dynamo of the set, Elizabeth Arden, who went through an endless number of trainers and managers, Mrs. Phipps was the model of old guard stability. In her forty-four years on the turf she had only three trainers, one of them, Sunny Jim Fitzsimmons, contributing his genius and a long list of classic winners for thirty-eight years.

Also, just as the Phippses are accustomed to having the details of ordinary life taken care of by an on-going managerial operation such as the "Office," so the day-to-day care of Mrs. Phipps' breeding stock was laid upon the shoulders of the very best breeding "office" in the business: the Claiborne Farm of Arthur "Bull" Hancock in Kentucky.

All of the Phipps family's stallions stand at Claiborne Farm along with the Phipps broodmares. They will have nothing to do with the annoying trivia of running their own farm.

The foals are raised by Hancock to yearlinghood, whereupon those that they want to be rid of are sold and those they choose to keep are placed in the hands of the Phipps trainers to be developed into racehorses. So Gladys Phipps herself was as departmentalized as any of the big business operations in the portfolios of Bessemer Securities. Her stallions were bred to her mares in Kentucky; her yearlings were trained in South Carolina; her two-year-olds raced in Maryland, Florida, Kentucky, New York, California—all over the U.S.—her older horses competed in the great racing classics of France and England. The sun rarely set on the racing colors of Gladys Phipps—purple for royalty, and gold for what almost everything the Phippses have touched has turned into.

Almost. The second and third generation Phippses have been known to have moments of not especially self-serving frugality. Occasionally, when moved by an impulse to rid themselves of a "washout" racehorse, they have lived to regret their parsimoniousness. This, despite all her good horse sense, happened to Gladys Mills Phipps herself in the case of a horse of her own breeding named Seabiscuit. The young racer had not been paying his way one season, so Mrs. Phipps decided to tighten the purse strings and get rid of him. Charles Howard of San Francisco bought him for $8,000. In Howard's stable Seabiscuit went on to become one of the world's leading money-winners, and in 1938 defeated War Admiral, Man o' War's greatest son, in a special match at Pimlico.

Gladys Phipps did not often run second. During her lifetime, her Wheatley Stable, named after a highway that ran by her mansion in Roslyn, Long Island, raced ninety stakes-winning horses (some in partnership with her husband, her son Ogden and her grandson, Ogden Mills Phipps). And in 1954 an event occurred that two years later was to mold the Phipps clan into a tighter group than ever before: the birth of the horse Bold Ruler.

Bold Ruler was bred by Mrs. Phipps and was foaled at Bull Hancock's Claiborne Farm. He had the typical bloodlines that a Phipps-bred horse would inevitably have, but at birth he seemed nothing unusual and was simply left in the capable hands of Mr. Bull Hancock. In fact, the son of imported Nasrullah and Miss Disco looked so sickly as a foal that Bull Hancock tried to keep him out of the sight of visitors.

"He was a very skinny foal, with a large hernia," he said. "We had the devil's own time trying to get him to look good, and I must say that I was never really pleased with his condition the whole time I had him."

In addition to his double hernia, Bold Ruler had a rheumatic condition that plagued him all his racing life. Nevertheless he always delivered his utmost in a race, always strained to be up in front with the leaders. He could accelerate in the manner of a fine racing car. "Bold Ruler could beat any horse in the world at any distance from six furlongs to a mile and an eighth," said Sunny Jim Fitzsimmons, his trainer.

Bold Ruler vindicated Sunny Jim's high regard by winning twenty-three of his thirty-three races, and managing four seconds, two thirds and a total of $764,000, including the title Horse of the Year for 1957. It was inevitable that he would be compared to William Woodward's Nashua, considered by many to be the greatest horse of his time; both were sired by Nasrullah, trained by Jim Fitzsimmons and ridden by Eddie Arcaro. "For the things he can do," said America's most famous jockey on the day that Bold Ruler won the Trenton Handicap from Gallant Man and Round Table in a tremendous burst of speed, "Bold Ruler is better than Nashua. As a matter of fact this horse is Grade A."

Things went well for the Phippses with their great champion. Retired to stud at the age of five, for seven seasons in a row Bold Ruler headed the American sire list, which translated into his progeny winning into more dollars on the racetrack than the sires of any other stud, a statistic perhaps not unrelated to the fact that the Phippses and others with the best stables and trainers had a monopoly on his stud services. When one considers that his stud fee (if one could manage to obtain his service) might run as high as $35,000 per service for an average of forty annual services over fifteen to twenty years, it becomes evident how lucrative it is to own a thoroughbred stallion.

In July of 1970, after ten years at stud, Bold Ruler finally began to fade a bit. At first he simply showed signs of difficulty in breathing. Bull Hancock called in his veterinarians and they administered antibiotics, hoping to forestall possible infection. But in a few days bleeding developed in the horse's nostrils, slight at first, then heavy. A veterinary surgeon was summoned. He performed a tracheotomy to make breathing easier, then probed and discovered inflamed tissue. Nothing as yet was known of the cause of the inflammation. A month later, having lost considerable weight, Bold Ruler was admitted to a veterinary hospital. There he had exploratory surgery, which revealed a large growth extending from the nasal passage to just below the brain. Biopsy found the tumor malignant; the question now was how close to the brain did it extend and was it accessible to cobalt treatment.

Gladys Mills Phipps also lay ailing—she was in her eighty-seventh year and now followed the activities of her racing empire not by plane or jeep but in the pages of the *Racing Form* and by reports from her family. She yielded to the advice of her son and his consultants to permit Bold Ruler to undergo cobalt treatment.

Bold Ruler was removed to the veterinary clinic at Auburn University in Auburn, Alabama, where a team of specialists planned and supervised the isotope therapy. It was the first time in history that any animal had been treated for cancer of this type. The malignancy was deep-seated and close to the brain; great skill and care was required to assure zeroing the radioactive cobalt in on the precise center of the tumor without endangering other vital tissues. But this, of course, was Bold Ruler and no expense or detail was spared.

The champion came through the ordeal with flying colors. He showed rapid detoxification, an encouraging return to normalcy and a regression of the tumor. In a few weeks, he was back in his paddock at Claiborne Farm with a new lease on life delivered by science and human skill. The following year, in the breeding season, he was even able to serve his full quota of thirty-seven mares, of which he got twenty-seven in foal. In May, X-ray examination showed nothing suspicious: he was active, eating well and carrying good weight. But in June he began to fall off, even though he continued to clean up his feed; by the end of the month he was still losing weight, vigor and mobility. Biopsy soon confirmed the suspicion: the malignancy had reactivated itself in a fresh and overwhelming crop of tumors and lesions that spread throughout the head, neck and chest. The virus of cancer had shown itself superior to that life force which had made Bold Ruler a link in the magnificent chain which runs all the way from Godolphin

Arabian to Secretariat. On July 12, 1971, Bold Ruler, in his sixteenth year, was quietly destroyed.

Gladys Mills Phipps had passed on the year before, just a week after she had been advised that Bold Ruler had been discharged from the hospital "with a new lease on life."

CHAPTER 17

Ogden Phipps (1908-)

"Emphasis will be placed on serving our customers, who in this instance are all those who make up the racing world."

—Ogden Phipps, upon taking chairmanship of The Jockey Club, *The New York Times*, January 8, 1964

THE PHIPPS DYNASTY ennobled its humble coal-country beginnings by much intermarriage with European aristocracy. Amy Phipps, for instance, daughter of the dynastic founder, married a dashing British nobleman, Captain Frederick E. Guest. Two of her children, however, preferred the French aristocracy to the British, son Raymond marrying Princess Caroline Murat and daughter Diana the Count Jean de la Valdene. Other third-generation Phippses did more of the same, another son allying himself with a Lady Pleydell-Bouverie, other daughters linking with a Hans C. Scheer-Thoss and one C. Sidamon-Eristoff.

Amy Phipps Guest's sons, Winston and Raymond, are both six-foot-plus, sinewy British types, aristocratic in appearance as the four-legged progeny of the dynasty. But when it comes to the Ogden Phipps branch of the family (Ogden is the only son of Gladys Mills Phipps) the physical characteristics fall somewhat short of the aristocratic stereotype. Despite the fact that he traces his ancestry, on his mother's side, back through a long, and lean, line of aristocratic Livingstons, Ogden Phipps has a tendency to plebian beefiness. Indeed, if his conformation bears any resemblance to an aristocracy it is to those German burgher-kings exemplified by the Hanoverian Georges, who acceeded to the British throne. Mr. Phipps does have the sky-blue eyes that seem inevitable in a Jockey Club chairman (his predecessor, George B. Widener, had even bluer eyes) and he moves with the grace of a man who has nine times been national champion of the royal sport of court tennis. Still, he does not possess the slim angular grace of his British cousins, the Guests, or even of his American counterparts, Cornelius Vanderbilt Whitney, for example.

Even in the next generation of Ogden Phippses the burgher quality is not softened, despite heritage. Ogden's son and namesake, Ogden Mills Phipps, in his twenties already a junior power in both The Jockey Club and on the racetrack, is a physical chip off the paternal block. In the more generous time of his avoirdupois career, he was a tow-haired replica of the late King Farouk. Now, in his thirties, he has already balded, as did his father.

Daughter Cynthia, also an outstanding horsewoman, is a debutante of 1963 whose $200,000 debut elicited a critical editorial from *The New York Times.* Though by no means unattractive, Cynthia is somewhat uncharacteristically ruddy-complexioned and large-boned; she might be more appropriate to a Breughel canvas than a painting by Sir Joshua Reynolds.

The other Phipps son, Henry Ogden Phipps, from a first marriage to Ruth Pruyn (later Mrs. Marshall Field) seems to have been something of a dropout from the family tradition. He was never much involved in the horsey scene. In 1962, at the age of thirty-one, he was found dead of an overdose of narcotics in a hotel on New York's Upper West Side. Despite his relative indifference to the world of horses, he too followed the Phipps pattern of marrying nobility, his wife being Diana Sternberg, daughter of Count Leopold Sternberg and a member of one of the oldest families in Czechoslovakia. Whether or not he would have approved, he was still considered enough of a Phipps to have the family cancel a horse race at Aqueduct on the day of his death.

With the exception of the deceased son, the Ogden Phipps branch of the family, despite any surface appearances, represents the horsiest group of people in America. His mother, with her Wheatley Stable and her Bold Ruler, operated the most powerful horsery in the country; he himself, besides being chairman of The Jockey Club, was only second behind his mother in the success of his own stable. He also co-owned with her the stallion Buckpasser, which was syndicated at a price of $4,800,000, the highest at the time; Mrs. Ogden Phipps, although by birth a Bostwick—itself a not inconsiderable horsey clan—has refined her tastes so that she races nothing but steeplechasers. Ogden's son, Ogden Mills Phipps, himself a stakes-winning stable owner, became a member of The Jockey Club when he was hardly out of his teens and also is currently one of the trustees of the New York Racing Association (which gives the Phippses two representations on that most prestigious overlord of race courses). Daughter Cynthia is a constant visitor at the thoroughbred auctions and has already been featured in the "*Dramatis Personae*" section of *The Blood-Horse,* on the debut of her purple and yellow racing silks.

With all the options that money, position and power can offer, one may wonder why the Phippses and their peers spend so much of their time (for some, practically all of it) breeding, buying, selling and watching racehorses? No other outlet? Ogden Phipps and his son, for example, also excelled at various participant sports, both indoor and outdoor. The nine championship awards of the senior Phipps in court tennis alone testify to athletic talent and excellence. Time on their hands? True, the ordinary need to earn a livelihood is not present. The point would seem to be that horse racing becomes a primary occupation, a kind of work-sport that, with its demands in the field of breeding, buying and selling, racing, following the races, administering the sport in which so much is invested, fills in both a sporting and commercial fashion all the free time of a participant. As José Ortega has said, "What does man do when he is free to do as he pleases? The greatly liberated man—the aristocrat—has always done the same thing: *raced horses.* . . . [italics mine]"

In today's world, there is also the reason of image. "There are a lot of people walking around with a pretty low opinion of themselves deep down inside," says Charles Hatton of *The Racing Form,* a well-known turf writer who has covered the sport for years. "They don't want to be known as just a multi-millionaire or the son or, for that matter, daughter of a multi-millionaire. They hate that image. Racing gives them a chance for another image. They get their name in the papers as the owner of this or the winner of that. It gives them a crack at a new self-identity. Look at Mrs. Tweedy with Riva Ridge and Secretariat—why she has had more TV exposure than Indira Gandhi?

Of course it doesn't always have to be on such a highly public scale. Some of them like the idea of just being known among their own rich friends as something more than a rich man or woman."

Exemplary of this is Ogden Phipps. He lists his occupation as investor, a label suggesting that, although involved in business to the extent of receiving income from it, he is not actively engaged in the direction of a business.

As a young man, Ogden attended St. Paul's Academy, which, with St. Marks, Middlesex and Groton comprise the so-called St. Grottlesex group of preparatory schools favored by the rich and well-known. In 1931 he graduated Harvard College, having achieved nothing especially outstanding either academically or in sports, although as an undergraduate he already owned more than one racehorse. A shy, introverted youth, whose every need was taken care of by the "Office" of the Phipps Trust, on leaving Harvard, he predictably entered the investment banking business.

Phipps also made no headlines on Wall Street. He contributed by associating his name, position, and money with operations such as the investment banking house of Smith Barney & Co., International Paper, and other oil and banking companies, including the family money-handler, Bessemer Trust Company.

Ogden Phipps was peculiarly suited to the world of the horse. In 1932 Phipps made the move that was to send him to the top in horse racing. He purchased the cream of the deceased Colonel E. R. Bradley's immensely successful racing stable, and in 1936 he won his first major stakes with White Cockade.

Even though he was now well on his way to being a fulltime horseman and getting good professional notices, horses didn't seem enough to satisfy his appetites. Polo was always available, but Ogden Phipps had never been outstanding in the active manipulation of horses. Besides, cousins Mike Phipps, Winnie and Ray Guest were making all the headlines in that sport. So Ogden found himself another outlet.

Court tennis proved to be an ideal medium for his personality. Court tennis is a game that has always been played in isolation. It originated in medieval France and was originally played in the moats of castles, from which the water had been drained before the contest. Later, indoor courts were constructed by the monarchs, such as the one at Henry VIII's Hampton Court, the palace itself taking its name from the fact that it contained a playing court. Another was built in the Jeu de Paume ("game of racquets"), the court of French kings in the Tuilleries. Today the sport continues to be a royal kind of one-to-one affair played in places such as the Racquet & Tennis Club, a kind of Renaissance edifice fronting an entire block on New York's Park Avenue. The game itself is a kind of combination ping-pong, tennis and handball, played with racquets that sent the ball crashing over the center net against the floor, walls and roof. Here, in his second area of competitiveness, Ogden Phipps began to be noticed by his peers and, to some extent, the larger public, both in the United States and abroad, which follows the affairs of the super-rich and social. His days alternated between Belmont paddocks and the "Racket" Club, on whose $250,000 imported courts he became national amateur champion nine times.

Meanwhile, although not actively engaged in a conventional business, Phipps was very much involved on the administrative side in the business-sport of racing. He became a member of The Jockey Club at the age of thirty, and a steward of the club ten years later. By 1949 he was ready to apply his experience and background to preserve the royal sport from encroachments by outsiders such as Jule Fink. Phipps was one of the two Jockey Club stewards who, despite the appearance of people such as Bernard Baruch as character witnesses for Fink, pressured the State Racing Commissioners to uphold the Jockey Club's denial of Fink's license to race. The democratic bounds of Ogden's life, spent on the royal tennis courts and the Turf & Field Clubs of Long Island, Saratoga and Palm Beach had not stretched to the district of a Jule Fink. But William C. Langely, Wall Street investment banker, and Ashley Trimble Cole, top flight corporate lawyer, and Jacob Swirbil, Grumann Aircraft president—the three comprising the State Racing Commission—he knew well. Jule Fink was denied his license.

Following that development, colleagues in The Jockey Club named Phipps vice-chairman under George D. Widener. When New York State's highest court ruled against The Jockey Club in the Fink case and abrogated its absolute powers, Phipps was able to find time to help restore the Club's position in somewhat more subtle fashion than theretofore.

Ogden Phipps

In 1964, at age fifty-six, Ogden Phipps became the sixth chairman of The Jockey Club, succeeding the retiring George D. Widener.

"We have no intention of simply defending the status quo simply because it is a status quo," announced Phipps to the press on his appointment, "but we also have no intention of ever losing sight of the main purpose of The Jockey Club—which is to preserve this sport as a sport."

Despite his brave words, The Jockey Club, comprising the oldest wealth and the purest bloodlines in the land, had, as previously with the British House of Lords, suffered a trimming of its powers. Gone were the days of open alliance between ruling class and ruling mechanism. The format of government had so radically changed that now its agents were compelled to pose, at least if not as enemies of privilege, then certainly as neutrals. Horseracing was no longer "the sport of kings but the sport of governors," observed one of the more sympathetic agents, New York Republican legislator, Paul A. Fino. "It is no longer used to test and breed better horses but to fatten state treasuries." So at this juncture when mayors, governors and even presidents, in their ever-growing need for more taxes, were forced occasionally to utilize their upper-class benefactors for additional sources of revenue, the shy, stammering Ogden Phipps in his role as chairman of The Jockey Club became one of the spokesmen for the horsey set.

This new provision in the tax structure created an ironic paradox. Whereas Phipps's predecessor, Jockey Club chairman George D. Widener, had taken court action in 1928 that established the breeding and racing of horses as a business (and therefore deductible from *federal* income taxes), three decades later Jockey Club chairman Ogden Phipps was declaring his intention of "keeping the sport a 'sport,'" admittedly for exactly the same reason: taxes. This time, however, it was to prevent *New York state* from "taxing the sport so much that it would be forced to become a commercial business."

The apex of Ogden Phipps' career was reached with Buckpasser, Horse of the Year 1966. Not only had he won that distinction at three, he was also champion colt at two, best of the older horses at four and the youngest horse to have been installed in Saratoga's Hall of Fame.

His pedigree left nothing to be desired in the way of fashion. His sire was Tom Fool, another Horse of the Year (1953) and also a champion at two. Busanda, a favorite Phipps broodmare, was his dam —a mare which among other accomplishments, had beaten colts in that great handicap test, the Suburban. And so on all the way back: the best bloodlines money could buy.

In conformation, Buckpasser was practically the perfect thoroughbred. Dr. Manuel Gilman, who has been inspecting horses at New York tracks since 1945 said, according to *The Blood-Horse* of August 8, 1970, ". . . I defy anybody to pick a flaw in Buckpasser."

Having the advantage of all this to start with, Buckpasser had the even more important advantage of being placed, successively, in the hands of two of the best trainers in modern racing, Bill Winfrey first, and then Eddie Neloy. Under these handlers he went on to win just about everything in sight, although cracked hooves kept him out of many important races. He wound up being retired to stud, after his fourth year, having won 25 of his 31 races, with earnings of $1,462,014. From an economic point of view, to say nothing of performance, Buckpasser had more than fulfilled his promise. But there was more in terms of dollars still to come. Syndication had now become the fashion and Phipps syndicated the horse for $4,800,000.

"Economics had nothing to do with my decision [to syndicate Buckpasser]," stated Mr. Phipps to David Alexander of *The Thoroughbred Record* on being questioned about the deal. "Syndication was a matter of convenience, of relieving pressure. I have a great many good friends with good mares, and if Buckpasser merely stood at a fee, they'd be after me. I'd hate to refuse any of them, so syndication might possibly be the solution and get me off the hook."

Syndication of a thoroughbred stallion also involves the prosaic of making sure of a tax-free dollar. Anyone fortunate enough to have a stallion from which he can realize $4,800,000 in one lump sum by syndicating him, as Ogden Phipps did with Buckpasser, would be somewhat foolish not to spread the risk. Suppose one kept him for himself and the stallion proved sterile, as so many have? One would be lucky to get $4,800. It's like a corporation "going public": get one's hands on the dollars and let the buyers take the risk (*caveat emptor* applies to horseflesh as well as less exalted goods). It also enhances the stock and the prestige of the stable if one can syndicate a horse for millions of dollars—to say nothing of the tax possibilities.

Third and fourth generation Phippses, particularly Ogden Phipps, are not so noteworthy for philanthropy as were, say, the Whitneys or even old Henry Phipps. Generally, the contemporary Phippses seem more at home on the receiving end, and no nonsense about it. It is a lifestyle that not only they but also those around them take for granted. It even applies to a game of golf, as David Alexander reported. Alexander had interviewed Phipps on his appointment as Jockey Club chairman and taken the opportunity to congratulate him on his golf prowess.

"You know, Eddie Neloy [Phipps' trainer] tells me you are quite a whiz on the links," said Alexander. "He says that every time he plays with you he loses ten bucks. But," he added, "Eddie says that he'd rather lose ten bucks than lose Buckpasser."

Mr. Phipps frowned. "If Eddie is throwing all those games to me, I'll fire him," he said. "I'm very proud of beating Eddie . . . Or maybe I'll just challenge him to a game of court tennis."

The Phipps court seems to have little room for jesters.

CHAPTER 18

Mrs. Ogden Phipps
(1906-)

"One can only feel flattered."

—Mrs. Ogden Phipps as she watched her Neji "sail over the fences at Belmont Park like a swallow" with 176 pounds on his back

CULTS OFTEN HAVE A WAY of fragmenting into subcults and supercults that often regard each other as anathema. There are socialists who consider communists heretics, even though both might follow Lenin; some fishermen would not be caught dead with a catfish while others look upon it as the prize among fish; the same for the red fox hunter and the gray, the softball player and the hard.

And so it is with the cult of the horse. Trotting or harness horses are considered lowly and plebian by many thoroughbred enthusiasts —"jugheads," they are called—and the jughead owners sneeringly refer to thoroughbred horses as "flats." There is also a faction within the horsey set (and indeed it is this faction which provides the stereotype of the "horsey" label in the public mind) that considers the steeplechase horse that jumps over obstacles as a far superior being to the flat-running horse that merely circumnavigates the conventional, unobstructed racecourse.

Mrs. Ogden Phipps, wife of the chairman of The Jockey Club, is such a person. As she is a sister of gentleman-jockey George H. "Pete" Bostwick, a diminutive aristocrat who nevertheless has managed to catapult countless large horses over countless countryside fences, including even those of England's Grand National Steeplechase, this is not surprising. Still, she has also long been a member of that most exclusive group that comprises the "hunting" set, a coterie that, in the enchanted horse Shangri-las of Virginia, South Carolina and Maryland, devotes itself to pursuit of the fox, either real or by drag hunt. This is a sport in which there is no fox, but instead the hounds follow the scent of a drag, an object containing the scent of fox that has previously been dragged over the countryside. The sport of steeplechasing (oddly enough, its ruling group—The National Steeplechase & Hunt Association—unlike The Jockey Club, does not exclude women) is closely allied to the foxhunt. Although steeplechasing on the racetrack does not involve pursuit of a fox, nor does it require an accompanying pack of hounds, it does necessitate the hurdling of fences, hedges and ditches, or, as racetrack vernacular has it: timber, brush, and hurdles. The sport gets its name from the fact that, originally, spirited young blades not satisfied wtih having run down a fox, would pick out the steeple of a distant church and challenge each other to race to the Lord's threshhold.

Today the racetrack version of steeplechasing is a dying sport, despite efforts of a few of the old guard to perpetuate it. William F. DuPont, Jr., built and maintained, up to his death in 1969, a private steeplechase course over his estates in Maryland, where each year he summoned the citizenry of the two-day Fair Hill jump races, as feudal lords once gathered the serfs at the manor at annual get-togethers. His octogenarian sister, Marian DuPont Scott, formerly married to cowboy movie actor Randolph Scott, still sponsors the Colonial Cup steeplechase meeting over her own lavish course in the horse country of South Carolina, a $100,000 event which, because of today's lack of competition, often sees Mrs. Scott presenting the winner's trophy to herself. The venerable Monmouth Hunt, which the Amory Haskells had for years sponsored over their New Jersey domain, also has been given up. And, lastly, the New York Racing Association, under Alfred G. Vanderbilt, the sixty-one-year-old "young Turk" of racing, has been forced to deliver what might eventually prove the *coup de grâce* to the old sport: in 1971 he cancelled steeplechasing at all NYRA courses except for the four-week season at Saratoga. No official reason was given for the move, except that there was a need for a change in the stakes program. Informed sources, however, suggested that the real reason was the need to increase the volume in betting: many bettors preferred not to risk wagering on a jumping horse.

But Lillian Bostwick Phipps persists. Despite having a family that includes a husband who is the number one flat-racing owner in the country, a mother-in-law who was flat racing's *grande dame,* a son and daughter who have flat-racing stables, and even a steeplechasing brother who also owns and trains his own flat-runners, Lillian still carries on the steeplechase tradition. In a career that has stretched nearly fifty years, all the way from riding to hounds with the Hartford Hunt to getting a winner over brush at the old Westchester-Biltmore course, with brother "Steeplechase Pete" in the saddle, she has never condescended to have a string of flat-racers.

Except for a few Clarks and DuPonts and Mellons, Mrs. Phipps is now almost alone in her pursuit of fence-jumping champions. Even Mrs. DuPont Scott and the Clarks race a few flat horses in addition to their jumpers. "Economics," says Mrs. Scott, one of the world's richest women. "I must race a few flat runners to make ends meet. But I really wish I didn't have to."

Mrs. Phipps is not so much interested in making ends meet (after all, the Phipps family did rather well with Bold Ruler and Buckpasser) as she is in causes. Steeplechasing is patronized by an elite body of gentlemen jockeys, trainers, and owners who are in a perpetual round of pilgrimages to ultra-social race meets throughout the world. Steeplechasing is far more symbolic of the old guard in the sport than are other phases of the game. And since steeplechasing is in danger of dying out, Mrs. Phipps has taken to herself the cause of seeing that it survives. It is her great passion, and accordingly, in pursuing her cause, she has, with typical Phipps energy, made herself a leading owner in the sport as well. She has won its outstanding award (the J. Ambrose Clark) and its most valuable race (the $100,000 Colonial Cup) in addition to producing Neji (a horse of the year and holder of the money-winning record). She was also successful in the campaign to prevent the release of photographs of spills that horses often take in going over hurdles.

"It gives the public a mistaken notion that steeplechasing is a cruel sport," she once told a reporter for The *Morning Telegraph.* "Actually I don't think I have had eight horses fall in the thirty years I have raced them. Photographs of spills also tend to create an impression there are extraordinary risks involved in wagering on steeplechasing." Not so, she advised in a kind of insider's tip to horseplayers: the percentage of winning favorites in jump races is consistently greater than in flat racing, a fact that few seem aware of.

But the sport of steeplechasing is not the only higher cause to which Lillian Phipps has given herself. Says Eugenia Sheppard: "Following the duchess pattern, Mrs. Phipps is full of good works. She has slaved for the Visiting Nurses Service and for the Metropolitan Opera. A dedicated Republican, she became seriously ill during the 1964 presidential campaign [slaving for Goldwater]" . . . It was in the latter pursuit that the courts peremptorily found a reason to exempt her and Jock Whitney from the law requiring political party officers (she was vice chairman of the Republican Party Finance Committee and Jock the chairman) to refrain from racing horses while holding office.

A few years ago Lillian Phipps decided that she wanted to improve the cultural life of Palm Beach by making fine art available to its residents during their long winters of isolation. She opened the Lillian Phipps Galleries on Phipps Plaza, the family's own private commons in that noted resort. She also commissioned the construction of what her neighbors describe as a "Moorish palace"—a place where she could conveniently keep an eye on the new venture.

"Mrs. Phipps has wanted the Galleries for five years," said Director Lee Kinsolving on opening day. "Even though some of her best friends own the Palm Beach Galleries, she passionately wanted her own." The old competitive drive, elsewhere released on the race course, was now let loose among the canvasses and oils and opening nights. For the friends involved in those competing Palm Beach Galleries were such as the horsey Mrs. "Laddie" Sanford, "Big Mom" Joan Whitney Payson, Sonny Whitney's sister, Barbara Headley, and Lillian's own cousin-in-law, Mrs. Michael Phipps.

Lillian Phipps did not really want to live in Florida. It was the doctor who suggested and the Galleries that demanded. "The Old Grover Loening house hardly knows itself as her new Moorish castle," reported peripatetic Eugenia Sheppard. "It's Moorish all the way through. The inside, according to Palm Beach, looks just like a harem. There are no chairs at all in the living room. Only floor couches—dozens of bright pillows and ledges to lean against.

"Lillian Phipps is nothing if not thorough," Eugenia Sheppard continues. "As a hostess, she plans to wear Moorish clothes. A friend brought her a genuine caftan and, on Seventh Avenue, Andrew Woods is designing an American version in turquoise and gold. After all, that independent streak goes a long way back. Her mother and father made plenty of headlines in the early 1900s when they crossed the Atlantic from Mamaroneck to Nice in their own auxiliary schooner."

Of such heady and hardy stock is Mrs. Lillian Phipps, a lady of prodigious spirit, descended.

CHAPTER 19

Other Phippses

"The Phippses . . . seldom run second—to other peoples' horses or to anything else."
—Whitney Tower, *Sports Illustrated*

THE PHIPPS DYNASTY is a large clan. It numbers with its Bostwick, Grace, Guest, Martin and Mills cousins well past one hundred. Considering its size and diversity, it is a surprisingly well-organized group. This is perhaps attributable to the fact that its members have a common interest: the $300,000,000 Bessemer Securities, the trust which takes care of all the family finances whether it be a bill for an ocean-going yacht, a horse blanket or a box of paper clips. Cohesion also derives from the fact that most of the clan has, in one way or another, found some part of its identity with the horse.

Even with its tendency to homogeneity, the Phipps Dynasty has had its share of originals—iconoclasts, mavericks, even dropouts. Consider, for instance, Amy Phipps (1872–1959). One of the five children of old Henry Phipps, the founder, Amy brought the Guest family into the clan by marrying Captain Frederick Edward Guest, first cousin of Winston Churchill and one of England's richest aristocrats. This was a union that not only absorbed into the American dynasty one of Britain's noblest families, but also produced the jetsetting Guest brothers, Raymond and Winston.

Members of The Jockey Club, Amy's two boys raced horses, pursued tigers and, in their spare time, bestrode the Anglo-Saxon world in a variety of roles, including the founding of airlines and serving as ambassadors to countries congenial to their set and its diversions. They also became top-drawer polo players—Winnie, despite his large six-foot-four frame and small pigeon-toed feet, drawing a 10-goal rating, and Raymond, only a shade shorter, managing a 6-goal handicap.

Amy Phipps Guest, however, did considerably more for society than Winnie and Raymond. She served as a kind of self-appointed roving ambassador, travelling anywhere she felt appropriate and giving embarrassed heads of state a piece of her mind about their delinquencies in discharging their responsibilities. She also had a habit of giving just the right diplomatic party at the right time in the right place: her houses in London, Paris, America and the African colonies.

She also added a few more millions to the Phipps account when she inherited the Guest fortune upon her husband's death. Her real estate holdings in Florida and New York alone were estimated in 1957 to be worth some $400,000,000. That, however, did not prevent her from taking the time and effort to personally return to a butcher for proper credit an unused duck that had been ordered for one of her parties.

One of the first women to pilot an airplane, Amy was planning a pioneer flight across the Atlantic in the 1920s when the family stepped in and managed to block it. She settled for backing Amelia Earhart in her first flight across the Atlantic. Amy never quite lived down the disappointment of not making her own flight. Later, when she was able to stand up to the family, she began her practice of flying about the world in her private plane to berate world leaders. In 1956, against her family's wishes, she made a flight to try to bring peace to the Middle East. At eighty-four years of age, she was rolled out of her plane in a wheelchair, first in Cairo and then in Tel Aviv, to point a reprimanding finger at both Nasser and Ben Gurion. She died at eighty-seven in 1959, still complaining about the way people did things, still nursing the disappointment of that first aborted flight across the Atlantic.

"People would have me take such care of myself," she said, "that I'd never do anything interesting."

Amy Phipps Guest did plenty of interesting things in her long life, not the least inconsiderable of which was to be the mother-in-law of Lucy "Cee Zee" Cochrane (1920–   ). Cee Zee was the prize that her son Winston pursued, captured and brought into the family fold. A stunning Boston Back Bay girl, Cee Zee captured the imagination of the male component of the horsey set not only with her blond beauty, but with her style in having at old guard conventions. She had the perfect credentials for her unconventionality: a show-business mother who had married a wealthy descendent of England's fifth Earl of Douglas, which mix, gave her a theatrical flair and sophistication together with the security that tends to come from a Boston Brahmin background.

Cee Zee slouched through Fermata, a social girls' school in Aiken, South Carolina, where, she admitted to friends, "I really spent most of my time riding." Back in Boston as a debutante after graduation, she was in and out of the newspaper society columns, always "democratic," according to her contemporaries, but never sufficiently so to have moved in the same circles as lesser-caste Jack Kennedy, whom she knew slightly when he was at Harvard.

Her coming-out party was old guard Boston's biggest social event of the year. But society was not enough. Presently she began spending time with the movie people, in particular with actor Victor Mature, who was stationed with the Coast Guard in Boston during the war. Lee Shubert, hypnotized by her patrician beauty, made room for her as a showgirl in his revival of the Ziegfeld Follies; later Darryl Zanuck saw to it that she had a screen test and Twentieth-Century-Fox signed her to a seven-year contract. However, despite her upper-class credentials distinctly turning on the moguls of Hollywood, she was never to be a professional success with them. After nine months of coaching she went home to Boston without a single screen credit.

None of this made any difference to Winston Frederick Churchill Guest. He saw one of Cee Zee's photographs and immediately lost his heart. He also saw another picture of her, the famous nude which Mexican artist Diego Rivera had made after meeting her in Mexico City, a painting that somehow ended up in Ciro's Bar in the Hotel Reforma. Winston lost no time. After a whirlwind courtship, complete with the old Phipps–Guest panache, he finally married Cee Zee in a ceremony at the Havana plantation of his old hunting friend, Ernest Hemingway, and haeded straight for the bar in Mexico City. Fifteen thousand pesos convinced the padrone to part with the nude painting of the North American blonde lady made by the world's greatest muralist.

Today, Cee Zee's reputation as a social leader is as secure as that of another former actress who married into the set, Mrs. August Belmont, the ninety-five-year-old lady who has attended so many parties for her favorite charity: the Metropolitan Opera Company. Even more secure: "Cee Zee Guest is so secure a member of International Society," says a reporter for *Time* (July 20, 1962), "that she can afford to stay at home because she feels like it. For Cee Zee there is no such thing as missing a party. Either she's there, or for her it doesn't exist."

At fifty-three, Mrs. Winston Frederick Churchill Guest is still very much with her horses, mostly in show and hunting. For years she went up to White Plains to take lessons from Gordon White on the techniques of ringmanship—feet, hands, and placement for the jumps—and she has skillfully led many hunters around the floor of the National Horse Show in New York. This, however, takes only part of her time in the city. She is also one of the leaders in the fashion and entertainment world. Never, however, would she go in for "those little female lunches at the Côte Basque. And I hate cocktail parties. We usually have people in or go out in the evening—to a dinner or a benefit or a ball. I'm not a great night-clubber, but of course, I've always turned up at El Morocco from time to time. One winter it was Le Club. I thought it was loads of fun."

THE VANDERBILT DYNASTY

CHAPTER 20

Cornelius Vanderbilt—The Founder (1794-1877)

"There never was any disagreement," said the Reverend J. O. Choules, Cornelius Vanderbilt's private chaplain, [*on debarking from one of the Commodore's round-the-world yachting trips with his quarreling family*]. *"The Commodore did the swearing and I did the praying."*

THERE IS A FAMILY NAME in America that is synonymous with social position, etiquette, and the breeding of fine horses. The man who gave his name to that family, Cornelius Vanderbilt, started life as the rough-cut son of a land squatter. His manners at the end of his life were, if anything, more abominable than in his youth, and the only breeding he was ever connected with were the twelve Vanderbilts he sired. These unlikely beginnings also gave birth to one of the greatest success stories in the history of American capitalism. It also created a family dynasty that has reigned socially supreme in this country for five generations.

Vanderbilt family origins were far humbler than most of the other American dynasties. The first known ancestor, Jan van Derbilt, was a Dutch farmer who came to the colonies in 1650 and squatted in a section of what is now Brooklyn, New York. Later he moved to New Dorp, Staten Island. For four generations, into the beginning of the nineteenth century, the van Derbilts remained poor squatters. In 1811,

Cornelius, the fourth of nine children, soured on farm life and persuaded his mother to lend him a hundred dollars to buy a two-masted, flat-bottomed sailing scow—called a *periauger*—which he planned to use as a ferry to Manhattan. She agreed to make the loan, a large sum for a landless farmer, on one condition: that in the thirty days remaining before his eighteenth birthday he plow, harrow and plant the eight-acre lot from which the family drew its sustenance. In the sanguine manner typical of his later business career, Cornelius immediately rounded up a gang of boys and, with promises of rides on his new ferry, inveigled them into doing the job.

At the tiller of his periauger, it was now "Captain" Cornelius Vanderbilt—unschooled, tobacco-spitting sea-salt. And, on the eve of the War of 1812, he was already ferrying passengers across the same waters that the State Island Ferry traverses to this day. By the time he was twenty-three, the lanky, blue-eyed Dutchman with a gift for inspired profanity had repaid his mother and acquired a $10,000 profit. He had also built a reputation for toughness, energy and imagination, if not for refinement. During the War of 1812 Vanderbilt operated as a privateer, a virtual civilian "pirate," on the New York–New Jersey waterways, trading blows with both the British and American forces if they dared interfere with his traffic. On one occasion he applied his bare fists to an American officer, who had dared board his ferry with drawn sword, and laid the fellow low with a right to the jaw. It was the kind of life in which he delighted. "I didn't feel as much satisfaction," he once said, "when I made two million on that Harlem corner as I did on that bright May morning sixty years before when I stepped into me own periauger, hoisted my own sail and put me hand on me own tiller."

A man of boundless virility (he sired twelve children in two marriages), the newly prosperous young ferryman now looked about for a bride. His uncouth manner did not attract the Astor or Livingston or Rhinelander women, so he settled for a first cousin: a hard-working uneducated domestic named Sophia Johnson whom he had known since his squatter days. Marriage and honeymoon were consummated in typically no-nonsense style. One evening, after docking his ferry for the night, the nineteen-year-old blood slipped off with his bride into the Staten Island twilight and was back to business on his dock the next morning at the usual six o'clock.

Above, left: Commodore Cornelius Vanderbilt, considered the richest man in the world in the mid-1800's.

Above, right: Youthful Alfred Vanderbilt examines track with Mr. and Mrs. C. S. Howard, the owners of Seabiscuit, prior to match race against War Admiral in the Pimlico Special of 1938.

Below: Seabiscuit, the "old warhorse," J. Pollard up. The Phipps family sold him for a small sum, but he went on to defeat War Admiral in Alfred Vanderbilt's match race and became one of the legends of horse racing.

Left: Alfred Vanderbilt with his "superhorse" of the 1950's, Native Dancer, Eric Guerin up.

Right: Chairman of the New York Racing Association, Alfred Vanderbilt, receives a trophy for a stakes race won in 1973 by his jockey, Robyn C. Smith.

Shortly after his marriage, the "Commodore," as he was now mockingly called around the waterfront, launched the first of the violent battles that eventually won him one the world's greatest fortunes. Steamboat transportation had just become a commercial reality as a result of Robert Fulton's sailing the *Clermont* up the Hudson River to Albany. The old colonial aristocracy, headed by the Livingstons, had long reigned over this waterway. Robert R. Livingston, then chancellor of the State of New York, now legitimatized his position with apparent due process by squeezing out of the legislature a monopoly on steamboat travel up the Hudson. Under this arrangement the Livingstons made claim to the entire width of the river over the urgent protest of the State of New Jersey. They also exacted tribute from any steamboat owner who sailed his vessel past the shores on which they had built their vast manors. For their own transport operations they built elegant steamboat palaces, such as the *Chancellor Livingston*, which carried the fashionable in splendor up the river to Albany and back. Supplemented by flotillas of less magnificence, which accommodated those of lower social standing, the Livingston river fleet churned up a continuous flood of profit.

Vanderbilt, the two-fisted, New Jersey, tobacco-chewing "pirate" could not resist the temptation of challenging the aristocratic Livingstons' right to his riverboat monopoly. A small "war of the states" ensued, with New York officers seeking in vain to serve legal writs on the elusive "Commodore," and New Jersey authorities threatening to jail Livingston. Vanderbilt's sleight-of-hand, ingenuity, and force kept the battle going until at last it was fought in the United States Supreme Court. No less a personage than Daniel Webster represented the Vanderbilt interests in a landmark case that broke the Livingston monopoly. After that it was a free-for-all; everybody got into the act. The Hudson River soon swarmed with steamboats and early steamboat racing on the Hudson provided an outlet for the aggressive instincts of men who were vying with each other for the prize of the river's domination. Victory in a boat race meant not only a victory for the ego but also publicity that would help to win business away from rivals. Carl Carmer in his book, *The Hudson*, writes:

> Steamboat racing on the Hudson began soon after competition was established. The *North America* and the *Champlain* and

> the *Nimrod* took to spurting whenever one drew alongside the other. Live-Oak George Law bet Commodore Vanderbilt a thousand dollars that his *Oregon*, which had come into the river with a broomstick tied to her smokestack as a symbol of her ability to "sweep the river," could beat the *Cornelius Vanderbilt*. He won the wager, though his crew, faced by fuel shortage, had thrown into the furnaces all the carved wooden furniture and most of the fancy woodwork. The Commodore in his excitement had wrenched the wheel from the hands of his pilot and had forgotten to slacken speed to make the upriver turn at Croton Point. The *Oregon* beat him back to the Battery by twelve hundred feet.

In a few more years the Commodore was running ships to Boston and Providence and then, with the advent of the California Gold Rush, he spread into international waters. Anticipating the Panama Canal by a half century, he pressured the Nicaraguan Government into permitting him to build docks on both coasts and connect them with a road. This, with his fleet of ocean-going steamers, gave him a transcontinental passage that cornered the exploding market in transit to the west coast of the United States. With this move he rose from the ranks of local river privateer to swashbuckling international corsair, and the booty was now counted in millions. Asked how he had managed to achieve his success, Vanderbilt replied, "Never tell nobody what yer goin' to do 'til yer do it, and don't never buy nothin' you don't want or sell nothin' you ain't got."

At fifty-two and an established success, Cornelius Vanderbilt made a characteristic assault on New York society. He built a mansion in the city at One Washington Place, but when his wife balked at leaving Staten Island he had her committed to an insane asylum until she managed to see things his way. At the same time he decided to erect a monument to himself in Central Park. It would be the tallest and most impressive in the city, a testimonial to the joint glory of two great Americans, Commodore Cornelius Vanderbilt and General George Washington (for whom he had named a son). His mother, a sober woman in her eighties and one to whom he always turned for help, suggested that it was perhaps Cornelius Vanderbilt and not his wife who should have been committed; the Commodore abandoned his idea for his statue. He agreed to release his wife from the asylum, if she "went obediently to her new home."

Rich and powerful as he was, Vanderbilt was still far from the paradigm of rags-to-riches that he later became. Despite his failure to impress New York old guard society, he was something of a figure in other sectors of the social scene. In Saratoga the Vanderbilt name was already associated with thoroughbred racing. The Commodore was a backer of John Morrissey, the ex-pugilist and politico, who initiated racing at the Spa racetrack. And even though Vanderbilt was not directly involved in breeding and running thoroughbreds he was an enthusiastic follower of the races. He would sit for hours on the great porch of the United States Hotel, surrounded by cronies and family, and make wagers with betting commissioners. Between times, he would look into the status of his other gambling interests.

One summer, seated in his wicker rocker among the whispers and the buzz of afternoon flies, he took the plunge that eventually made him the richest man in the world. The mechanics of the entire operation involved nothing much more than the swift dispatch of cables, messages, and couriers from a Saratoga hotel porch, while ladies were delighting themselves with chatter and tea. A masterwork of skulduggery matched by nothing in the history of the nineteenth-century robber barons, the taking of the New York Central Railroad involved the bullying, blackmailing, and cajoling of a group of quarrelling local railroads into becoming one big happy family—under, of course, the guardianship of Cornelius Vanderbilt.

First, he attended to the twin New York & Harlem and the New York & Hudson companies and, in a characteristic nineteenth-century stock-market operation, beat down their shares to the breaking points, whereupon he promptly bought them. Now he had two railways, both of which connected to points west at the Albany terminal of the New York Central line. At Albany, Central passengers from the West continued south on Vanderbilt's two roads only when the Hudson River was frozen and Central's boat lines were inoperative.

The old river pirate smelled blood and plunder. He bullied not only his own passengers, but also New York Central's, by stopping his trains two miles short of their terminal, thereby making a hike across the icy bridge necessary for passengers going either way. When Central demanded that he run his trains across the bridge, Vanderbilt pointed to an old statute stipulating that no Hudson train, that is, his own, could cross the bridge into Central's territory. The result was that New York Central's business started to fade away, and when its stock reached bottom, the Commodore moved in. He now had a network of railroads that was the second largest in the country.

As a self-reward, the father of the first through-service from New York to Chicago assumed the Central's presidency, issued himself $6,000,000 in cash and $20,000,000 in new stock, which, with his original $18,000,000 in shares, made him the railroad baron of the world. Having won the contest and the purse, he now required the trophy. This he received from himself in the form of an heroic bronze statue of himself which he placed in front of the New York Central depot on Hudson Street. The city's mayor, A. Oakley Hall, memorialized the victory with a celebration and a dedication. "Stand there, familiar image of an honored man!" the mayor said. "Stand there and breast the winds . . ." And there the statue stood for sixty years, until time and progress in 1929 moved it further north to the Park Avenue ramp entrance of the new Grand Central Terminal at 42nd Street. Layered with green patina, forty-five years later it is still looking south toward the Staten Island waters where its inspiration made his first nickel.

One story, reported in *The Saratogan,* reveals well the clue to the character that was sufficiently uninhibited and unabashed to grapple with the Livingstons and other aristocratic pillars of industrial and social empire. One afternoon in his usual spot on the United States Hotel porch, Vanderbilt flung aside his cigar, got up from his rocker and rushed down to the street. He threw his arms around an elderly woman apple-peddler who was hawking her wares. His two daughters, now well on their way to becoming proper members of society, were aghast as they watched their father embrace the woman before the eyes of the elite "porch gallery."

"Father!" one of the daughters said. "How horrible of you in front of everyone! How could you embrace that old apple woman!"

"Why, girls," replied their father, "the woman is an old friend of mine. When I worked the Staten Island ferry she and her friend had the pushcarts. Ah, they were the prettiest girls. One hawked apples and the other oysters. And, me dears"—here the Commodore deliberately raised his voice loud enough for the rocking-chair brigade to hear—"except that I liked oysters better than apples, that woman might have been yer mother."

Cornelius Vanderbilt died in 1877 at the age of eighty-two. He had been married twice, first to a cousin who stayed with him for some fifty years and later, in his seventies, to a woman less than half his age. He was the father of twelve children. Throughout his life, his virility was such that it was difficult to keep female help in the house. Yet, despite unmannered braggadoccio, he was a man shrewdly aware of his limitations. When near the end of his life he gave $500,000 to Vanderbilt University, he said, "Folks may say I don't care about education, but it ain't true. I've been to England and seen them lords and other fellows, and I know that I had twice as much brains as they had. And yet I had to keep still for fear I'd expose meself, damn it."

He also never forgot the cost of a dollar—though he tended at times to overdo it. In his last illness his physician prescribed a glass of champagne every morning. "Champagne!" said perhaps the then richest man in the world. "*Every* morning? Damn it, I tell you, Doc, I can't afford it. Won't sody water do?"

A hundred years later, the nearly six hundred living descendants of Commodore Cornelius Vanderbilt, having inherited the proceeds of a fortune that by today's values would be worth billions, had fragmented into separate and often hostile groups. Individual Vanderbilts had intermingled over the years to form a dynasty that extended all the way from Britain's Duke of Marlborough to the son of Broadway's Ruth Gordon and Jed Harris. The great railroad complex that made their fortune had been lost to a brash commoner, Robert R. Young, in the same kind of stock squeeze that had won it for the founder. Later the railroad itself crumbled into bankruptcy. The old New York Central Building, now called the New York General Building, symbol of the Vanderbilt century of power as it bestrode Park Avenue, is no longer itself as the Pan-Am Building now sits on top of the terminal. The pigeon-stained statue of the old Commodore still breasts the winds in his bulwark above the Park Avenue ramp, but inside the Pan-Am Building, carefully sheltered from the birds and the wind and the rain, a spanking new statue has been set in place. It is the bust of another and newer brash entrepreneur, Erwin Wolfson, Originator and Builder. It keeps a hard eye on its piece of turf wrested from the Vanderbilts, staked out with a marker flung fifty stories above their monument.

"What does a Vanderbilt do?" the author once heard a tourist ask out on the avenue named for the dynasty's founder. "*Who* is a Vanderbilt? . . . is there really any such a thing?"

There will probably always be a Vanderbilt. There certainly is Alfred Gwynne Vanderbilt. He keeps the name of Vanderbilt alive. Consider the lilies of the field. They spin not, neither do thy toil. And so with the Vanderbilts. Of all the six hundred extant members of that most energetic of American families most are now just faces in the crowd. But not Alfred Gwynne Vanderbilt. Mostly, one suspects, because he alone of all of them races horses.

CHAPTER 21

Alfred Gwynne Vanderbilt (1912-)

"Maybe we're a little spoiled. I wonder how many pillars of the turf would keep coming out to the track regularly if they had to park their cars in some distant lot and walk to the entrance."
—Alfred Gwynne Vanderbilt to Steve Cady of *The New York Times*

"I HAVE ALWAYS BEEN IN LOVE with racing," sixty-one-year old Alfred Gwynne Vanderbilt declared, motioning inclusively around the chairman's office at Belmont Park. "This is my life!" At this point one might almost expect the This-Is-Your-Life crew to invade Mr. Vanderbilt's office and overwhelm him with the ghosts of Native Dancer, Discovery, and other racehorses that have kept his name in the society columns since the early twenties. The idea is not altogether inappropriate: The great-great-grandson of Cornelius Vanderbilt, in addition to being matinee-idol handsome, has always had a taste for the theatrical. Two of his three wives were debutantes who had brushes with dramatics, the third he met in Hollywood, and his putative latter-day passion is a jockey who was once a movie starlet. Alfred Gwynne Vanderbilt has been something of a national institution for forty years: "America's Most Eligible Bachelor" in his twenties, "Rich-boy PT Boat Commander" in his thirties, owner of Native Dancer in his forties, "Young Turk of Racing" in his fifties, and now, in his sixties, the blue-blood "radical" who not only aided women's lib by providing a female jockey with horses that had a chance of winning, but also levelled class lines by escorting her—even against the objections of some old guard associates in The Jockey Club. Small wonder that the press and racing fraternity alike refer to him as "Alfred," with the kind of populist intimacy appropriate to a democratic prince.

Alfred Gwynne Vanderbilt II (he dropped the "II" some years ago) represents for his set the same sort of anti-Establishment "radical" who can work with the "masses" and still remain a part of the Establishment that John F. Kennedy and John Lindsay represented for politics. He has the boyish good looks, charm and élan that characterized the late President and the New York mayor. Having been about horses nearly from the day he was born, he was as expert as any in the Old Establishment and so perhaps the perfect "white knight" to popularize and democratize the sport of racing.

Alfred comes from a line that, on the male side, extends directly back to the old Commodore. Cornelius begat William H., who begat Cornelius II, who begat Alfred Gwynne I, who, before he went down on the *Lusitania* in 1915, begat the symbolic, if not actual, leader of the current clan: Alfred Gwynne II. Were it not for a headache-and-hangover remedy called Bromo Seltzer, the reputation of the Vanderbilts would in these days be tied to trouble-ridden railroads, nostalgic calling cards, popularized etiquette books and not especially top-drawer primitive paintings, instead of to a sort of New Frontier style for the sport of kings. It was the Bromo Seltzer fortune of Alfred's maternal grandfather, and not Vanderbilt tradition, that put him into racing. Up to Alfred's time, except for William K., no Vanderbilt had interested himself in racing outside of occasional visits to the track. They spent their time chasing Sir Thomas Lipton in expensive sailboats down the Eastern sea lanes in search of the America Cup, or getting into and out of costly marriages and grand manses.

The millions that Captain Isaac E. Emerson, the Baltimore apothecary who mixed up Bromo Seltzer, accumulated from the headaches of losers at racetracks were turned to other purposes. Some of this money financed a farm called Sagamore, just outside Baltimore, which was turned over to Emerson's daughter Margaret, the mother of Alfred. She installed a band of thoroughbred stallions and broodmares on the premises and soon blooded yearlings were cavorting in the Maryland sunshine and a real racing stable was in the making.

Alfred G. Vanderbilt was born amid the whirlwinds of family

safaris to far corners of the earth. His mother—"one of the last surviving social leaders of the gilded era preceding World War I"—circumnavigated the globe no less than eight times, pausing in 1912 to give birth to Alfred in a fashionable section of London.

"There was no particular reason why I should have been born abroad," Alfred has said. "Mother was generally a pretty well-organized person. I guess in this case her timing must have been off a bit." Margaret Emerson was also well-organized in other areas, as for instance her trips to Reno, where she maintained a permanent residence to accommodate her during divorce season. Her first journey there was for the purpose of divorcing Dr. Smith H. McKim, a physician of modest means who had been a guest on one of her father's round-the-world cruises. The case was a sensation of the early 1900s. It had Mrs. Margaret Emerson McKim, the acknowledged leader of society's "Four Hundred," charging in open court that her husband had beaten her many times when he was in a drunken rage. Dr. McKim, the now ex–co-leader of the Four Hundred, countered with that legal anachronism that generally appears only where large amounts of money are involved: the alienation-of-affection suit. He filed it against Alfred G. Vanderbilt I, heir to some $80,000,000, whereupon the doctor received $150,000, Margaret got her divorce, and Alfred got Margaret.

After the senior Alfred went down on the *Lusitania,* the junior Alfred, with his younger brother George, was brought to America and settled on an estate in Lennox, Massachusetts, where his mother devoted herself to raising horses. Next, she married the Secretary of the Mint, Raymond T. Baker. He was a man who had been a rival to Alfred, Sr., in alienating her affection from McKim. This union produced a half sister for Alfred: Gloria Baker. But in ten years Mrs. Margaret Emerson McKim Vanderbilt Baker was once more ensconced in her Reno residence. Charles Minot Amory now became the next candidate, remaining wed to her for six years, whereupon Margaret once again visited her western headquarters. After that she was content to be just plain Mrs. Margaret Emerson and remained so until her death.

The net result of all this marital gerrymandering was to provide Alfred with rather a special view of the potentialities of breeding. "I have a full brother," he once observed ironically, "a half brother and a half sister, but the half brother and half sister are not even related to each other." Many of his friends feel that such complex genealogy had a significant role in producing the overcautious, rather suspicious, quick-to-be-hurt man that Vanderbilt tends to appear to be even to this day. There is a whole repertoire of stories about the Vanderbilt fear of being "taken."

A rather widely circulated story that points up how financially vulnerable Vanderbilt feels himself to be the one in which an associate was recounting all the many lavish contributions that Jock Whitney had made to various charities. "Humph," remarked Vanderbilt, the heir to a $20,000,000 estate. "If I had Jock's money I would too."

Perhaps a further clue to how Alfred feels about himself is reflected in what the psychologists would call his body language. Again, it is interesting to compare him with Whitney, especially as they move about the Belmont paddock. Alfred Vanderbilt invariably has his hands buried in his pockets or his arms folded in a shield across his chest, while Jock stands like a cocksure general, his arms hanging openly and expansively at his sides. Alfred tends to slouch about; Jock strides across.

In his celebrated psychoanalysis of "Little Hans," Sigmund Freud reported that the entire future life of a particular child was affected by seeing a horse fall while walking in a Vienna street with his mother. The boy, according to Freud, identified his father with the horse, and, as a result of his unconscious Oedipal wishes, had a phobic fear of horses. When he saw the horse fall he experienced an overwhelming guilt reaction, since the fallen horse symbolized his wish for his father's downfall. Some say that Little Hans went on to become Sir Rudolf Bing, the longtime general manager of the Metropolitan Opera Company. Whether or not this is true only Freud and Sir Rudolf know. But what is known is that Alfred Vanderbilt's life was irrevocably influenced by seeing, not a fallen horse, but a triumphant one, while sitting in his mother's box at the Pimlico Racetrack in Baltimore. In the 1923 Preakness, Alfred, only ten, made a bet on a horse called Tall Timber, which ran fifth. Having lost his first bet, he was about to conclude that going out on a limb, as he had just done with his first dollar, was a risky business in life, when his mother's betting commissioner came up to the box and put $5.50 in his hand. Tall Timber had been coupled in the betting with Vigil, the horse which had won the race, and Alfred was therefore entitled to the winnings. This meant that, in the very first horserace in which he had ever been involved, he had actually wrested victory from apparently sure defeat. He was forthwith to be hooked on racing for life. He went on to become president of the racetrack and a dedicated promoter of the very race—the Preakness—that had been his baptism.

When he turned fourteen, Alfred was sent off to St. Paul's Academy in New Hampshire, where he early showed signs of his later iconoclasm. Raised among the horsiest of the hunt set, he loathed hunting and riding; brought up in the tradition of upper-class devotion to rugged participant sports, he shunned varsity rowing and soccer. He was an intellectual, gangly and skinny, a pallid forerunner of "America's Most Eligible Bachelor," which he was later to be dubbed.

But though he loathed riding he loved racing. This fact was documented by the regular appearance in the school's mailroom of parcels wrapped in brown paper and marked to the attention of Alfred G. Vanderbilt, Esq. Later investigation by a curious dean revealed them to be not clandestine mailings of *The Diary of a French Stenographer,* as suspected, but copies of the *Daily Racing Form.* The future owner of the greatest thoroughbred of his time had nothing if not a sense of mission: other boys could fritter away their time over pornography, but his reading material would apply strictly to business.

Besides, the *Daily Racing Form* was essential to his school activities. *Making* bets on horses was a sucker's game, he had long ago concluded, despite the miracle of Tall Timber in the 1923 Preakness. To this day, he does not bet. But *taking* bets on the horses . . . that is quite another matter. While the rest of the class was declining Ovid and Virgil, Alfred, in his role of underground school bookie, was perusing past performances of horses in the *Racing Form* secreted in his lap under the desk. In 1929 he made book on the Kentucky Derby, taking his classmates' allowance money in bets at odds highly favorable to himself. He achieved a killing when a horse named Clyde Van Dusen, on whom none of the innocents had thought to bet, won the race. Despite the satisfaction of victory over his peers, to say nothing of his cash return, the incident isolated Vanderbilt even more. Even as his contemporaries looked down on the old Commodore for his vulgarity, so Alfred's classmates now looked down on the little bookie in their midst. He was lonely and unhappy . . . he folded his arms and pocketed his hands more than ever; the decrepit old hat—which he later sported and which for him became symbolic of an elegant, rebellious loner—began to appear.

At Yale the picture was not much different. Calculus, chemistry and the history of Eastern civilizations seemed of questionable practical use to a man whose life was to be spent in contesting such matters as the colossal weight handicaps that would be placed on his horses—especially his beloved Discovery—and who one day would preside as King Alfred of Saratoga/Camelot. Also, there were no horse courses at Yale. After a year and a half of inner searching, he dropped out on Christmas, 1933, just after his twenty-first birthday.

"I quit because I thought I knew what I wanted to do," Alfred said (his mother had just given him a birthday present of a fully equipped thoroughbred farm and racing stable). "And fortunately I was right. I wanted racetrack."

Racetrack was what he got, or at least racehorse. But first he indulged himself in that other fashionable diversion of the super-rich: journeying to the Dark Continent in pursuit of lion, elephant and other four-legged adversaries, and along the trail he met up with the prototype of man-against-nature *machismo,* Ernest Hemingway. However, it was an encounter with two rhinoceroses that furnished more substantial motive for a turning point in his life.

"We had two white hunters," Vanderbilt explained, "and I was as safe as anybody could be in that country. But we'd shot some guinea fowl for food, and the gunbearers had gone over to pick them up. I looked around and there were two rhinos looking at me. No gun. So I started to run, and so did they. I could hear them pounding, and I had a notion just where that horn was going to hit me. Then I remembered hearing that a rhino can't see very well, and that sometimes you think they're running after you when they're just running. So I ran around a bush. The hunters had dropped one of them, but the other ran around the bush too. The next bush I came to, I jumped in the middle, and the rhino kept going. You never saw two hunters more relieved when I came back around that bush. They thought they'd lost a client."

Alfred Vanderbilt decided to return permanently to his involvement with *non*-participant sports. In the future his running would be confined to horses carrying his colors on the racetrack.

The present that his mother, the Bromo Seltzer heiress, had set aside for her eldest son on his twenty-first birthday (younger son, William H., preferred politics to horses and became governor of Rhode Island) spread over six hundred acres of Maryland's lushest countryside just outside Baltimore. Sagamore Farm was the Calumet Farm of the east, a showplace underwritten by the accumulated tremors of millions of American hangovers, just as Calumet had been built on the profits from the baking powder of the same name. There were no Man o' Wars on the farm. Although Mrs. Emerson's Sagamore Stable had once been quite successful, it was now in decline and the only reason she maintained it at all was because her son was fascinated by racing. Alfred began his career, therefore, with only a few mediocre horses-in-training, some broodmares, yearlings and foals. But now, master of his own farm and possessor of the first share of his father's estate (he was to receive the balance in three installments), the twenty-one-year-old Yale dropout went to work. He began to buy racing and breeding stock and to expand his stable facilities on such a scale that he soon had one of the largest thoroughbred operations in the country. In 1935 he had one hundred seventy-five thoroughbreds, seven workhorses and two mules. A full-scale, traditional thoroughbred operation was being run by a twenty-one-year-old neophyte. Thomas Sugrue, a writer of the time with *American Magazine,* described it in this fashion in his article "A Kingdom for a Horse" (August 1936):

"By five-thirty or six the races are over. Then young Alfred returns to the farm, eats dinner, figures out the next day's schedule, and gets to bed. By two o'clock there are ghostly goings-on in the barns. The horses get breakfast at two, so that by five-thirty they have digested the meal and are ready for work. At five-thirty young Alfred is up.

"That is life at Sagamore Farm. The horses rule, the men serve. There are seventy-five men employees in all, and no women. Of these, twenty-four are exercise boys, who ride the horses in their workouts, and four are jockeys. There are eight foremen, two blacksmiths, a veterinarian, a bookkeeper, and the grooms, cooks, and stable workers of various kinds.

"The horses give the men little rest. Foaling comes along in the spring, weaning in October. Then, the next July, or perhaps in June, the youngsters are broken. First, saddles are put on them in their stalls. When they become accustomed to this burden the girth is tightened. Then, if they are going to buck, they do it. They do not often give trouble when first ridden.

"The puzzle is when they will understand what they are supposed to do on a track. Some never learn. Airflame knew the first time what he was supposed to do. He loves to run, and insists on being ahead of every other horse—a good habit.

"After that, exercise comes regularly, without a chance for dividends until the next January. All horses have their birthdays on January 1, so that on the New Year's Day following the summer in which they are broken they become two-year-olds. Then they can race.

"Meanwhile they have to be named, a painful process which entails submitting a list of names in order of preference to The Jockey Club in New York, which sends back the one that is accepted. No name which has been registered in the last ten years can be taken. With a static population of over 5,000 registered thoroughbreds [last year over 27,000 new thoroughbreds were registered] try to pick a name that hasn't been used in ten years!

"Meanwhile, too, they are eating up an average of ten quarts of feed a day. There are at present one hundred seventy-five horses on the farm, one hundred sixty-six of these being thoroughbreds. They eat 1,750 quarts of feed a day, or 19,961 bushels of feed a year.

"This, of course, is but one item of the expense. There are the board and lodging of the seventy-five men, plus their salaries; there are the salaries and commissions (percentages of winnings) of Stotler and the jockeys, the salaries of the other employees, including the farmhands, and the general running charges for heat, light, water, care of tracks and grounds, horseshoes, medical supplies, rent of stables at tracks, transportation, entry fees for stake races, jockeys' uniforms, etc. It takes well over $200,000 [today, close to $1,000,000] to run the business for a year."

Little was spared to turn the ordinary accomplishments of Margaret Emerson into the brilliant achievements of Alfred Gwynne

Vanderbilt, all in the understated style that was to achieve for him the "democratic" label of his later years.

"I daresay," said Audax Minor (writing as George T. F. Ryall) in *Country Life* of January 1936, "that no manor house, if you could call it that, of any racing stud in the country is quite so unpretentious as that at Sagamore Farm. It is a seven-room, two-story, white frame building, the sort that might do well enough for a second gardener, or a small family in quite moderate circumstances in the suburbs. As a matter of fact, originally, it was the kitchen of Sagamore Farm. Kitchen, by the way, is a generic racetrack term for any building, big or little, where grooms, and exercise boys eat and sleep.

"It takes forty-five men and boys to maintain the machine-like regularity of the establishment," continued Ryall. "They live in a kitchen that is Mr. Vanderbilt's particular pride, for he had a lot to do with its designing. It is in two sections, one for the white and another for the Negro grooms and exercise boys, and they are furnished exactly alike. I might say it is probably the only racetrack kitchen hung with Currier and Ives prints."

The drop-out heir to perhaps America's most social name was well on his way to becoming a maverick latter-day Lord Baltimore, whose box score in less than three years read like this:

	1932	*1933*	*1934*	*1935*
Races	8	24	139	569
Firsts	1	8	28	88
Seconds	0	6	21	69
Thirds	2	2	18	72
Winnings	$725	$6,650	$70,752	$303,705

The chief reason for this impressive record (he led the owners' list in 1935 and even showed a profit of $50,000 for the year) was the great horse Discovery. Like Columbus searching for India, Vanderbilt was convinced that somewhere out there was a great horse and he set out to find him; he found Discovery. Up to this point, Mr. Vanderbilt had bred nothing of his own of special note. Discovery was somebody else's two-year-old, and Mr. Vanderbilt bought him for $25,000. Whatever it was that makes for success in a racehorse—pedigree, training, luck—Discovery most assuredly had it. In his three-year-old season he suddenly emerged as a top-flight racehorse, although to Alfred Vanderbilt's great disappointment he always trailed his nemesis, Cavalcade, in the great classics such as the Kentucky Derby. To this day, Mr. Vanderbilt has never won a Derby.

But it was in his four- and five-year-old season that Discovery reached his peak. He became one of the great handicap horses of all times, a Hercules of horses—that is, one that could carry weight over a distance; appropriately enough, he became known as the "iron horse." He won stake race after stake race, bearing the ever-increasing poundage that the handicappers placed on him. In his fifth year he toted 143 pounds in one race, which he lost—the largest weight ever carried by a racehorse in modern times. Eventually his legs gave way and, as racing historian John Hervey said, "The handicappers had won their battle. They had at length sent him from the race course not only beaten but limping, his steel-and-whipcord underpinning finally yielding under the inordinate strain they had imposed upon it. They had converted him into a target for bitter animadversions in lieu of the eulogies formerly lavished upon him wherever he went and whatever he did. In the combat of the one against the many he had gone down." In Discovery's fifth year, Alfred Vanderbilt finally gave him his well-earned rest and retired him to stud. A racehorse had opened a whole new world for Mr. Vanderbilt, a fortuitous buy in the horse market and the great courage of a thoroughbred had made him the boy wonder of racing.

By 1936 the Volstead Act had been repealed for nearly three years, but in the executive suite of the 192-year-old Maryland Jockey Club at Pimlico Racetrack in Baltimore, where alcoholic beverages had never been sold, the directors were still arguing should they or shouldn't they go along. On the wall hung a portrait of ex-President Andrew Jackson, a Maryland Jockey Club member who had had the gumption to recess a session of the United States Congress so that its members could attend the Pimlico races with him, and his earthy appetites seemed to come through the expression in his painting to vote "yea." But still to be heard from was the old guard from the South, in the person of the secretary of the club, Matt Daiger. Since 1743 the club had run the local racing as a kind of high fashion show for Maryland's elite. Daiger wanted no part of any such common traffic as selling whiskey on the premises. One by one the other directors announced where they stood and why. A young Maryland newcomer, only recently elected to the board on the basis of his eminent family connections and the outstanding achievements of his racing stable, had waited quietly and respectfully until all the older men had spoken.

"And what about you, Alfred?" he was asked.

"They seem to want it," said Vanderbilt, casting his decisive vote in a tie. "Better to have a bar, or even several bars, on the track than to go tripping over empty bottles all over the place."

Vice-president Robert J. Walden resigned on the spot. Secretary Daiger shouted in gentlemanly tones, "I'll sell all my stock in this track right now for $150 a share!"

Getting no takers, he shouted again, "For $125, then!"

"Sold," said Vanderbilt, and the twenty-four-year-old director wound up with a block of nine hundred shares, to which he later added enough additional holdings to give him controlling interest in America's oldest racing organization.

That was not the end of it. Before long, Vanderbilt was elected vice-president and then president of the track. But he was still in the minor leagues as far as racetrack officialdom was concerned. Pimlico, notwithstanding all of its tradition and turn-of-the-century charm, was known nationally for but one day of racing: that day in May when it presented the Preakness, the second leg of the Triple Crown. Still, Vanderbilt had at least one foot in the door of racing's big leagues. He had already been admitted to membership in The Jockey Club—the youngest ever accepted up to that date—and his racing stable had already moved quickly to the front ranks. Now, with Pimlico Racetrack as his own domain, the socially registered drop-out from Yale took steps to establish his reputation as the people's sportsman. The first thing he did was to install an electronic public-address system so that the ordinary bettor who was always relegated to witnessing a race from subterranean levels could at least hear its progress, if not see it. He revived classic old races and established new ones, substantially raising the quality of the local sport with his "stake-a-day" program. He further automated the facilities with a Puett mechanical starting-gate, a device to get all of the horses in a race off at the same time, a considerable improvement over the European practice of assembling them in front of a tape barrier and then dropping it.

But it was the case of the "mountain made low" that brought him into the most direct of his conflicts with the Dixie pharisees. There had been since time immemorial at "Old Hilltop," as Pimlico was popularly known, a hillock in the infield that presented no problem of vision to those comfortably seated up in the private boxes; but, for the customer down on the concrete, that small Himalaya—which tradition seemed to demand should forever remain directly in his line of view—meant that the backstretch part of the race might just as well be taking place in India, for the horses suddenly disappeared from view behind the hill, never to be seen again until they emerged into the homestretch. To the horror of the Maryland racing establishment, which had already had its fill of this class renegade, young Alfred Vanderbilt proceeded to level the offending mountain. One sunny morning the rough voice of the steamshovel was heard in the land and, some $80,000 later, the mountain was laid low. So were two more outraged members of the Pimlico old guard: General Lawrenson A. Riggs and Racing Secretary Frank J. Bryan, who marched off the premises in a proper huff.

In his operation of Pimlico, Vanderbilt also displayed some of the showmanship of the old Commodore. His great-grandfather had often piloted the *Commodore Vanderbilt* up the Hudson River in races with rival steamboats that were such sensational, no-stops pulled, winner-take-all contests that the victor's prize was tantamount to using the river as his own private waterway. Four generations later Alfred did something of the same with a horserace. The Seabiscuit–War Admiral contest of 1938 was a sensational match race between two thoroughbreds that Alfred managed to run on what was in effect his own private racetrack.

War Admiral was the most famous son of Man o' War and was also the champion three-year-old of 1937. He was owned by Samuel D. Riddle, who also owned his famous sire. Seabiscuit was the cull that the Phippses had considered unworthy of keeping and had sold for a paltry sum. He was now five years of age, had been through the racing wars and become the grizzled old handicap king under the silks of Charles S. Howard, a West Coast millionaire.

The entire turf world debated with passion the relative merits of the two contenders—one a fresh young gladiator in his prime, the other an old hero bruised by work and time. In addition, the race would be a contest between East and West. Belmont Park management decided to settle the issue with a match race for a purse of $100,000 winner-take-all. For days sports writers haunted the stalls of the two turf stars to report on their activities, as boxing writers might chronicle the progress of contenders in a heavy-weight championship match. Public interest had reached a fever pitch when, three days before the race, Seabiscuit injured his hip and the race had to be cancelled. When the horse recovered, every racing management in the country tried to revive the match. But Riddle had lost interest. Finally everybody gave up—everybody except Vanderbilt. He went to work on Howard.

"You feel your horse can beat War Admiral," he said. "I know the size of the purse doesn't matter to you. Let me make the match for Pimlico and put up a $15,000 purse."

"All right," Howard unexpectedly agreed, "but I'm not sure you can get Riddle now. If you can, it's a deal."

Vanderbilt was in New York at the time. He telephoned Riddle at his home in Philadelphia and learned that the owner of War Admiral was on a train to New York. Vanderbilt met the train and talked fast for about five minutes. He took out an envelope, wrote the terms of the race on its back, and Riddle, amused at the young man's persistence, signed it. The match of the century was on once again.

No one who witnessed that race in November 1938 will ever forget it. It became a permanent part of American folklore, recorded for posterity by all the arts: painting, photography, radio, literature, and eventually crowned by a Hollywood movie. Grantland Rice, dean of American sports writers, was present to record it in the *Baltimore Sunpapers* of May 12, 1938:

> The drama and melodrama of this match race, held before a record crowd keyed to the highest tension I have ever seen in sport, set an alltime mark.
>
> You must get the picture from the start to absorb the thrill of this perfect autumn day over a perfect track. As the two thoroughbreds paraded to the post there was no emotional outburst. The

big crowd was too full of tension, the type of tension that locks the human throat.

You looked at the odds flashed upon the mutuel board—War Admiral one to four, Seabiscuit two to one. Even those backing War Admiral, the great majority of the crowd, felt their pity for the son of Hard Tack and Swing On [Seabiscuit], who had come along the hard way and had churned up the dust of almost every track from the Great Lakes to the Gulf, from the Atlantic to the Pacific.

After two false walking starts, they were off. But it wasn't the fast-flying War Admiral who took the lead. It was Seabiscuit, taking the whip from Woolf, who got the jump. It was Seabiscuit who had a full-length lead as they passed the first furlong. The Admiral's supporters were dazed as the 'Biscuit not only held this lead, but increased it to two lengths before they passed the first quarter.

The 'Biscuit was moving along as smoothly as a southern breeze. And then the first roar of the big crowd swept over Maryland. The Admiral was moving up. Stride by stride. Man o' War's favorite offspring was closing up the open gap. You could hear the roar from thousands of throats—"Here he comes, here he comes!"

And the Admiral was under full steam. He cut away a length. He cut away another length as they came to the half-mile post—and now they were running head and head. The Admiral looked Seabiscuit in the eye at the three-quarters—but Seabiscuit never got the look. He was too busy running with his shorter, faster stride.

For almost a half mile they ran as one horse, painted against the green, red and orange foliage of a Maryland countryside. They were neck and neck—head and head—nose and nose.

The great Admiral had thrown his challenge. You could see that he expected Seabiscuit to quit and curl up. But Seabiscuit has never been that brand of horse. I had seen him before in two $100,000 races at Santa Anita, boxed out, knocked to his knees, taking the worst of all the racing luck—almost everything except facing a firing squad or a machine-gun nest—and yet, through all this barrage of trouble, Seabiscuit was always there, challenging at the wire. I saw him run the fastest half-mile ever run at Santa Anita last March, when he had to do it in his pursuit of Stagehand.

So, when War Admiral moved up on even terms and 40,000 throats poured out their tribute to the Admiral, I still knew that the 'Biscuit would be alongside at the finish. The 'Biscuit had come up the hard way. That happens to be the only way worth while. The Admiral had known only the softer years—the softer type of competition. He had never before met a combination of a grizzly bear and a running fool.

Head and head they came to the mile. There wasn't a short conceded putt between them. It was a question now of the horse that had the heart. Seabiscuit had lost his two-length margin. His velvet had been shot away. He was on his own where all races are won—down the stretch.

He had come to the great kingdom of all sport—the kingdom of the heart.

The Admiral had shown his reserve speed. From two lengths away he was now on even terms. But, as they passed the mile post with three-sixteenths left—the vital test—the stretch that always tells the story—where 40,000 looked for the fleet War Admiral to move away—there was another story. Seabiscuit was still hanging on. Seabiscuit hadn't quit. With barely more than a final furlong left, the hard-way son of Hard Tack must have said to the Admiral—"Now let's start running. Let's see who is the better horse."

Foot by foot and yard by yard, Woolf and Seabiscuit started moving away. Charlie Kurtzinger gave the Admiral the whip. But you could see from the stands that the Admiral suddenly knew he had nothing left in heart or feet to match this crazy five-year-old who all his life had known only the uphill, knockdown devil-take-the-loser route, any track—any distance—any weight—any time. And who the hell are you?

War Admiral had no answer. Down the final furlong the great-hearted 'Biscuit put on extra speed. He moved on by. Then he opened a small gap. Forty thousand expected the Admiral to move up, close the gap again. But the Admiral was through. He had run against two many plow horses and platers in his soft, easy life. He had never tackled a Seabiscuit before.

He had never met a horse who could look him in the eye down the stretch and say to him, in horse language, "Now let's start traveling, kid. How do you feel? I feel great. This is down my alley."

Yard by yard Seabiscuit moved on ahead. Then it was length by length. Seabiscuit left the Admiral so far behind that it wasn't even a contest down the stretch. War Admiral might just as well have been chasing a will-o-the-wisp in a midnight swamp. He might just as well have been a fat poodle chasing a meat wagon. He had been outrun and outgamed—he had been run off the track by a battered five-year-old who had more speed and heart.

The race, they say, isn't to the swift. But it is always to the swift and the game. It so happened that Seabiscuit had these two

> important qualities in deep abundance. War Admiral could match neither flying feet nor fighting heart. Man o' War's brilliant son hung on with all he had until it came to the big showdown—to the point when the hard-way thoroughbred, the horse from the wrong side of the track, began really to run.

As a result of the match race the old Seabiscuit became symbolic of the invincible old war horse. He moved up to second place for total lifetime winnings, just a shade behind Sun Beau, and he made the Phippses, who had rejected him, look more ridiculous than ever. When all the results were in, Alfred Gwynne Vanderbilt had also moved up to be the boy wonder of the racing world.

Alfred was no longer a mere underweight reject from varsity athletic teams. He was now a young adult—still underweight, to be sure, but nevertheless the projector, with the aid of an adoring press, of a glamorous man-of-the-world image. When he slouched across the paddock green in his calculatedly slow, catlike gait, it was "America's most eligible bachelor" on parade. His pale thin face, capped by a jazz-age widow's peak, seemed out of a Noel Coward drawing-room comedy and it monopolized the rotogravures, generally accompanied by some well-endowed starlet's full wide smile. He was lionized by Cholly Knickerbocker, panegyrized by *Men's Wear* and eulogized by *Town & Country*.

But, for a young man of such potential, he remained in a state of eligibility an inordinately long time. Alfred was a late starter. It was as though the young man whose over-caution made him shy away from a stranger's extended hand was loath to break away from the lifestyle that he had been comfortable with since boyhood. Horse racing was a way of life for which he had, in the words of a contemporary witness, "given up everything else: wine, women, song, the city, business, pleasure." He was a man "whom you could like but only as far as he'd let you," said the reporters.

In 1938, at the age of twenty-six, Alfred made the break from the eligible bachelor's life. It was the first of his three marriages, and he stayed fairly well within the realm of the horsey world. She was Manuela Hudson, a cousin of Mrs. Charles S. Howard, whose husband owned Seabiscuit and who had been instrumental in getting him to agree to the match race with War Admiral. Manuela was a young woman of some social status, a fancier of horses and horse racing. Alfred had, in fact, met her in her cousin's box at Santa Anita Racetrack. This mutual affinity notwithstanding, the marriage was a rather pallid affair. At twenty-nine, Alfred was back in circulation and the only note of consequence resulting from his first marriage seems to have been the addition of another Vanderbilt (Wendy) to the Social Register.

After that Alfred was smitten by women with a passion for the theater rather than by belles of the horsey set. Both his next two wives and his great romantic interest of the 1970s all had at least tried their hand as thespians, even if none of them had won much more than notices in society gossip columns.

Jeanne Lourdes Murray, his second wife, whom he married in 1945, is the daughter of one of the first commissioners of the New York–New Jersey Port Authority, a granddaughter of a famous inventor, and a cousin of Mrs. Henry Ford II. She had worked, in pursuit of her ambition for the theater, as a press agent for a night club. Alfred was dropped from the Social Register for this marriage which so amused him that he named one of his best horses Social Outcast.

In addition, the new Mrs. Vanderbilt, a slim, attractive brunette with Irish coloring, played in such productions as *Mr. Roberts* and the TV version of the *The Women.* She had little taste for the racetrack, being able to "take it or leave it," as she was fond of saying. Eventually she did just that, leaving both Alfred and the horses in 1956 and taking with her two more Vanderbilts, their children Heidi and Alfred, Jr. She kept the prestigious name of Mrs. Murray Vanderbilt, and became a talent scout for the now defunct David Frost TV show.

Alfred's third wife hailed from Chicago: Jean Harvey, a tall twenty-year-old blonde, a member of a midwest restaurant clan. Alfred could have been listed, once again, in the Social Register, for his wife was not only a Harvey but also a member of the Cudahy meat-packing family. She too was of the theater, having been in the middle of dramatic studies in New York City in preparation for a stage career when Alfred met her. He was forty-four, more than twice her age, when he married her in Mexico City in 1957.

Jean dutifully accompanied Alfred to the racetrack, graced his appearances at the track and generally made herself a decorative wife. The marriage moved along at an even pace for some ten years, when

Alfred once again became restless. Separation rather than divorce had taken place at last report but he at least got, in addition to another young Vanderbilt, a practical piece of information out of the experience: "I learned from my wife's family that I didn't have to sneak around the racetrack incognito checking up on things," he told a reporter. "They're in the restaurant business, you know. They told me there's a service that you can get to do that job for you."

In 1940 Alfred Gwynne Vanderbilt was brought to Belmont Park to succeed ailing Joe Widener as its new president. This created some raised eyebrows. It was generally assumed that the job would go to Joe's nephew, George D. Widener, who in addition to being one of the conservative members of the establishment was also a leading thoroughbred owner. Moreover, the idea of someone as liberal as Alfred running America's most prestigious racetrack was anathema to many who feared "that young snippet" would do to them in New York what he'd done to them in Maryland. He was a renegade, no different than that man in the White House. And indeed his position in racing was akin to that other "traitor to his class," Franklin D. Roosevelt, whose political concern for their very own system had brought down on his head the enmity of the same groups. But just as wiser political heads saw that Roosevelt's New Deal policies would save capitalism for the aristocracy, even over their own blind opposition, sober racetrack minds realized that Vanderbilt's maverick policies would do the same for their control of horseracing. In Maryland, under Vanderbilt's aegis, Pimlico, rather than having been "ruined," had been rescued and was now functioning prosperously, still under control of the most aristocratic name in America. In New York, much of the same kind of "New Deal" was needed. The Jule Fink case of 1952 was still twelve years off; racing under Jockey Club rule was still in the Middle Ages, with not the slightest hint of reform.

And so another maverick by the name of Vanderbilt—Cornelius Vanderbilt "Sonny" Whitney—stepped into the picture. Sonny Whitney, who incidentally is not only a cousin of Alfred's but was also a Roosevelt Democrat, used his leverage as the controlling stockholder in Belmont to get Alfred the job as president. After all, as a child, Alfred had played on the lawns of Saratoga while his mother raced one of the best stables in the country. Even The Jockey Club had recognized that he belonged when they made him a member at twenty-four.

In New York, right at the outset as he had done at Pimlico, Alfred repeated his old pattern: outraging the entrenched by doing things that they considered nothing less than Bolshevik. The Widener Chute at Belmont, for instance, was an arrogant example of contempt for the general public, the common bettor whom they invited to their racetrack to provide dividends on their stock investment and as an audience for the performance of their horses. Named after Joseph E. Widener, Alfred's predecessor as Belmont's president, the Chute was a 6½ furlong straightaway (a race course with no turns in it) which turf writers had described as a "long-hated, vision-defying abomination that bisects Belmont's beautiful infield, drives form players daffy and reduces chart-callers to raving maniacs." Nobody, particularly the nobodies in the grandstand section, could see what was happening in the far end of the Chute, and even less could the common bettor see what happened at the finish. But that made little difference to those who sat up in the boxes with their powerful binoculars. What was really important, they contended, was that a straight dash without any curves provided the best and truest test for young horses. And horses, after all, was what racing was all about.

Alfred saw it differently. The twenty-eight-year-old young Turk seemed to take a special delight in seeing things differently from the old guard of his class. He always seemed to think and do the unthinkable. As his first significant act of office he junked the Widener Chute. George D. Widener, one of the most diehard proponents of the Chute, almost had apoplexy; the conservatives of The Jockey Club fumed at themselves for every having voted the upstart into membership, and a general feeling of despair settled over the green pastures of Long Island. But Vanderbilt, being a Vanderbilt, was able to get away with it. He was even able to install a chute of his own—the Vanderbilt Chute. But he was careful not to push things too far. Although his chute did at least have one bend in it, and the ordinary bettor could see what was happening, he never was so sacrilegious as to run the old guard's hallowed Futurity race over it.

In other areas he was also unconventional. The young "radical" blitzed his way through the ancient citadel of the old order. Drama and color was mounted in every nook and cranny of the staid old track. Fashion shows blossomed in the patios, string orchestras amid the potted palms of the dining terraces, wreaths of gardenias on the withers of Belmont Stakes winners. He even allocated a section of the sacrosanct Turf & Field Club to the bourgeoisie in the clubhouse section. As always he was lavish with management's money and tight-fisted with his own—the "poor" Vanderbilt who envied his richer peers for their greater millions yet rejected them for their backward ideas. He wouldn't blink an eye at spending Belmont dollars on glamorizing the winner's circle, yet he also expected free photographs of his own winning horses that reached the circle. For Belmont Park, price was no object; Alfred Gwynne Vanderbilt, however, was still wary. His attitude about money can be summed up by his reaction to a newspaper report when one of his children was in an automobile accident. The headline read: VANDERBILT CHILD SHAKEN UP. "That's the first time," he remarked testily, "that I've read about a Vanderbilt not being shaken down."

In 1942, at the end of his second year as president of Belmont, Alfred Vanderbilt went to work at his first fulltime job outside of racing: the United States Navy. George D. Widener, who had been waiting in the wings, finally got the job that he had so coveted. The first thing he did as president of Belmont Park was to restore the Widener Chute and it remained in use until 1958. At that time, The Jockey Club's old and faithful servant, Marshall Cassidy, was able to prevail upon the membership that abandonment of the Chute was really in their long-term interest.

Aristocracy has had a long tradition of choosing certain regiments for its tour of military service, as for instance the fashionable Guards Regiments favored by the scions of British first families. There was something of an American parallel in the fancy of rich young Americans for the elite flotilla of PT boats which patrolled Pacific waters during World War II. Anthony Drexel Duke had one (about which he later printed a lavish private edition of its and his exploits). John F. Kennedy had another, and Alfred Gwynne Vanderbilt was to have one, too.

But first Alfred rid himself of Manuela, his first wife, and the major part of his racing stable. Next he went looking for a uniform. The incident was recorded in *Newsweek* (June 8, 1942):

> COMMODORE'S SCION—Boatswain Alfred Gwynne Vanderbilt took up "flunky duty" at the Navy Department last week preparatory to going to sea. The Navy finally rewarded his persistence (his gorging on bananas and water to make poundage) by waiving the weight requirement. But it showed less tolerance when the heir to a $20,000,000 New York Central fortune reported for duty in an unaltered ready-made uniform. This he had snatched up in a lower Broadway store after his own swank tailor confessed that the specifications of a bo'sun's uniform were beyond his ken. Vanderbilt's first order was to march to the nearest tailor and "have that rig cut down to size!"

One wonders not unreasonably, considering Alfred's constant love affair with the dollar, if the story behind the story was not that Alfred saw a chance to pick up a bargain by wearing his lower Broadway sailing togs "as is" off the rack rather than sending them uptown as a model for the guidance of his expensive tailor.

Alfred stayed in Washington until fall of 1942, then went to the PT school in Rhode Island and, in spring of 1943, reached the Pacific. "It must have been May," he said, "because racing was at Belmont." He served on some forty combat patrols until September, 1944, when he developed a fungus growth on his foot and spent a month in the hospital. The trouble cleared up as soon as he left the New Guinea area, and he was certified as unfit for tropical duty. For about six months he was on a cruiser in the Aleutians, and at the end of the war was studying in a combat-intelligence school at Honolulu. "I was," he said, "literally the first man home from the Pacific when the war was over."

Like so many of the rich young men who served in the war, Alfred Vanderbilt came out of it with a new attitude toward life. Jock Whitney had discovered a "fundamental block in our educational system," that deep down "American soldiers did not believe they had any more freedom than the Germans have," and he decided to spend some of his money to convince them otherwise. Peter A. B. Widener II was converted to "militant democracy" as a result of having been re-educated in Army soup kitchens, and he progressed far beyond having Tiffany custom-made sterling silver bars upon his promotion to lieutenancy. Alfred too returned home a changed man. Horseracing no longer seemed the most important thing in life. "You just can't get Alfred to do anything," some of his colleagues complained. He spent a good six months probing himself, reserving decisions, standing, as it were, on the razor's edge.

But, as Alfred Vanderbilt had been fond of saying, "I had always raced horses because I loved it. I loved the scene, the life, the action, the excitement. But that did not mean that I was necessarily crazy about horses. Kids can like the circus without being nuts about elephants. It's the same with me: I *like* horses but I *love* racing."

The sport had always been a way of life for Alfred, a habit that gave his existence the love and the meaning it might otherwise have lacked. Its renunciation, even partial, would have meant the abandonment of a large part of himself. The postwar period he spent contemplating proved relatively fruitless. He had now just turned forty. How was he, in Ortega's words, to "fill the terrifying emptiness of life?"

"Maybe I should have sued under the G.I. Bill of Rights for the return of my old job at Belmont," Alfred said in the nasal tone he reserves for jest. But it wasn't a joke. George D. Widener, another lifelong horseman, also needed to fill his time and wasn't about to relinquish his office. Alfred didn't even have the solace of Jock Whitney's words the night that someone had cut in on him at the Belmont Ball: "Don't take it so hard, Alfred . . . you still have Discovery," for the truth was that Discovery had long since given up his duties as stud. The mood of the moment was etched in the appearance of the man: Alfred Gwynne Vanderbilt was appearing at the country's racetracks looking more like the man in the song, "Sam, You Made the Pants Too Long," than as "America's Best-Dressed Man."

Something wonderful beyond human calculation was needed. It was to happen years later in 1970 to Mrs. Helen Tweedy, daughter of Jockey clubsman Christopher T. Chenery, with the birth of a foal called Secretariat whose wondrous exploits on the turf three years later transformed a pleasant, obscure Smith College graduate into a national television luminary. It happened now, miraculously, to Alfred Vanderbilt. Even while he was in retreat, Vanderbilt had not totally removed himself from the thoroughbred scene. He had taken time out to breed one of his mares, a daughter of Discovery named Geisha, and in 1950, in Lexington, Kentucky, Native Dancer was born.

Geisha was about as unlikely a prospect to foal an equine wonder of the decade as could be imagined. She had won one race in her eleven starts and had earned $4,120. Her own dam had won a few races here and there—nothing much—and her maternal grandsire was John P. Grier, who had "had his heart broken at the eighth pole" by Man o' War, in revenge for the only defeat of his career by a Grier stablemate, Upset.

As for the sire, Polynesian had no doubt been an excellent performer. He was also Widener-owned and traced back through his own sire to Sickle, a Lord Derby stallion. Discovery, one of the grandsires, was one of the princes of the turf, and related through his grandsire, Fair Play, to Man o' War. But then who was not related to Man o' War through the countless cousins that resulted from his bloodlines after he became the wonder horse of the century? The conclusion is that there was really nothing in the pedigree of Native Dancer that could not also be found in the bloodlines of any thoroughbred which made its way into the Stud Book of The Jockey Club, a fact acknowledged by Vanderbilt himself:

"All I know about breeding," he once said, "can be said in a minute or two. If you breed a mare of ability to a stallion of ability, you've got a better chance of getting a horse of ability than if you don't. In other words, if you want to breed better horses, get better mares or better stallions or, better still, get both."

In Native Dancer's case, the mare Geisha admittedly did not qualify as "a mare of ability." But she was a Discovery mare, and at the time Vanderbilt's total breeding formula was contained in his policy of, as he put it, "simply breeding to a Discovery mare." This was what he did in the mating of Polynesian with Geisha. He demolished the whole mystique of the relationship of pedigree to racing ability with a random mating—an act of pure luck by his own admission—that produced the most able horse in several decades. On pedigree alone, as *The Blood-Horse* observed, "any number of two-year-olds in the spring of 1952 might have seemed better candidates for greatness than Vanderbilt's gray [Native Dancer]."

Now, Jock Whitney might say, "Don't worry, Alfred, you now have Native Dancer," as he had once said, "Don't worry, Alfred, you still have Discovery."

Vanderbilt emerged from the limbo of his postwar years. The timing of Native Dancer's arrival was perfect. He was a gray horse, something that set him apart from most of the great horses of both past and present. He also appeared on the scene simultaneously with the expansion of television into a major national medium. He succeeded in becoming one of the first national TV idols, even to millions who had little interest in racing. The sight of the ghostly gray form coming from way back in a field of rivals and sweeping to victory across the Saturday TV screens brought viewers to their feet in their own living rooms. When Alfred proudly led the hero into the winner's circle, in race after race across the racetracks of America (Dancer won twenty-one of his twenty-two starts), it was almost as Caesar returning in triumph under the great arch of Rome. Once again he was at the center of the stage.

The story of Native Dancer is one of the great romances of modern times, woven through with chivalry and symbolism. The gray phantom won his first race in 1952, his debut year, by 4½ lengths, and four days later was already a stakes winner as he romped home by six lengths in the Hopeful Stakes. Then he proceeded to demolish the entire two-year-old competition by winning stake race after stake race, always coming from way behind to win by tremendous margins. He wound up the season matching the world's record for 6½ furlongs and breaking the long-standing record for winnings as a two-year-old. He won all nine of his starts and was chosen juvenile champion as well as Horse of the Year.

In the meantime Alfred Vanderbilt had had a renaissance both as an individual and as a horseman. The petulant expression and crossed arms of the limbo years relaxed. Even his clothes seemed less unstylish. For the first time in his career, he had the prospect of a Kentucky Derby winner, despite the fact that no individual in Native Dancer's female family line had ever done anything past the age of two.

The Dancer came to the Derby with an eleven-for-eleven racing record and went off at the incredibly low odds of three to ten. Then came one of the biggest and most controversial upsets in sporting history.

The Derby went off typically enough, with Native Dancer staying off the pace—biding his time for his great stretch run. "At the clubhouse turn," trainer Bill Winfrey later told *Sports Illustrated*, "Eric Guerin had him far back. There Money Broker shut him off—perhaps intentionally, but I have no reason to believe it was. Now, being keyed up, Eric might have had his judgment affected. Anyway, down the backstretch Native Dancer ran like a wild horse, and he got [a good] position going into that far turn. There Eric dropped onto the rail, and they were third, turning for home. Dark Star was two lengths in front and about fifteen feet out from the rail. Correspondent was a length in front of us, and Native Dancer was on the inside. If every horse had held position it would have been one thing, but as Dark Star came over to the rail Eric pulled Native Dancer out and had to start his run all over again. He missed Dark Star by a head. The point is this: being shut off by Money Broker didn't in itself mean defeat, but it led to subsequent events. If we hadn't been shut off, Native Dancer might have won by four or five lengths. I was crestfallen, not for me, because the game owed me nothing, but I felt sorry for Mr. Vanderbilt and for the horse—and for everyone else."

The great horse, which had come like a messiah to save Alfred Vanderbilt, had been betrayed by a Money Broker! And, as if that were not symbolism enough, in the only defeat of his career, he had been undone by a Dark Star. Even as Man o' War, some twenty years ago, had been defeated in his only loss by a horse named Upset. For Alfred Vanderbilt, who made much of his knack for choosing names for his horses, the whole business of names must now have been a bitterly ironic one.

But that was the least of it. The laying low of his idol and near alter ego drew from Vanderbilt a display of petulance as he raised a small storm in the press postmortems on the Derby. When a reporter suggested that Eric Guerin's handling of Native Dancer might have been the ultimate cause of his having lost the race, Vanderbilt retorted, "I can't see what he did wrong. Eric had no way of knowing that he was going to be hit by a horse deliberately going after him and getting him at the first turn." Earlier Vanderbilt had told another reporter that he did not so much mind losing the Derby as the fact "that one horse was out to get Native Dancer. The trouble on the first turn was obviously deliberate. They came looking for him, and Money Broker deliberately fouled him."

Later Mr. Vanderbilt said he was misquoted. The incident did, though, seem rather of a piece with his lifelong tendency to feel put-upon and plotted against, always vulnerable.

Native Dancer, however, delivered in great style in his next race: the Preakness at Pimlico. He won by four lengths at 1 to 20 odds, and sent Dark Star off into retirement with a bowed tendon. He went on performing in the same grand style for the rest of his career, until he himself was retired at the age of four with twenty victories out of twenty-one starts. He was in the company of the gods, a peer of Citation and Count Fleet. He had inspired a reverence that had been felt only for immortals such as Babe Ruth and Jim Thorpe and Man o' War. Thousands of devotees did not cash their winning tickets, saving them instead for souvenirs. Jock Whitney admitted that for the first time in his life he could not bring himself to wish the defeat of another man's horse, even in the contest of his own Straight Face against Native Dancer. Most important of all—at least for Alfred Gwynne Vanderbilt—the name of Vanderbilt had become synonymous with Native Dancer and Native Dancer with Vanderbilt. The dynasty had been rescued.

After Native Dancer retired to stud in 1954, no other horse of exceptional worth appeared on the scene, and it would be at least a couple of years before Dancer's progeny would be ready to assault the barricades. Racing stables, or at least parts of them, had been sold out before. Generally this is done in order to show a profit in the specified period that tax laws require for qualifying the stable as a business (thereby subject to beneficial deductions) and not a hobby. In these instances the owners often buy right back in and start all over, taking tax deductions for another loss period. Or often a horse is sold, as in the instance of the 1972 syndication of Secretariat for $6,080,000, to defray expenses of settlement of an estate, usually at some tax advantage. In extreme cases, a stable temporarily closes down, as Lord Derby's did in the 1930s, to ride out an economic storm until a more friendly ambience develops.

Which of these reasons was behind Alfred Vanderbilt's sale in 1956 is up to conjecture. Almost simultaneously with his divorce from his second wife and mother of two of his children (whereupon he quickly married his third wife) he disposed of the greater part of his racing stable. The official reason given for the sale was that "The demands of various outside activities [his presidency of the World Veterans Fund] have taken me outside the country for increasing periods of time during the last few years," and that the time required for carrying out future missions for the Fund was too much for the continuance of an active racing establishment. Nevertheless, Sagamore Farm was held onto as was Native Dancer and the more valuable racing and breeding stock.

During this period the structure of the ruling group in American racing was being leavened somewhat by the introduction of new blood from up-and-coming tyros of the military-industrial world getting into positions of prominence in the New York hierarchy and in other areas as well (more about this so-called New Crowd is included in chapter 24). Men like John Galbreath, Christopher T. Chenery (father of Mrs. Helen Tweedy) and John W. Hanes were beginning to edge just a bit the Phippses and Whitneys. A Guggenheim (it was Harry Guggenheim's Dark Star who gave Native Dancer his only defeat—in the Kentucky Derby) had moved into a position of power in The Jockey Club; a Jew, Jack Dreyfus (of the mutual fund), had been admitted into the Club; Cohens and Kellys were sprouting all over the lot in Maryland and New Jersey; John Schapiro took over some of the limelight with his International Classic at Laurel—a race to which the most prestigious owners in Europe eventually would send horses. It was perhaps time for the return of Alfred Vanderbilt. "Their turf" did seem in some danger of becoming "anybody's turf."

Alfred returned in 1963 with his ascension to the presidency of the American Thoroughbred Owners and Breeders Association. Suddenly he was flying about the country in discharge of his duties and responsibilities—though apparently still concerned about his finances.

"I am not a rich man," he would complain to his trainer on finding himself booked into a hundred-dollar suite in a Florida hotel for the debut of his new stable. "Please keep that in mind. A fifty-dollar room would have done as well."

"By God, you know, there's a man with one of the richest names in the world," said the trainer. "Has the most expensive horses, flies his own planes, dished out to three wives. And he worries about a thing like fifty dollars for a suite of rooms. People say work teaches the value of a dollar. With Alfred, I guess it isn't work as much as no work that makes him so aware of the buck."

By the middle sixties Alfred was once again at the head of a highly organized racing and breeding establishment. There wasn't a horse to match the caliber of Native Dancer in his new string, but he had an estimable stable nevertheless. Sagamore Farm functioned both as his own stud and as a commercial farm—a center for boarding and training thoroughbreds for the industry. He was doing well.

In 1970 he reached the apex of his career. A graying fifty-eight, but still looking (and acting) every bit "America's most eligible bachelor," he was offered the chairmanship of the board of trustees of the New York Racing Association. The Jockey Club, with its infusion of bankers, builders, and Wall Street operators, yielded stoically to the times. Widener Chutes could no longer be thrust upon the public; Jockey Clubs could operate, at best, as shadow governments well behind the scenes, and a semblance of a new spirit had to be displayed if the sport of kings was to last even into the next decade. Alfred Vanderbilt was the answer. After all, he wore his hair relatively long, had a liberal aura, and even though he might be something of a nuisance, he was one of their own.

Alfred accepted and immediately was in the center of controversy. He fired Tommy Trotter, one of the nation's most popular and capable racing secretaries. He angered the old guard steeplechase crowd by eliminating their jump races at Aqueduct and Belmont, claiming that the track sold more hot dogs than mutuel tickets during those events. He effected changes that were, as he said, "in the interest of making racing a more exciting show," but nevertheless, always seemed to rub the Establishment the wrong way. Even the annual Belmont Ball, a society charity fixture that promoted the Belmont Stakes, was cancelled after he took office, an act for which he never publicly assumed responsibility.

And now, Alfred Vanderbilt once again sits at the head of New York racing, the only Vanderbilt of a long line coming down from the old Commodore, who still races horses. No Joseph E. Widener, yearning for the blueblood across the tracks, Alfred Gwynne Vanderbilt is rather the reverse: an old-line American aristocrat with the air of the newly rich outsider who finally made it. His lifestyle has filtered down to his children. Daughter Heidi married the son of Broadway's antic Jed Harris and the septuagenarian pixie Ruth Gordon; Wendy, the first daughter, joined with a Lehman, a descendant of the Jewish "Our Crowd," and Orin Lehman is one of its more hip members. Son Butch

(Alfred, Jr.) grew his hair long, sprouted a Fu Manchu mustache and, eyes shuttered by groovy dark shades, appeared with his new commoner bride in *Town & Country's* "Other Young Couples To Watch," along with the Ted Kennedys, George Plimptons and Gianni Uziellis. For a while Alfred Sr., thought he might have to watch Butch at the Fillmore East when he announced he was devoting his life to leading a rock-and-roll combo. But then he settled for working in the mix department of Mercury Records, for which his father has said that he is "quite happy."

It was in the romantic area of his own life that father Alfred Vanderbilt was to create the most waves among the solons of The Jockey Club and the New York Racing Association. In 1969, Robyn C. Smith, a tall, slim girl who had once been a Hollywood starlet (she was in the employ of MGM at about the same time as the luckless Sharon Tate), undertook to become a jockey. This was a commitment that required courage, for jockeying had always been a man's game, and no woman of real ability had ever broken through. Robyn worked third-rate Western tracks and the county-fair circuit for six months, serving a tough apprenticeship before she set out for the big time. Up against prejudice and discrimination on all sides—male jockeys, conservative trainers, stiff-necked management—she nevertheless succeeded in becoming a firstline rider in New York and Florida. By the end of 1971 she had won a total of forty-two races, become an exemplar of women's liberation, and opened race-riding to women, by her record of will, persistence and performance.

Alfred Vanderbilt was sixty, Robyn Smith in her mid-twenties. Alfred was still a man-about-town. Jean Harvey, his third wife, had just retired from the scene, noting that, as one gossip reported, "Alfred is always so enormously busy with the horses." Robyn was also of the theater, always a factor in Vanderbilt's choice of women; like himself she was involved in controversy, an annoyance to traditionalists. In boots and riding gear she might have appeared boyish, but in a dress she was a most strikingly stylish and feminine beauty. Not only did Alfred date Robyn but he also gave her the choicest of his horses to ride, thereby creating an unheard-of scandal: a Jockey Club member dating his jockey!

There was a heavy backlash. Fingers pointed at slavering gossip columns and columnists. Rumors circulated that Alfred was in danger of losing his job as chairman of NYRA; "no comment" was the standard response to inquiries about what was going on. Suddenly the 1972 Belmont Ball, the traditional and brilliant social fixture that annually promoted the Belmont Stakes for the benefit of the National Racing Museum in Saratoga, was cancelled. No one could find out exactly why it had been done. Mrs. John A. Morris (wife of one of the twenty NYRA trustees and chairwoman of the 1971 Ball) said to *The New York Times,* "I just plain don't know. I asked Mr. Morris, 'Well, what about this?' but he just said, 'It was Al's decision,' so I said to myself, 'That's that!' "

Another observer, however, suggested that "it was the wives [of the trustees] who really did it," implying that those ladies would rather have had their racing museum rot than see Vanderbilt bring his jockey to the ball, which they were certain he would. Commenting on the whole Vanderbilt furor, Robyn herself told the Washington *Post*, "My real problem is trainers who are afraid of their wives. And if there's anybody who doesn't fool around, it's me. My two best features are rating a horse and pushing a horse. I don't think I'm very good with young horses. Young horses like to play around with me. I get along best with old class horses, the old pros. They like me." *The New York Times* concluded that the dominant theory about cancellation of the ball was that it "simply got caught in the middle of a power struggle among trustees over how the NYRA should be run —and who will run it."

Whatever the resolution of the struggle, Alfred Vanderbilt did not lose his job, but by the end of the 1972 season Robyn Smith was no longer riding Vanderbilt horses. Other stables, notably the Hobeau Stable of Jack Dreyfus (who is also a Jockey Club member and Vanderbilt's predecessor as NYRA chairman), came to her rescue with mounts of high quality. She pressed on, showing her mettle as a person and as a jockey.

With the advent of the 1973 season, Robyn was back riding Vanderbilt's best horses, winning big stakes races. Her shiny red Jaguar was once more wending its way on Saratoga mornings to his stables for the exchange of pleasantries. To questions of "what happened," Alfred replied to the author, "I find that offensive! None of your business!"

The Belmont Ball for 1973 conspicuously returned to the agenda, and a noticeable détente was in the air. Who had chastised whom?

Which group had been the victor? What compromises had been made behind the scenes? Where would it all eventually lead? No one seemed to know.

The smart money, though, was on the likelihood that Alfred Gwynne Vanderbilt would go his own way in his own fashion, in the best tradition of his great-great-grandfather, the "Commodore."

CHAPTER 22

Breeding and Bloodlines: The Myth of Pedigree

"Mr. Phipps [chairman of The Jockey Club] says that the magic formula for success in breeding thoroughbreds is very simple. It's a thing called luck."

—From an interview with Ogden Phipps by David Alexander in *The Thoroughbred Record,* April 8, 1967

IN THE EARLY PART OF 1973, even before he had won the Triple Crown, a three-year-old racehorse was syndicated for the staggering sum of $6,080,000, an all-time high for the price of a thoroughbred. This literally made that particular 1,100 pounds of horse worth nearly four times his weight in gold at the market price, which was then $70 an ounce. In a human comparison, it put a horse in a class with the portly old Aga Khan, who used to be periodically weighed in for his measure in precious gems and metals, and it made a single animal worth more than half the price that nine fine young men brought when CBS sold its New York Yankees for $10,000,000.

Put more precisely, it was not the racehorse Secretariat that was syndicated but rather his sperm. The terms of the syndication agreement gave holders of the thirty-two shares only the right to send their mares to Secretariat for breeding, but in no way provided for participation in his racetrack winnings. Those were to go to his original owner until the end of the year, at which time Secretariat would be retired to stud.

What is there, the question now arises, in the semen of a three-year-old racehorse that it should command a price of six million dollars? And why would the transaction take the form of syndication?

The answer to the first of these questions is that monopoly control can inflate the price of semen as effectively as it does that of oil; to the second, that syndication is a device that permits realizing a profit from the inflated price while at the same time retaining control of the monopoly that inflated it in the first place. And, of course, there is also the built-in tax shelter.

The word syndicate means, among other things, "to combine for the purpose of carrying out a particular transaction." Two of its best-known usages are found on Wall Street, where groups of underwriters syndicate securities issues in order to raise large amounts of money quickly, and on whatever street the Mafia (which really popularized the word) syndicates for the purpose of controlling profits in commercial crime. Some even believe there are parallels to these usages that go into racehorse syndication.

In Secretariat's case there was the stated need to raise a large amount of money quickly. The horse's owner, Christopher T. Chenery, who had risen from railroad engineer to a large utilities fortune, had died, leaving huge tax levies on his estate. His daughter, Mrs. Helen "Penny" Tweedy, pressed by the tax collector, was considering sale of the family heirlooms in order to pay off the mortgage on the old homestead. "We probably could have sold the horses and invested the money in stocks," said Penny, an attractive, fiftyish, Westchester housewife in a newspaper interview, "but we knew that Dad wouldn't want us to give up the horses. So I don't think we had a moral right to do it."

Syndication of racehorses is a technique that now has taken its place alongside the charitable foundation as a fashionable tax ameliorative for the super-rich. When men with nine-figure bank accounts start availing themselves of the device—such as Charles Englehard, who syndicated Nijinsky for $5,440,000 in 1970; or Ogden Phipps, who syndicated Buckpasser for $4,800,000 in 1966—it becomes obvious that there is more involved in the syndication of racehorses than the sudden need for succor from merciless creditors. Chiefly, these considerations revolve about the old business of tax deduction and capital gain.

But perhaps even more importantly, syndication is a device that implements the determination of the horsey aristocracy to retain its tight control over breeding and bloodlines in the sport of kings. When considered from the perspective of racing's long history, syndication is a relatively new element in the business. It came into practice just after World War II with the expansion of racing and breeding in this country and the start of the inflationary trend that increased the income potential from a fashionable stallion's breeding services. Syndication offers the stallion's owner the opportunity of selling shares in his property, just as a private company does when "going public" (except that the stallion goes "private," and always among a very select group) while retaining either partial ownership, control or both. "Tax advantages also present themselves," observes John O. Humphries in his summation of racing law, published by the National Association of State Racing Commissioners. The arrangement generally involves from thirty-two to forty shares, or an amount equal to the number of mares that the stallion will presumably be able to service in a year. Of this number the owner usually retains several (enough for service to his own mares) while the remainder are sold to other breeders, usually, in the case of an especially desirable stallion, to the top strata of the horsey set. To keep the blood of the stallion in the hands of this closed group, provision is generally made for giving first refusal to the original promoting group in the event of resale of the shares. This not only monopolizes the blood of the stallion for the special group, in addition to providing "tax advantages" for the promoters, but also, and perhaps more important, inflates the value not only of the horse but also his every cousin, uncle, and grandfather.

When a horse named Carry Back, for example, won the Derby and Preakness in 1961, the syndicators suddenly descended on Saggy, his tired old sire who was living out his advanced age in peaceful obscurity in the lush grasses of a stud farm. The seventeen-year-old, near-senile fellow was primped up, hormoned, and otherwise prepared, for the promoters were sure they could market his services on the dream of his siring another Carry Back. Fortunately Saggy did not read the *Racing Form*. Otherwise he would have discovered that his syndicated progeny proved about as worthless as most of the new issues of corporate stocks that went public during the stock market fantasies of the 1960s.

The syndicators, however, did all right. If a thoroughbred stallion can be made fashionable, the income potential can be enormous, as witness the price tag fixed on Secretariat, who comes from the ultra-fashionable Bold Ruler line, a stallion owned by the equally fashionable Phippses. Even if a stallion is not syndicated, the gross can reach a breathtaking high. An owner of a horse with the right pedigree, particularly if he has a good record on the track, can get as high as $40,000 for the stallion's services. Multiply this figure by forty services a season and you have $1,600,000 a year, which, over the stallion's fertile life of, say, fifteen years, makes a gross value of $24,000,000. With grosses on this scale possible in the breeding business it becomes necessary to invent criteria to make stallions fashionable—and also to see to it that these vast grosses stay in the proper bank accounts.

This has led to a situation in the horseflesh market that parallels in many ways, the whole spectrum of super-salesmanship, insider deals and tax ploys that prevails in the security market. The entire edifice rests on the single myth of bloodlines. If stallion A is bred to mare B, the peddlers of pedigree assure us, there is a high chance that the output will be a fine racehorse. Or, more convincingly put, the pitch is that the sons, daughters and even remote cousins of certain bloodlines will get you to the winner's circle at Belmont, perhaps even the Kentucky Derby. Even most of the insiders—the first families of racing—passionately believe that pedigree can deliver the racehorse they dream of (and, if not, the formidable prices they get for exchanging stud services with each other at least as a capital gains advantage that takes care of the tax problem). But it is for the general investor, the relatively *nouveau* big-time spender who comes into the market seeking at least a financial association with the first families, that bloodlines have the most effective appeal.

Feeding this myth of bloodlines (and also being fed by it) are intricate compilations of scholarly statistics that painstakingly detail every move that every offspring of every stallion has made in every contest all the way back to practically the very Adam and Eve of thoroughbreds. These records are the work of an army of experts funded by interests concerned with the "improvement of the breed," such as the professional journals, trade press, industry organizations, and sales companies. The earning indexes they produce on thoroughbred bloodstock—all of which are supposed to act as guidelines for the purchase or breeding of future racehorses—would put to shame the technical charts of the most respected Wall Street securities analyst. If one desires a colt that can run seven furlongs in the mud with blinkers off at Belmont, one simply consults *The Blood-Horse* or *The Thoroughbred Record*, those *Standard & Poors* of the horse market, and there one will allegedly find exactly the right stallion—or at the very least, a cousin of just the right stallion. Within the year, if one has enough patience and capital, one's investment will without doubt be rewarded by a fine blue-chip foal.

If, on the other hand, one does not have the investment experience, then one may go to any of the myriad investment advisors that dot the horse terrain. (The Whitneys and the Phippses have no need of this since they and their syndicators *make* the blue chips in horses, as once they did in stocks.) These investment advisors are the men who are the super-salesmen, the turf consultants who tout the bloodlines and help build the multi-billion dollar myth that is the breeding business. They use luck, smooth talk, the age-old need of the believer to believe, and the ability to manipulate a statistic. If a Secretariat, a son of Bold Ruler, wins the 1¼ mile Kentucky Derby, the victory finally disposes of the cynics. It proves that Bold Rulers really can go a mile-and-a-quarter. If Secretariat loses, well, most of us knew Bold Rulers had speed but no mile-and-a-quarter stamina. These men are for the most part based in the Kentucky bluegrass area. They are called "hardboots," a term used to describe southerners, particularly Kentuckians, who in the course of wide travels through farmlands and backroads pick up mud and clay on their boots. Today, the word has also come to mean a horse-trader and especially a shrewd one.

Leslie Combs II, of Lexington, Kentucky, is not only exemplary of hardboot, he is also one of the best practitioners of hard sell. From the day, some thirty-five years ago, when he moved from the insurance business into that of thoroughbred breeder and advisor, his horse market has been nothing but bullish. He took 127 acres of bluegrass farm at $400 an acre and escalated it into over 6,000 acres at $8,000 an acre. In 1947 he acquired the stallion Beau Pere from Hollywood's Louis B. Mayer and promptly syndicated him at a considerable profit. This established him not only as the father of syndication but also as the world's most successful commercial breeder of thoroughbreds. Today he stands more than thirty of the most fashionable stallions among the five hundred horses that annually populate his Spendthrift Farm. The name Spendthrift is an apt one; Cousin Leslie, as he refers to himself, got his hands upon a substantial portion of the dollars that paid for the farm from the new-rich spendthrifts who bought the yearlings that had his stamp of approval, as well as from the wealthy old-line stallion owners that followed him into syndicates.

If you really want to get into racing the *right* way, not just some itty-bitty hit-or-miss operation that will probably lose you all your money anyway, you've got to be prepared for a four-year program and spend a million dollars. This is fairly typical of the Combs approach, followed by the conclusion that, in order to avoid getting into the business the wrong way, you'd naturally want to come and buy your horses and get advice from good old Cousin Leslie.

In his seventies and undoubtedly one of the shrewdest of all horse-traders, Combs has built a reputation for himself as a man who possesses clairvoyance in the matter of breeding winners. This is an image which he has carefully cultivated, but nature also collaborated by providing him with a smooth pate, aquiline nose and squinty eyes —the effect being to give him the look of a wise old owl. When, additionally, he releases pronunciamentoes in his thick bourbon accent, hardly a prospective horse-buyer alive can resist the feeling that he is in the presence of at least a domestic oracle . . . the Oracle of Kentucky.

Actually, Combs's success is largely attributable to riding shrewdly the crest of the great boom in horseracing and breeding in much the same way as stockbrokers recognize and take full and proper advantage of sudden public interest in stocks. In the 1950s nearly every $100-a-week clerk had a broker handling his "investments" on Wall Street; since World War II legions of new millionaires have sprung up, hungering to racehorses with the Whitneys and Vanderbilts. Combs was as skillful in catering to these horsey ambitions as was Merrill Lynch in "making every American an investor in America." And with just as much success in skimming—legitimately, of course—his piece of the action off the top. He had a yearling to sell that would fit the limitations of almost any purse, and all with the implied warranty that Cousin Leslie has the goods, y'all can bet yuh boots

. . . a taste of that good old Spendthrift water will move up any horse. He presided over the disposition of the millions that Elizabeth Arden poured into horses after she had made her fortune in cosmetics, sharing her delight when she had an occasional winner and quoting consoling statistics when she became depressed over her long list of losers. His Spendthrift Farm was graced with a number of new foals every year, many of which brought six-figure prices from other novitiates as rich as Elizabeth Arden, some winning their investment back, most not.

On the other hand, there is no disputing that Combs knows the horse business even as, for example, Merrill Lynch knows the stock market, and he also operates as a kind of broker and advisor to some of the oldest names in racing. First, as the man who originated syndication, he functions as the prime syndicator for the establishment, with the result that many of the most fashionable stallions wind up standing at Spendthrift Farm. Nashua, owned by the late Jockey Club chairman William Woodward, the first racehorse syndicated for over a million dollars, is among those Combs has on his farm. Other breeders such as George D. Widener, another Jockey Club chairman, and Harry Guggenheim also preferred to let Combs handle the day-to-day problems of both breeding their bloodstock and raising the foals on his farm, operations for which Spendthrift is admirably equipped. Many of these big operators even went into partnership with him on a certain number of their horses. Thus, Leslie Combs formed associations with the very top level of the horsey set, and the advantage of having these connections perhaps overshadows even his ability at breeding winners in the origins of his success. Woodward and Widener and Guggenheim stock *bred* at Spendthrift Farm go into the stables of the world's leading owners. These stables have the best facilities, the best trainers, the best of everything. Obviously many of these horses have a built-in head start toward the winner's circle. Yearlings which Combs breeds for *sale*, by virtue of his reputation for the highest prices, end up perforce with well-financed establishments, again giving Combs-bred stock a high likelihood of success. A commercial breeder such as Combs puts a large number of new thoroughbreds onto the racetrack each year, almost all of them in the silks of the topmost stables. As a result, not so unlike a fortune-teller foreseeing that a lovely rich female client will soon have a new man in her life, he is bound to have some impressive results. The successes are always well publicized. The failures . . . The real test would seem to be not who is America's most successful commercial *breeder,* as Combs advertises himself, but rather how many so-called worthless horses has one turned into stakes-winners in the manner of trainers such as Hirsch Jacobs or Allen Jerkens. (It was Jerkens-trained Onion of Jack Dreyfus' Hobeau Farm that beat Secretariat in the Whitney at Saratoga in August of 1973. *That* was an achievement.) It also takes no special prescience to decide to breed a mare to Bold Ruler or any other of the stallions on the leading sire list (although the results are by no means automatically wonderful). Alfred Vanderbilt once said that in planning the breeding of Native Dancer he "gave the mating of Geisha to Polynesian a great deal of thought and study and the somewhat nebulous value of twenty years of experience and, lo and behold, here comes Native Dancer. Quite naturally, I'm not going to tell you I have given a great deal of study and thought and my background of twenty years' breeding experience to the mating of all my other horses, many of which could not get out of their own way." Ogden Phipps, owner of Bold Ruler, sire of some of the world's best racehorses, has gone much further in telling a reporter from *The Thoroughbred Record,* "the magic formula for success in breeding can be summed up in one word: luck."

Nevertheless, new money keeps coming into the market, much of it flowing to Leslie Combs's reputation. And Cousin Leslie, like your friendly stockbroker, continues to scoop his take off the top—sometimes both ways—whether the new money gets burned or not. A case in point is Majestic Prince, which won the 1969 Kentucky Derby, one of those instances when Combs indeed hit the jackpot.

On that occasion the *Thoroughbred Record,* organ of The Jockey Club, one of the media through which Combs's near-mystique has been built, immediately reported:

"It is virtually impossible to determine the capability of a horse in advance, but—ONE MAN 'KNEW,'" declared the publication that collects reams of statistics suggesting fixed equations between heredity and performance. "Leslie Combs II, owner of Spendthrift Farm, and one of the most knowledgeable horsemen in the world, picked one colt out of his 1966 crop of weanlings, however, and he 'knew.' Now we know he knew, because the colt was Majestic Prince. He was high on the colt from the start and, before the colt was sold to Frank McMahon for a world record price of $250,000 at the 1967 Keeneland Summer Sales, Mr. Combs had already told some people that he thought the colt was one of the best, if not *the* best, horses he had ever bred. Today, the facts are bearing him out."

This immediately started a stampede on the sire of Majestic Prince—not unrelated to an investors' rush on a hot stock in Wall Street—with all manner of technical pedigree reports to demonstrate how it was inevitable that such bloodlines would produce a Derby winner, particularly since Cousin Leslie "knew."

"Mr. Combs was not just high on the yearling because he was such a good-looking colt," emphasized the *Thoroughbred Record.* "Majestic Prince was sired by Raise A Native, which had been a record-breaking horse in his own right." (And a horse that Mr. Combs had syndicated for a record sum of $2,625,000, thereby assuring that his progeny would go to the best stables). When Majestic Prince's full brother, a horse from exactly the same breeding, was ready for the sales ring in 1970, Combs announced:

"I thought Majestic Prince was the best colt I ever raised. But now I've changed my mind. His brother is the best-looking young colt I've ever *seen.* When he comes into that sales ring next summer, it's going to be something. I'm going to announce that Frank McMahon [who bought Majestic Prince] owns half the dam and further state that both of us may bid. I just want Frank to have his chips ready, because old Cousin Leslie might wind up buying this colt himself!"

The colt—later named Crowned Prince—lived up to Cousin Leslie's predictions. He was sold at auction for a record price of $510,000 before he even set foot on a racetrack. The buyer was once again oil multimillionaire Frank McMahon. This time, McMahon's purchase was sent to England to be trained and raced. But Crowned Prince returned only $41,140 of his purchase price—the total coming from the two races he won as a two-year-old. After finishing a poor fourth in his debut as a three-year-old he was retired from competition, the reason being, according to his owners, that he had an enlarged soft palate. This time, however, there was little fanfare about the yearling on which Mr. Combs had been so "high," and certainly no mention that Cousin Leslie once again "knew." Nevertheless, Crowned Prince was sold to a partnership for $1,200,000, to pass on his fashionable blood at a stud in Ireland.

Pedigree is of very limited use in predetermining how a future thoroughbred will perform on the racetrack. Admittedly, genetic factors in the ancestry control physical characteristics of the progeny; in accordance with Mendelian law a breeder can, with some certainty, predict the coloring and conformation and even, to some extent, the disposition of a particular foal. But to attribute Secretariat's success as a racehorse to the fact that he was sired by Bold Ruler is to confuse science with good fortune—also known as luck.

The story of how Mrs. Tweedy became the owner of Secretariat is literally one that turns on luck—she got him by tossing a half-dollar piece with Ogden Phipps in the office of Alfred Gwynne Vanderbilt. "It was all part of a very complicated arrangement that father had made years before with Ogden Phipps," said Mrs. Tweedy. "They had agreed that each season Mr. Phipps's great sire, Bold Ruler, would be bred to two of my father's broodmares. Every two years they flipped a coin. The winner had first choice of the two foals that year, and the loser had first choice the year after."

Mrs. Tweedy decided, on assuming management of her deceased father's stable, that the arrangement with Phipps was not a good business deal for her, but agreed to "go on with it for two more years and then be through with it." At the time of her final coin toss with Phipps in 1969, she lost, and the chairman of The Jockey Club had the first choice. He selected the foal by his Bold Ruler out of her mare Somethingroyal. Having been the loser, next year Mrs. Tweedy was now entitled to first choice. But there was no choice, since only one of the two 1970 mares had foaled, and Mrs. Tweedy had to take whatever the one pregnant mare dropped. That happened also to be a foal by Bold Ruler out of Somethingroyal. The result was that Ogden Phipps's choice of 1969—something by the name of The Bride—could not, as one wag put it, "beat a fat man running downhill"; Penny Tweedy's no-alternative choice became a horse named Secretariat.

What came out of the mating of Bold Ruler with Somethingroyal was clearly about as controllable as the honest toss of a coin; and Ogden Phipps, the foremost breeder in the country, and Helen Tweedy, racing's leading owner, could predict the outcome of a breeding with about as much prescience as a blackjack player in a Las Vegas casino can have concerning the denomination of the next card.

So far as Triple Crown winner Secretariat's ability to transmit his own racing prowess to his progeny—an expectation backed by the $6,080,000 invested in his syndication—that would seem another of the horse world's fairy tales. The eight previous Triple Crown winners from Sir Barton in 1919 to Citation in 1948 for the most part produced nothing out of the ordinary in the stud. Considering the high rating of both their pedigree and their performance on the racetrack, they did a most disappointing job of passing on their class. At this point one can anticipate a chorus of raised voices: "Triple Crown winner Count Fleet sired Kentucky Derby winner Count Turf . . . Triple Crown winner Gallant Fox sired Omaha, another Triple Crown winner. . . ."

To which one feels constrained to reply: A cheap $1,200 yearling by the name of Canonero II also became a Derby and Preakness winner, just missing the Triple Crown. As for Triple Crown winner Omaha; his progeny performed so wretchedly on the racetrack that owner William Woodward gave him away to a group of obscure dairy farmers. And Robert Kleberg's Triple Crown winner, Assault, was so worthless as a thoroughbred sire that he was finally consigned to the ignominy of servicing King Ranch's quarter-horse mares.

Nonetheless pedigree in thoroughbreds is big business. When the shareholders invested in the Secretariat syndicate, they were investing in themselves and in the business they control. The list of shareholders reads like the roster of The Jockey Club: Alfred Vanderbilt, Ogden Phipps, John Hay Whitney, Robert Kleberg, Paul Mellon . . . which means that the 1973 Triple Crown winner's offspring will go into the hands of owners with superior facilities, top trainers, powerful connections and sufficient capital to wait until a horse is ready to give his best—in effect, "money going to money." With that kind of up-front support, and given reasonable good luck, the sons and daughters of Secretariat are reasonably assured of better-than-average success. The fact that an obscure stallion like Saggy sired a Carry Back, or a $700 buy like Alsab, in the hands of a skillful trainer, won over $350,000, or a $1,200 cull like Canonero II just missed winning the Triple Crown does not change the establishment's continued emphasis on fashionable ancestry. The owners of fashionable stallions continue to make millions in stud fees by inflating the price with the mythology of pedigree—even if they occasionally must contribute to the general industry pot by subscribing to a painfully high syndication. Soon enough, it will be their own turn to make a multimillion-dollar syndication.

That pedigree is a sometime affair of fashion and control is attested to by John Hervey ("Salvator"), one of the most respected names in the thoroughbred world, the author of the *Encyclopedia Britannica*'s section on breeding and of a volume in The Jockey Club's monumental *Racing in America* series. In a *Blood-Horse* article, January 17, 1942, dealing with the then prevalent fad of making imported horses fashionable, Hervey says:

"In the making of horses, and bloodlines, fashionable, it is, speaking practically, money rather than merit which tips the scales. It has now reached that point in this country where it is very difficult to make a native-bred stallion fashionable. To verify this one has only to consult the stud-cards of our leading breeding establishments for it is they, and, it might almost be said, they alone, which set the fashion and are its arbiters." A case in point, continued Hervey, was that of a stallion which was "imported at a cost of $225,000, plus other expenses reported to have totalized at above $250,000. To import him a syndicate of multimillionaires was formed. At the time, it was asserted—and not denied—that the combined wealth of the importers was in excess of one billion dollars ($1,000,000,000). The stallion was placed at the head of the largest and most select stud in America. A fee of $2,500 was placed upon his services, but in reality he was limited to mares owned or booked to him by members of the syndicate. These gentlemen, among them, own a small army of the choicest broodmares in this country, of which the very *crème de la crème* was skimmed off to breed to him. If, in certain cases, a member did not think his available material "good enough to breed to such a horse," he either tried to buy something ultra-select for the purpose or arranged with the owner of some exquisitely bred or already famous matron to mate her with the stallion. On their parts owners of such mares outside the syndicate made strenuous efforts to perfect such arrangements. Favored by such extraordinary assistance, the stallion climbed to the top of the sires' list the second season that his get raced in this country.

"It is, therefore, as naïve to ask why the imported stallion's winners top those of the native sires as to enquire why there are more diamond tiaras scattered along a few blocks of Park Avenue than throughout all the rest of America. Or why the names of their wearers are daily paraded in the public prints while those of Mrs. Bill Smith of Skaneateles, or Mrs. Tom Jones of Paducah, though the latter ladies may be fairer to look upon and more delightful to encounter, remain unheralded and unsung.

"Yet from the Smith-Jones strata of the breeding world there keep coming to the top such things as Alsab and Market Wise and so on and on and on. Fashionable? Good heavens, no! Never, until by sheer force of merit and a dauntless struggle up from the bottom they have made themselves so. . . . After which we will be treated to learned digressions upon the number of times that the names of animals which appear in fashionable pedigrees appear also in theirs. And that therefrom all their greatness springs."

To help support the pedigree argument, very complex theories and experiments have been devised. They are as legion as the investment advisory letters on Wall Street, supported by as occult a statistical ideology and for the most part are similarly unrewarding. One such is the "theory of dosages," developed by a Frenchman, Lt. Col. J. Vuillier, who, because certain families were more numerous and hence tended to produce more horses of exceptional class, ascribed various qualities to different families and suggested combining certain proportions of these strains (dosages) to get the kind of animal one desired. Many other breeders, on the other hand, states Hervey in his *Encyclopedia Britannica* article, "place their hopes upon the repetition or approximation of a 'nick' or combination of bloodlines which already has produced one or more good horses. Such practice gradually gave way before a growing comprehension of the elementary principles of genetics. Only one thoroughly scientific attempt to estimate the complicated probabilities in race-horse breeding was made in the first half of the 20th century—at the Eugenics Records offices of the Carnegie institution at Cold Spring Harbor, Long Island, N.Y., in the 1920s under the direction of Dr. H. H. Laughlin. Most breeders remained unaware of the conclusions reached, and would find it difficult to apply them if they were understood."

But the guide that has the greatest authority for most breeders is the Progeny Index developed in the offices of the American Thoroughbred Breeders Association in Lexington, Kentucky. This theory of predicting genetic probability is based on the assumption that relative earning power provides an approximate measure of a horse's class, constitution and soundness, the principal factors which its proponents claim are significant in quantitative measurement of the inheritance of racing ability. The basis for all calculations is the average monetary distribution per runner in a given year (if 1,000 horses raced in 1970 for $1,000,000 in purses, then the average monetary distribution is $1,000 per runner); and the performance of any runner in that year is expressed as a ratio to this "average expectancy." Given this ratio, or earnings index of the parent, one can then measure the probable earning power of the offspring, for it is claimed there is a directly proportional relationship between these two statistics "within the limits provided by the chance assortment of genes and by environmental factors."

The Jockey Club has gone to the great trouble and expense of setting up in Lexington a compu-statistical center for gathering this kind of data on every thoroughbred nearly all the way back to the Godolphin Arabian. When complete, the file will embrace enough ancestral bloodline and earnings information on each horse so that all one need do is push a button and the printout will provide the protocol on who should cohabit with whom. But here again the issue seems as confused as before. To whose earning-index, in practice, should the desired progeny's probable earning power really relate? To the sire's, as suggested in all that data so painstakenly collected? Or to the particular stable's, as represented in the owner's Dun & Bradstreet rating and in the trainer-jockey standing on the performance list?

Perhaps the breeding theory which approaches nearest to the actual truth is the non-theory of Angel Cordero, Jr., the sensational black Puerto Rican jockey who rides top flight racehorses.

"Prior to the running of the recent Cowdin Stakes," reported Teddy Cox in the *Racing Form* of October 13, 1970, "Angel Cordero, Jr., found himself weighing offers from several trainers who were without riders for their charges. The colorful Puerto Rican even considered putting numbers into a hat.

"'There wasn't really much choice between the colts who were open,' Cordero recalled. 'Then I got to thinking that it was foolish for me to be taking pot luck when Allen Jerkens was among the trainers on the list. I said to myself that there shouldn't be a choice when I have a chance to string along with perhaps the finest horseman in the world. As a matter of fact, the man is absolutely amazing. Take Step Nicely, for example. He is by a sire [Watch Your Step] who certainly hasn't shown much and is out of a Beau Gar mare. If you put a colt of that breeding in a yearling sale he wouldn't bring the first bid, but that's the kind Jerkens makes into stakes winners. One time I heard a man say that Hirsch Jacobs made his own breeding. I think that is also true of Jerkens.

"'Those of us who ride for him learn quickly never to sell him short, which is precisely why I chose Step Nicely in the Cowdin when I could have decided on more fashionably-bred colts.'"

In other words, a young jockey who with his own body has felt the bones and sinews of thousands of racehorses grinding under him down dozens of racetracks in quest of numberless victories is saying that it is the trainer (and training facilities) that makes the racehorse —not his bloodlines.

In an article in the *Morning Telegraph*, December 2, 1949, H. J. McGuire quotes Peter A. B. Widener III as saying, "Fully aware that the theory is at variance with the accepted belief of many breeders, I feel that environment governs the success of a thoroughbred in racing to a greater extent than heredity. It follows that I believe that ability to run fast is developed rather than inherited.

"The theory of environment over heredity is now practiced at Elmendorf, and you can tell any prospective buyers of our colts and fillies that they have been bred in the accepted manner of my father and grandfather of breeding the best to the best. When I decide to test my beliefs, the experiment will not be at the expense of buyers of Elmendorf stock, but will be a separate undertaking."

"I do not mean to imply that all characteristics of a thoroughbred are due to environment and neither do I maintain that the theory would hold good for horses suffering from some inherited weaknesses.

Color, soundness, action, characteristic heads, temperament, and other features are obviously inherited. But ability to run fast is not inherited. It must be taught. There is no guarantee that the mating of the quickest sire with the fleetest dam will produce the speediest foal. Sometimes the opposite is the result."

At this point, McGuire asked, "Would you say, then, that a mediocre stallion and mare would have the same chance to produce a foal with ability to run as those now considered top-bracket?"

"Yes," said Widener, "provided of course, that there was no hereditary disease or ailment involved and the foals were given equal treatment in rearing and racing. Individual cases cannot be accepted to either prove or disprove the theory. It must be remembered that many of the foals of mediocre sires and dams never get the benefits of rearing that are given automatically to the top foals and thus the record of top foals might appear brighter.

"Consider the hypothetical case of a renowned concert pianist who married a girl equally talented with the piano. If, for any reason, there was not a piano in their home or where they visited for any length of time, it is unlikely that their children would inherit the ability of playing the piano. They would have to be taught."

Widener went on with a grin: "Horse people are wonderful but at times are stubborn. You would be surprised at the number of people who will accept the theory of environment for every other animal, but deny it to the thoroughbred. Yet these same people would be insistent that a recently purchased weanling or yearling be placed in capable hands, which means suitable environment, for training."

His position put Peter A. B. Widener very much at variance with the established ideas about breeding held by the great majority of thoroughbred people with whom he grew up and still moves. The Jockey Club with its monopoly of bloodlines continues its tight control over the breeding of thoroughbred racehorses and thereby, in effect, over racing itself. No thoroughbred may race on any recognized American racetrack unless it is registered in the American Stud Book, which is owned and maintained by The Jockey Club. In the manner of an international cartel, no American thoroughbred may race on the courses of the other great racing nations unless their Stud Books are reciprocally recognized.

This presented something of a problem for American racing interests in 1958 when, for the first time, the Soviet Government was invited to send its best thoroughbred to compete in the Washington, D.C. International. Racehorses in the Soviet Union are owned by the state, and horses in the Russian Stud Book do not have automatic eligibility to race on American tracks, as do those in the English, French and Italian Registries. But the promoters of the Washington International were anxious for publicity purposes to have the Russians in their race, the first regularly scheduled international classic in the United States. And so there was the spectacle of two Soviet thoroughbreds named Garnir and Zaryad who, despite the fact that their bloodlines traced back to the purest of English thoroughbreds, had in effect to be declared honorary Americans by The Jockey Club before they were permitted to race on American turf—an irony when one recalls that only ten years previously the American horsey set was itself in practically the same position with respect to the British Jockey Club. The keepers of the pedigree in London still tended to look down their noses at the Colonies' descendants. Many American racehorses were halfbreds according to the racing lords at Newmarket, and their bloodlines considered inadmissible to the British Stud Book. However, because the pressing economic need for international control of the burgeoning bloodline market was beginning to embarrass the two breeding superpowers, The British Jockey Club repealed its "Jersey Act," a policy that had made even some of Man o' War's progeny "halfbred" and thus ineligible to race on British courses. Finally in 1948 the British Jockey Club relented and thereby legitimitized the American Declaration of Independence.

Many kinds of safeguards are employed to protect the precious sperm which carries on the bloodlines that come down to the modern racehorse from three stallions—Godolphin Barb, Darley Arabian, and Byerly Turk—all of which were imported into England from the Near East and, together with native English mares, created the thoroughbred line which was eventually brought to this country. Each of the hundreds of thousands of thoroughbreds living today trace their origin, through various progenitors, back to one or the other of these three founding fathers.

The Jockey Club keeps a tight control over this exclusive roster.

No individual may enter its Registry unless there is documentary proof certifying that stallion A was bred to mare B on such-and-such a date at such-and-such a place, producing, eleven months later, such-and-such a foal.

In practice on the farm, the act of breeding thoroughbreds bears little resemblance to the spectacle of wild and exquisite beauty so beloved of painters and poets. First, there is no such thing as a thoroughbred stallion running free with his mares. Thoroughbred breeding is a highly mechanical operation, compartmentalized and businesslike. Those magnificent stallions whose portraits grace the walls of manor houses of the great studs are segregated from their kind for most of their lives. Thirty to forty times a year the horse is led from his stall to make contact with a selected mare. And even then he knows nothing of pursuit and seduction of the female. This exciting (and frustrating) task is assigned to an unfortunate known as the "teaser," a worthless, usually halfbred stallion which is employed to nuzzle and fondle the mare but then is led away at the critical moment so that she may be mounted by the thoroughbred horse. This procedure is employed to determine if the mare is in season, so as not to waste the precious semen of the pedigreed stallion. If the mare responds to the teaser she is ready, if not, the stallion is kept in his stall.

Another sperm-saving device is the "ring." This is a gadget that is placed over the penis of a stallion while the organ is in a relaxed state. By causing pain when the penis enlarges on stimulation, it discourages erection and hence possible masturbation while the horse is in isolation. Such is judged necessary in a corporate structure where thoroughbred semen is worth $40,000 to $50,000 an emission, as in the instance of Secretariat.

Another production technique used on some breeding farms is the practice of altering less desirable stallions in a way that leaves them with a desire for sex but at the same time disables them from fulfilling it. Fitted with a marking harness, such horses are turned out with a group of mares which they can mount but with which they cannot copulate. Mares found with a mark on their back are in season and ready for breeding; the altered stallion goes on in his futile search for relief.

Even in the actual mating, restraint, manhandling, plasticity—anything but natural freedom—is the order of the day. Thoroughbred breeders are businessmen, not nature-lovers or poets. Controlled mating in breeding sheds produces some thirty-five percent more pregnancies than does free breeding in pastures. So the mare is led from her home barn to the breeding shed. There, her legs are secured in leather hobbles to restrain her from protest (kicking might damage the stallion's testicles). A "twitch" or rope loop is then inserted in her nose, pressure upon which urges compliance to the business at hand, and several men close in on her to push, shove and guide her to the stallion's penis. When copulation is completed a veterinarian, who all the while has been poised on the sidelines with a porcelain vessel at the ready, moves in to catch the residue of the semen as the stallion dismounts after discharge. The veterinarian makes sure that fertilization is achieved by manually applying some of the recovered semen into the mare's cervix and shoving it up the orifice to the full length of his arm. This is what The Jockey Club calls the "natural service" that is required in breeding every foal that enters their thoroughbred Stud Book.

Artificial insemination as a breeding practice, despite its obvious usefulness in simplifying the breeding business, is anathema to The Jockey Club. There are a number of highly regarded horsemen who for reasons of efficiency favor at least a limited policy of artificial insemination. There is also a sizeable body of breeding interests that would welcome the practice for the personal economic gain that an expanded market would yield. But the word at this juncture remains with the elite group that sits in The Jockey Club and controls the American Stud Book.

In general The Jockey Club justifies its opposition to the artificial insemination of thoroughbreds with the rationale that, apart from the danger of human error and possible fraud inherent in the practice, it is a gross violation of delicately tuned natural animal instincts.

"There is a tendency in these times of computerized society to substitute cold numbers for all the emotional drives of warm creatures of flesh and blood," Jockey Club Executive Secretary John F. Kennedy said in expressing the American Stud Book's policy on artificial insemination in 1968. "It is suggested here that even though men are but years away from treading on the moon, a good deal of the mystique and dynamism inherent in the earth's creatures continues to remain the Lord's business."

How this sentiment is to be reconciled with using flesh-and-blood teasers, the mares who are hobbled and twitched, and the marking stallions who get altered is perhaps also the business of the Lord. Or perhaps more appropriately a question for the sophist.

In any case it surely required a romanticist to come up with a theory in support of the official position against artificial insemination. Such was Signor Federico Tesio of Italy, a man who owned some of the most expensive bloodstock in history and concluded from his observation of the birds and the bees that artificial insemination was but an ineffectual man-made copy of nature's way of pollinating plant life. The winged creatures were simply carriers of pollen from one plant to another as man would carry semen from one horse to another. But the difference, observed Signor Tesio, is that plants are a lower order of life than animals. Plants have no nervous system and, therefore, a mechanical, impersonal mode of reproduction is perfectly suited to them. Animals on the other hand, having highly developed nervous systems, require for conception a sexual act that is accompanied by the discharge of violent nervous energy. Particularly is this necessary if the offspring is to have a fully consummated will; there is a definite relationship, says Signor Tesio, between the nervous energy committed to the sexual act and the willpower that the resulting individual will possess.

"The atmosphere of intense sexual urge—which artificial insemination fails to provide—" he wrote, "was intended by nature to accumulate a powerful charge of nervous energy which alone, when released through the sexual act, can result in an animal richer in will power than his fellows, winner of all his battles and a successful producer."

And in his book, *Breeding the Racehorse,* Signor Tesio dramatizes his hypothesis with a charming story that he claims "although fantastically romantic, is none the less true." True or not, it provides a touching brief for a less than sentimentally motivated position.

The Story of Signorinetta

In 1880 or thereabouts a Neapolitan gentleman, Cavaliere Ginistrelli, moved his thoroughbred breeding stock from Portici, near Naples, to Newmarket, with the intention of defeating the English on their own ground.

Cavaliere Ginistrelli was a "character" with original ideas. He immediately achieved a clamorous success by breeding a beautiful filly who was given the name of Signorina and who became a top star in her field. In 1892 Signorina, by then a five-year-old, was retired as a broodmare.

In the meantime the busy little Neapolitan had built himself a house at Newmarket, in which his bedroom adjoined the loose-box of his favourite. A window near the head of his bed enabled him to keep an eye on her at any hour of the day or night.

In spite of these attentions the beautiful Signorina was beginning to grow old without having given birth to a single colt of real quality, although bred to the most famous sires of her day.

In the spring of 1904 Cavaliere Ginistrelli had arranged to wed Signorina to the great Isinglass, whose services were in high demand at a fee of 300 guineas to be paid at the time of the betrothal.

Both the stallion and his bride-to-be were living in the town of Newmarket at opposite ends of a long, wide street called—I need hardly say—the High Street. During the breeding season it was the custom to promenade the third-class stallions, victims of unemployment, up and down this thoroughfare with their names in large letters seductively embroidered on their blankets.

On a certain morning in April the comely Signorina was on her way down the High Street to become the bride of the renowned Isinglass. She was led by a stable boy and followed on foot by Cavaliere Ginistrelli, who never let her out of his sight on these occasions. Thus she met coming toward her one of those humble thoroughbred stallions with his name, "Chaleureux," on his blanket.

Chaleureux proved worthy of the name. Stopping to savour Signorina's scent, he at once gave signs of a violent infatuation and refused to move another step. Signorina looked upon him with equal favor and also refused to move on. No amount of tugging or pleading had any effect and an amused crowd soon began to gather.

But Ginistrelli, who was a psychologist as well as a biologist, sized up the situation at a glance.

"They love!" he exclaimed. "A love match it shall be."

And so the proud Isinglass pocketed the 300 guineas, but waited in vain for his assignation with the fair Signorina.

Eleven months later Signorina gave birth to a filly who was given the name of Signorinetta.

The experts, convinced that Ginistrelli was out of his mind, were openly scornful of Chaleureux's love-child. But Signorinetta grew up to be one of the greatest fillies of all time, winning the

> Epsom Derby and—two days later—the Oaks, a double feat which only two fillies since 1780 had been able to accomplish.
>
> These facts are true and I [Tesio] was personally acquainted with all five of the individuals involved: Ginistrelli, Isinglass, Chaleureux, Signorina and Signorinetta.

Signor Tesio goes on to say that skeptics might argue that the results would have been the same if Signorina had been routinely bred to Chaleureux in the first place without all the ardor created by the love triangle with Isinglass. And in fact such an event did take place two years after, producing the Star of Naples, a filly indeed much more beautiful than her famous sister. But the Star of Naples never succeeded in winning a race.

"Thus in the case of Signorinetta it is not unlikely that the issue was affected by the circumstances of the unplanned encounter between her parents," says Signor Tesio. "The arrows of an equine cupid roused the sexual urge to a maximum of tension, which endowed the resulting individual with exceptional energy."

Who but the most cold-hearted could not respond to the story of Signorina and her passionate Chaleureux? But one need not be against true love to question that any convincing breeding theories flow therefrom. Nobody, one feels reasonably safe in asserting, has yet heard of a horse-breeder forfeiting a stud fee for equine romance, as Ginistrelli did with the 300 guineas originally put up for Isinglass' service. And how, given Signor Tesio's example of the disappointment coming from the second "arranged" mating, was a horse like Secretariat able to be born of an arranged match such as produced him in Virginia? And why, if it is possible to get a Secretariat from a controlled breeding, is The Jockey Club so opposed to the use of one of the most effective of all controls: artificial insemination?

That the answer, rather than being the professed respect for the "Lord's business," is really a wish to control market supply—and thereby price—can be reasonably deduced from the following excerpt from a Jockey Club Round Table discussion on breeding in which, despite the fact that the late Bull Hancock, one of the country's leading breeders, makes a case for artificial insemination in order to increase pregnancies, there is little encouragement from the establishment figures present.

SEVENTEENTH ANNUAL ROUND TABLE DISCUSSION ON MATTERS PERTAINING TO RACING HELD BY THE JOCKEY CLUB—AUGUST 10, 1969

Mr. Bull Hancock: One of the things we might take up, all of us have got one job and that is to try to get every mare on the farm in foal. We have four months to do it, and we have a lot of problems, as all our owners know. If we get seventy-five percent we think we've done pretty well. I think we could do better. I believe we could increase our percentage ten percent if we were allowed to artificially inseminate. I know it is dangerous and there is thought against it, but I believe if every farm or every stallion manager was required to send The Jockey Club a list of forty-five or fifty mares, whatever The Jockey Club wants us to limit it to, and then we were allowed to artificially inseminate those mares ourselves, we could do a better job, we could raise better horses in the end and probably step up the number of mares we have to a horse. We could certainly step up our percentage of pregnancies. By that I mean, for instance, most farms don't tease on Sunday. Say on Monday, May 1st, you tease and there are two mares which have come in season to one stallion. All right, they follicle [give hormones to] them and they're supposed to be bred on Tuesday. Well, you know you can't breed them both on Tuesday. So what you could do is you could breed one of them on Tuesday morning and inseminate the other. Then the next morning, which is not as good, supposedly, we could breed the other mare and inseminate the first mare, the mare we bred the day before.

Mr. O'Farrell: You're giving the mare an actual cover [copulation] but you are removing enough semen to inseminate the next day.

Mr. Hancock: I don't know how long the semen lives and I don't think any of the veterinarians can tell me. I have had one mare in my life that stayed in season for nine days after we bred her and she caught. So that semen had to live pretty near nine days. I think this other would do a great job for us, and be a big help to us.

Mr. O'Farrell: It would be in the same heat period, wouldn't it?

Mr. Hancock: Oh yes, the same heat period.

Colonel Koester: I think it is something that ought to be made the subject of an official study.

Mr. Hancock: That's the reason I brought it up.

Mr. O'Farrell: Actually I think we've already studied it enough when you are trying to get five hundred or six hundred mares in foal every year. There's no doubt in the world that Bull is is telling the actual fact. Many times you have three and four mares that should be bred the same day to a busy stud. What are you going to do? You've got a possibility of breeding one animal and if you require an actual cover and allow the semen to be used on another mare and breed the other mare the next day, you'd be able to vary it and have a much better chance of conception, I'm quite sure.

Mr. Green: I think you'd probably get more mares in foal but it looks to me that there might be many things that might pop up that couldn't be controlled. One might be, suppose you impregnate a mare today and you intend to breed her tomorrow, and tomorrow she's out [out of season] and you can't breed her but she gets in foal.

Mr. Hancock: That could happen.

Mr. Green: I don't say I would do it or wouldn't do it, but you've got that semen and a man goes around putting it in a mare and, you don't know, he might put it in some mare he's not supposed to put it in. Of course that could happen right now.

Mr. Hancock: It's based on faith anyway.

Mr. Green: I think it just offers a bit more temptation.

Mr. O'Farrell: The only thing you could do is govern the number of mares bred to any one sire. At least you could eliminate the possibility of breeding, say, seventy-five mares to one sire as the standardbred [horse] people have done in the past. But you could put on a hard and fast rule, say forty-five mares. I can see, Bob, what you are talking about, but actually you can do that now if you want to do it. Of course, it's unethical.

Mr. Green: Well, you just don't run around putting it in a mare now, but if you had it you might. I do know that as far as reinforcing the mating itself, in helping the mare get in foal, along with the actual cover, we stopped that entirely.

Mr. Hancock: I think you're probably right. You're just working for one owner, but I've got to please a lot of them. I think I would stop it. I have noticed we have more twins and more slips from mares that have been impregnated than otherwise.

MR. O'FARRELL: I stopped it two years ago. Only in very odd cases do I use it.

MR. HANCOCK: We don't impregnate until the first of May and routinely after the first of May we impregnate.

MR. GREEN: What about lights? Are you using the lights [to simulate spring, the breeding season]?

MR. HANCOCK: Yes. I don't think I've got a good enough sample yet to be sure, but last year I had one barn and tried to put equal mares on either side. There were twelve mares on either side of the barn. I got ten on both sides in foal. This year it looks like I got a few more mares in foal under the lights and they too are a little earlier. So I am spending some money putting lights in all my barren mares' stalls now.

MR. O'FARRELL: Bull, I've been doing this for about five or six years now religiously. The first year I thought it was the greatest thing in the world. I set up an automatic light system, and put them under December twenty-first and went on from there where we would give them the same daylight hours as, say, March twenty-first. I got thirty-two out of forty-two hard-to-get-in-foal mares in foal the first year. So I thought it was a godsend. You do get the mare into season earlier and you have a better chance of getting her in foal, but that seems to be probably the only result I have gotten.

MR. HANCOCK: The thing that is discouraging about it a little bit is that the Japanese were the first to take this up, but they have abandoned it I hear over there.

MR. O'FARRELL: I'm about getting ready to abandon it myself.

MR. HANCOCK: Does anybody have anything else?

MR. KENNEDY [Jockey Club]: Thank you very much, gentlemen, for a very interesting discussion. *In the matter of insemination I would like to ask Mr. Finney what he thinks the impact on the industry would be if we had more foals by certain popular sires.* [author's italics]

MR. FINNEY [Horse Salesman]: If we could get two hundred Bold Rulers to sell any year the impact would be wonderful for a while, but eventually it wouldn't be so good. Actually I think if ever artificial insemination is allowed it has got to be regulated to a reasonable number. Nearly fifty years ago in Michigan I was raising draft horses and we used to breed one mare and inseminate six or seven. Maybe you'd get two or three in foal out of those and it didn't make much difference then, but it surely would in this thoroughbred game. Personally I would hate to see the situation where only five or six top stallions' semen was used at all, and that could happen.

MR. KENNEDY: Thank you. Any other comments from the floor on this subject, or anything related?

MR. HANCOCK: Jack, the first thing that I said was that this would have to be regulated. A list of forty-five or fifty mares, or whatever limit of mares The Jockey Club would want to put on it for any stallion would have to be sent in and adhered to.

MR. KENNEDY: We all realize, Bull, that it is a matter of integrity and control. . . .

To determine how artificial insemination works among other breeds of horses where it is permitted, such as Tennessee walking-horses and standardbred harness horses, the editor of the *Thoroughbred Record* questioned a veterinarian and a stallion owner. He found that a split exists along basically the same lines. In general, the stallion owner felt that artificial insemination was more convenient, profitable, and sanitary.

"However, the veterinarian," said *Thoroughbred Record,* "while conceding some advantages, said that, taking all factors into consideration, he is against artificial insemination of horses, and 'vociferously' against it over a period of time and/or without some limit on books, say, fifty mares. Breeders tend to concentrate too much on too few popular sires, he said, and 'kill the goose that lays the golden eggs.' The value of the stallion's services 'goes to pot.'" [He raises the specter of abuse as a logic against controlled use.]

Syndication of the fashionable stallions among themselves; inflated stud fees, control of the Stud Book; perpetuation of the mystique of pedigree, and prohibition of artificial insemination—all combine to enable the entrenched to maintain control of breeding.

A supplemental tactic—perhaps the cruelest—is the plain old-fashioned cold-shoulder, which was tried and failed in the spring of 1971 when a three-year-old colt owned by an obscure Venezuelan family by the name of Baptista was flown into Louisville to compete in the ninety-seventh running of the Kentucky Derby. The horse had been sold at the Lexington auctions for a mere $1,200; his bloodlines, being sprinkled more or less with the general collection of names common to thousands of thoroughbreds, were anything but fashionable; he had won no stake of importance in Venezuela as a three-year-old, nor had his career as a juvenile in California been extraordinary. The horse's name was Canonero II. He was trained by Juan Arias, a black man.

This was a combination of negatives that would be enough to downgrade a racehorse's credentials for the tenth race on the night card at a county fair, to say nothing of the world's most famous horse race, the Kentucky Derby. Accordingly, the big bay colt from the hills of Caracas, despite his good looks, was considered just another classless upstart who had bought a ticket to a stylish ball to hobnob with his betters. He was placed in the "field," that is, in that grouping of horses of which nothing more is expected than that they will get in the way of everybody and spoil the party for the more classy contenders. In this particular Derby there were six such "platers," among them Canonero II, and a bettor could have the whole lot run for him on the purchase of but a single two-dollar ticket. The odds, too, reflected the low regard in which this field of six social climbers was held: 500 to 1 in Caliente's Winter Book and 30 to 1 in the early odds at Churchill Downs.

Added to Canonero's lack of prestige were his very real troubles. On the trip from Venezuela to Miami engine trouble forced his plane back twice. In Florida he was quarantined for four days without exercise. On release, he was confined to a van which bumped about for twenty-four hours on the 1,100-mile trip to Churchill Downs, where he arrived only five days before Derby Day—feverish, bruised, and fifty-one pounds underweight. This succeeded, according to the experts, in handicapping his chances in the Derby down to absolute zero.

But that is not how they felt about him in Venezuela. Compatriots formed to the size of a regiment, flashing tri-colored flags, Latin exuberance and good will, descended on Churchill Downs to cheer their 30 to 1 shot "gunner" on to success. Gustavo Avilo, Venezuela's leading jockey, who had piloted Canonero to three straight victories in Caracas, was brought to Kentucky to ride him. The entire population of the country sweated out days and dollars waiting for that Saturday afternoon in May.

In the race itself, witnessed by one of the largest crowds ever to attend an American horse race—123,284 jam-packed individuals—twenty horses broke out of the gate in a clean start. Sons of Bold Ruler, Fleet Nasrullah and other fashionable stallions immediately went to the front. Going into the far turn, Bold And Able and Eastern Fleet, the Calumet Farm entries, were in the lead, with the favorite, Unconscious, sprinting up to challenge. Canonero, way in back of the pack, stepped on nobody's toes nor got in anybody's way. But before the race had gone a quarter of a mile he shifted to the far outside, suddenly unleashed a wild burst of speed and came down from seventeenth place to fourth. Moving past tiring horses he maintained his strong drive all the way through the homestretch to win by four lengths over Jim French, Bold Reason, and Eastern Fleet, the class horses in the race.

In Venezuela the victory of the "classless" horse was enough to quiet Latin class-conflict, at least for the moment. Celebrations took on the quality of a national holiday; on-going battles between students and police suddenly stopped as both factions made off to collect their winning tickets; the nation's president cabled jockey Avila that "the great victory will stimulate Venezuela's progress in all its efforts."

But as Whitney Tower of *Sports Illustrated* later reported: "The first Triple Crown race of the year . . . was wishfully regarded by most horsemen as a joke. Twenty three-year-olds thrashing around Churchill Downs, the better ones stumbling over one another on the inside while some lucky field horse named Canonero II caught up with them in the stretch to win in slowpoke time, leaving thousands of sour-grapes losers moaning at the absurdity of the scene and openly suggesting that the injured Hoist The Flag, cast and all, could have whipped the whole bloody lot. That was the establishment version. The Derby-winning usurper from Caracas would get his comeuppance at the Preakness, was the word."

Yes, agreed the hardboots, when the chips were really down in Baltimore the change in altitude from Venezuela would indeed catch up with that $1,200 fluke.

"They made me feel like I was at the Derby to be a clown," said trainer Juan Arias through an interpreter. "They made fun of us at parties. There have been times when I wanted to tell the press to go to the devil, but I contained myself."

Perhaps the sorriest aspect of all was the unsportsmanlike way the old guard of racing behaved. Here was a thoroughbred which had captured public imagination as had no racehorse since Mrs. Richard DuPont's Kelso retired. The thoroughbred from Venezuela was a colt millions of people looked upon as the "people's horse" because of his plebian connections. He was also an animal that would give the sport its biggest boost at the turnstiles since Native Dancer, and yet the traditional Derby victory celebration held after the race at Churchill Downs was deliberately snubbed by the establishment.

In the Preakness, the next leg of the Triple Crown, Canonero, now a heavy sentimental favorite with the public, not only once again put all his classy rivals to shame, he also wrote racing history. He clipped three-fifths of a second off the track record which had been held by former Jockey Club chairman William Woodward's Nashua for sixteen years—a feat which Bold Ruler, Northern Dancer, Majestic Prince, and other fashionable horses had been unable to achieve. In the Belmont, the third leg of the Triple Crown, Canonero missed, finishing fourth to Pass Catcher.

But failing to capture the Triple Crown is hardly something to be ashamed of. Some of the greatest horses in history, including Alfred Vanderbilt's Native Dancer, failed at that—and without the onus of snobbish condescension. Indeed, the establishment, at least realistic about the dollar, decided it was time to take over for itself what it couldn't defeat. It now considered Canonero a good investment and made him a member of the club. Robert J. Kleberg of King Ranch bought the colt at a price of $1,000,000 for use as a stallion. He now stands in Kentucky, where fashionable stallions are supposed to stand.

CHAPTER 23

Saratoga, Also Camelot: Paradise Lost, Almost Regained

"If the visitor really belongs to the Saratoga circle, he will bring an entourage of fifteen to twenty servants, and probably arrive in his private railroad car. In these days of automobiles, when half a dozen friends are likely to drop in on any weekend, it is convenient to have the car in the railroad."

—James C. Young, *The New York Times,* August, 1930

ONCE EACH YEAR, Alfred Vanderbilt and the members of The Jockey Club make their annual pilgrimage to Saratoga. There, nestled amid the ancient elms that spread cool shade across a verdant Adirondack valley, thoroughbred racing is ensconced during the torrid month of August for twenty-four sultry, midsummer days. During the season at Saratoga the business of horseracing becomes more an affair of the heart than a matter of the privy purse.

Saratoga inaugurated its long history of thoroughbred racing August 3, 1863, on a patch of green called Horse Haven, just off what is now Union Avenue, pausing only for the Hughes anti-gambling law (1911–13) and a brief period during World War II. Casualties of the Battle of Gettysburg were still being buried when the field of thoroughbreds went to the post to amuse the fashionable families bored with sipping mineral waters in the great baroque hotels. The inaugural race of America's oldest racetrack—in which a filly named Lizzie W., with a one-eyed jockey, beat a colt named Captain Moore—was concerned with the more weighty business of laying the foundation, according to *Wilkes' Spirit of the Times:* August, 1863,

> . . . for a great fashionable race meeting like that at Ascot. . . . There was tremendous excitement among the sportsmen in the evening during the selling of the pools. . . . It was a busy and gay time at the United States Hotel. Upstairs in the grand ballroom there was a magnificent display of female loveliness, in costly ornaments and sumptuous attire, moving to stirring music in the mazy dance. Below, the stentorian bids of the betting men and the voice of Dr. Underwood [the pool seller] was heard through the clamors of the crowd.

In addition to the sport of kings and mineral waters, historic settings and cultural activities, Saratoga offered gambling casinos and sporting diversions of every conceivable variety. There was faro, poker, bacarrat, roulette, craps, wagering on horses, and any other kind of hazard to fortune the imagination could conjure up. Hotels in size and splendor to rival Versailles catered to every whim of men who could easily have bought the whole city several times over.

The Saratoga Racetrack that Alfred Vanderbilt and his Jockey Club board of trustees preside over today, as one of the three NYRA courses, was started by an ex-pugilist, a man who had once been the bare-knuckle heavyweight boxing champion of America—John Morrisey. Having made a fortune from the losses of the millionaire society patrons of his casino tables, Morrisey decided to invest in the up-and-coming sport of thoroughbred racing. Not having the kind of social credentials required for the sport of kings, he enlisted the support of two pillars of respectability, William R. Travers and John R. Hunter. With Morrisey money and Travers–Hunter sponsorship, the future of horseracing at Saratoga was solidly launched.

Of the three founders, John R. Hunter went on eventually to become the first chairman of The Jockey Club. William R. Travers in the following year, 1864, had a race named after himself, which he won with a horse in partnership with Hunter, and which is still the oldest continuously run stakes race in America.

John Morrisey achieved an immortality more appropriate to his social position. Having become a member of Congress as a result of his gambling-political connections, the bare-knuckle heavyweight champion of the United States, during the course of a heated debate, entered into the *Congressional Record* what was probably the least challenged remark in the Congress' history: an offer to "lick any man in the House." None, according to the archives, found occasion to take issue with the words of the distinguished member from New York.

Meantime the Civil War had ended, and Saratoga Springs became *the* place in which to display the fortunes stockpiled by those who had profited during the War.

The Spa already had a long history as one of the country's leading resorts. Ever since the day in 1802, when the pioneer Gideon Putnam built a tavern on an acre of land around the high-spouting geyser of Congress Spring, people poured in, attracted by the medicinal qualities of the waters. Some stayed on to settle, and found Putnam ready to sell them lots adjacent to "the first commodious hotel for the accommodation of visitors." Saratoga Springs was built around a tavern and continued to grow as a result of the building of increasingly grander taverns.

What Gideon Putnam had done was simply to make a commercial package of the natural product about which the local Indians had long known. Except that the Indians, relatively free of the white man's problems with his stomach, came not to take the waters, but the animals which drank from them. Each summer, over the centuries, the Oneida and the Mohawk had built hunting lodges near the geyser to catch the large numbers of game which were attracted by the saline properties of the water. To the Indian tribes, *Saraghoga* ("place of swift water") was as well known as modern Saratoga is to the white man today. One of its springs—the High Rock—was revered as the "Medicine Spring of the Great Spirit."

As early as 1643, Father Isaac Joques, a Jesuit missionary and explorer, became the first white man to set foot in the area. He tasted the waters and the exquisite fish that thrived in the lakes, but paid with his head for his attempts to turn the natives from their pagan ways. Later, after the land had been appropriated by the white man, he was rewarded for his labors with the first sainthood in North America. In 1767 Sir William Johnson, His Majesty's Superintendent of Indian Affairs, was carried by Mohawk braves on a stretcher to the springs so that he might benefit from the waters. Some years back Sir William, again aided by members of the Mohawk nation, had defeated the French at Lac du Saint Sacrement. For his efforts, Sir William was rewarded by his king with a baronetcy . . . and 100,000 acres of the Mohawk's land. In turn he changed the name of Lac du Saint Sacrement to Lake George, and made a practice of regularly visiting the magic waters of the Mohawk.

The first actual resident of the Spa was a Dutchman by the name of Dirck Schouten. In 1775 he built himself a cabin near the High Rock spring. But his tenure was rather short, for he heeded Indian warnings to move away from the Abode of the Great Spirit.

After the Revolutionary War had divested the Tory landowners of the acres they had expropirated from the Indians—to say nothing of the acres onto which the Mohawks had until then managed to hold—the stage was set for buy-and-sell and build. In August of 1783, while still a private citizen, George Washington visited the High Rock spring and was so impressed that he attempted to buy it and some adjacent springs. He never acquired the properties, but his interest in Saratoga helped to inspire visionaries such as Gideon Putnam. In the half century that followed, Saratoga mushroomed from Putnam's acre-in-the-woods to a thriving Spa with an international reputation.

With the introduction of thoroughbred racing, an era of golden flamboyance descended on what was up to this point a resort where wealthy and proper families came to take the waters and discreetly show off their eligible daughters. Now an astonishing admixture of elegant adventurer, brash tycoon, and international cut-up flooded in to join the "better class" which traditionally patronized the Spa. It was one of the most opulent and, at the same time, most vulgar periods in American history, which would last through the Gay Nineties.

Men such as Colonel James Fisk, Jr., helped turn staid and fashionable Saratoga Springs into the circus that it sometimes became. Jim Fisk had, in fact, started life as a circus barker, with a flamboyant con-man's talent for suckering millions of people—even titans as unassailable as Commodore Vanderbilt, from whom he stole the Erie Railroad and milked it dry as the current Penn Central. In between times he hustled contraband Confederate cotton northward during the War, created the "Black Friday" panic on Wall Street by attempting to corner the gold market (with Jay Gould) and generally kicked the country's economy about at will.

Where other war profiteers took their loot to church or to art or to "the poor workingman," Fisk prided himself on never having fallen for such a sucker's game. The ex-circus barker preferred instead to subsidize social institutions such as the 9th National Guard Regiment of New York with military trappings, brass bands and public relations tours around the state. This secured him his colonelcy and the gaudiest staff officer's uniform this side of the Austro-Hungarian empire. One August day, the short, fat Fisk—sprouting waxed mustachios a foot long and red spitcurls that bounced about his temples—placed himself at the head of his regiment and strutted on down Saratoga's main boulevard like the warlord of the province of New York.

Saratoga's old guard tried to avert their eyes from Fisk's flaunting of his wealth. But his huge diamonds outshone the crystal chandeliers in the lobbies of the hostelries they patronized, and his perfume overwhelmed the fragrance of the petunias in the summer gardens. Besides, he was too powerful and dangerous to affront.

But it was his affair with Helen (Josie) Mansfield, whom he openly paraded on the promenade, that most offended the proper Saratogans —perhaps out of envy—for she was one of the most striking beauties in a place where the elegance of one's horse-drawn carriage was only less important than the shapeliness of the lady who occupied it. Josie Mansfield was an "innocent" in her twenties aspiring to become an actress when Fisk met her. He was hypnotized by her voluptuous figure, flashing eyes and air of innocence, even though theatrical impresarios apparently were not. Fisk rescued her from the alternative of the storied "fate worse than death," and, although he had a wife, set her up in a fine mansion in New York.

In the Saratoga summer of 1869, the Colonel introduced Josie to his partner, Edward S. Stokes, a tall, handsome patrician who was always heavily in debt to the bookies at the racetrack. He "borrowed," first, the partnership's funds and eventually his partner's mistress.

The triangle between the portly bourgeois, the elegant patrician, and the "innocent" young thing created a vehicle for publicity beyond any tabloid's dreams. One of the results was that, one evening, Jay Gould, the puritanical ogre of Wall Street, and Fisk's superior, ordered the hotel band to play his usual dinnertime request—"Lead, Kindly Light"—and thereupon got up from his brandied peaches to send a telegram, an order that resulted in forcing Fisk out of his vice-presidency of the Erie Railroad. Not long after, the Colonel of the 9th New York National Guard Regiment was dealt a final blow. Edward Stokes, in a quarrel over Josie Mansfield, shot him dead in a New York hotel. Stokes received a light prison sentence.

Exhibitionistic displays were regular fare at Saratoga during the high period of the post-Civil War decades. Hotels, such as the United States—which stretched over a quarter-mile in length—had more than one thousand wicker rocking chairs on its two verandas. In 1874, an even grander establishment arose on the skyline. A. T. Stewart, a Scotch-Irish immigrant who had parlayed a pushcart of Irish lace into the world's largest retail store, celebrated his good fortune by dedicating himself to providing Saratoga with the world's largest and most lavish hotel. A million-dollar reconstruction of Gideon Putnam's original Union Hall—itself so pretentious for its day as to be labelled "Putnam's Folly"—the new Grand Union occupied almost a city block. It was five stories high, with a three-story piazza extending across the entire Broadway front, and two wings jutting back nearly a quarter of a mile. The interior courtyard, the size of a city park, had a promenade veranda running along three sides where guests could stroll, or sit and gossip in the glow of gaily lit fountains. Inside, there were 824 guest rooms and suites—all on a royal scale—a dining hall where 250 waiters served fourteen hundred patrons at a sitting, two miles of corridors, twelve acres of carpeting, and an acre of marble that glinted in the lobby, ballrooms, and on top of bedroom bureaus. Victor Herbert conducted an orchestra for dining and dancing, the brothers Otis provided steam-engine elevators for the convenience of guests not disposed to use the magnificent black walnut staircases, and mahogany cottages were available for those fastidious ones who required the ultimate in comfort and privacy. When the Grand Union Hotel opened for business in 1874 it was the world's largest and most lavish pleasure palace.

With the new Grand Union, Saratoga was embarked on a career of self-conscious opulence. Into its sumptuous parlors came the greatest names in American society—including presidents and cabinet members—followed by an even greater flood of wealthy and flamboyant operators such as Jim Fisk.

Bon vivants from abroad began to desert the old European spas for the new Saratoga, among them Squire Abingdon Baird, the English dandy who orchestrated his wardrobe with a $10,000 collection of walking sticks. He also raced a stable of thoroughbreds and escorted Lilly Langtry, the English society actress, around the Spa. One day at the Saratoga racetrack the Squire had a quarrel with Charley Mitchell, a British boxer who had once fought John L. Sullivan to a three-hour draw. Baird punched Mitchell in the face and, to the astonishment of onlookers, the pugilist did nothing in return. The same scene was repeated night after night in bars around the town, and received such wide publicity that it became an international item. Finally a friend asked Mitchell how he could tolerate being punched about by a fop. The boxer smiled and replied: "The Squire likes it. He pays me a hundred dollars for every blow he lands. And the truth is I rather enjoy it myself."

Another coxcomb whose highly publicized antics made Saratoga a national word during this period was Berry Wall. His specialty was waging sartorial battles with rivals at the racetrack, in the ballrooms, and on the promenades of Saratoga. Besides winning a national reputation as "king of the dudes," Wall was responsible, in a backhanded way, for a permanent addition to the lexicon of fashion. This came about as a result of his being snubbed when he showed up at an evening function in the Grand Union in a jacket without tails. When, in anger he removed himself to the rival resort of Tuxedo Park—still without the traditional white tie and tails—his new tailless jacket became such a sensation that henceforth it was called the "tuxedo."

Berry Wall's supreme challenge—which tended to characterize Saratoga during the Gay Nineties—was his announcement that he would in one day appear in forty complete changes of dress. Immediately the bookmakers were swamped with huge bets both for and against his ability to make good his boast. The crowds that gathered in front of the Grand Union saw him show up for breakfast dressed in black and white. Then, after eating a leisurely meal, he disappeared and, moments later, returned for a stroll, garbed in immaculate white linen. This routine continued throughout the day: one dazzling change after another, interspersed with walks around the block, stops for drinks at the bar, pauses for chats with friends—always with a return to his suite where his valet, like an aide to a quick-change artist, slipped him into a new costume complete to the nines. Finally, at dinnertime, John L. Sullivan, who had been one of the bookies to the ever-growing crowd, erupted into a "Hip! Hip! Hooray!" The band struck up "Hail the Conquering Hero Comes," and Berry Wall appeared in his fortieth change of the day: a Prince Albert, white tie, boiled shirt and poke collar.

A few years before, another fashion plate and a literary genius who was to become one of America's most eminent expatriates—visited the Spa. Henry James had small regard for the gingerbread architectural "monsters which stand facing each other," and even less for the manners of the American new-rich. In an article for *The Nation,* he wrote:

> They suggest to my fancy the swarming vastness—the multifarious possibilities and activities—of our young civilization. . . . As they sit with their white hats tilted forward, and their chairs tilted back, and their feet tilted up, and their cigars and toothpicks forming various angles with these various lines, I seem to see in their faces a tacit reference to the affairs of a continent. . . . They are not the mellow fruit of a society which has walked hand-in-hand with tradition and culture; they are hard nuts, which have grown and ripened as they could. When they talk among themselves, I seem to hear the cracking of the shells.

As for the ladies, James had this to say:

> . . . Saratoga is famous, I believe, as the place of all places in America where women adorn themselves most, or as the place, at least, where the greatest amount of dressing may be seen by the greatest number of people. . . . Every woman you meet, young or old, is attired with a certain amount of richness, and with whatever good taste may be compatible with such a mode of life. You behold an interesting, indeed a quite momentous spectacle: the democratization of elegance. If I am to believe what I hear—in fact, I may say what I overhear—many of these sumptuous persons have enjoyed neither the advantages of a careful education nor the privileges of an introduction to society. She walks more or less of a queen, however, each uninitiated nobody.

By the end of the 1890s, the "hard nuts" and "uninitiated nobodies" had almost sent the Queen of Spas to her grave with the richness of their indulgences. Saratoga faro now far surpassed Saratoga vichy as a village resource. Brothels commanded prices higher than the rates of suites in the most elegant hotels; the racetrack had degenerated into a workshop for touts and fixers—a place which even offered a special room where children could bet.

Reformers finally moved to stem the "tide of Sodom." Anthony Comstock, of the New York Society for the Suppression of Vice—Satan's principal adversary on earth—came and left without success. Prestigious summer visitors, such as Spencer Trask, owner of the Saratoga *Union* (he eventually turned his vast estate into the artist colony of Yaddo), fought the gambling interests and lost. None of the clean-up crusades seemed to avail. Saratogans, even the clergy, apparently preferred the prosperity that untrammeled gambling brought; the big-time operations were too well entrenched.

Finally, Nellie Bly, a reporter for the *New York World* who had become a national heroine by beating Phileas Foggs's time for his trip around the world in eighty days, came to have a look. It required considerably less than eighty days for her practiced eye to "case the joints" of the upstate Babylon. Under the banner headline, OUR WICKEDEST SUMMER RESORT, she reported how "Reputable and Disreputable Women/Solid Merchants, Bankers, Sports/Touts, Criminals and Race-Track Riff-Raff" had been "Crazed by the Mania for Gold."

> This town has gone mad with the mania for gambling. From the Carlsbad of America, Saratoga has become its Monte Carlo—a Monte Carlo with the reckless law-breaking of Leadville combined with the vulgarity of the Bowery.
>
> Gambling is in the atmosphere. Formerly men of wealth and social position, statesmen, philosophers, students and artists gathered here to drink the waters that nature forces through a hundred fissures, and enjoy the crisp, invigorating air and the picturesque scenery which have united in making Saratoga America's most famous summer resort. They came to ride, to drive, to dress and to secure that freedom from business and domestic care that gives perfect rest and brings back bodily health and vigor.
>
> Now the great summer population of Saratoga is largely composed of those gathered here to gamble or to live off those who do gamble. From one of the most reputable and most exclusive of American watering places, it has been transformed into the wickedest and the wildest.

That was the beginning of the end of Saratoga's turn-of-the-century, free-for-all era. The fashionable Broadway promenade was cleared of gaming houses; the riff-raff was shunted underground; negotiations were commenced by a syndicate of impeccable sportsmen, headed by William Collins Whitney, to acquire the racetrack.

When W. C. Whitney and his associates took over the moribund Saratoga Racing Association at the turn of the century and turned it into the Saratoga Association for the Improvement of the Breed, the Spa emerged into its golden age. The track was refurbished in grand style, but it retained all of its former old-world dignity. The fashionable racing stables, which had avoided the racetrack during its period of degeneracy, now returned with the best horses in the country. The Jockey Club, formed in 1894, came under the chairmanship of August Belmont II, and was now in complete control of the sport. The Whitney thoroughbred empire had just been founded; Phipps, Widener, and Vanderbilt turf dynasties were already in the making, and the formation of other racing clans was not far behind. The horsey set was being stabilized and defined, Saratoga was designated its Camelot, and the month of August the time of exaltation. Once again the ancient elms would make a shady court for the "dowager queen of the American turf."

After 1907, when Canfield's Casino, with its magnificently appointed dining rooms, was closed, the racetrack became the center where the fashionable gathered to do their gambling. Turf society now became the style-setter for the rest of the nation. Through this period into the 1920s the village itself began to take on the image that has most persisted in the public mind: an odd mix of conservative American first family with free-wheeling big-time spender, Broadway celebrity and black-coated Hassidic Jew. It would have come as no surprise to find Mrs. Helen Hay Whitney elbowing for space at the Hathorn Spring with James Buchanan ("Diamond Jim") Brady, Damon Runyon, and Moishe Rabinowitz from Ocean Parkway in Brooklyn—the three first-named personages being at the Queen of Spas primarily for the horses, while the last hoped to "greps up" on one long weekend the ravages of a year-long diet of pastrami and pickles.

Everybody had his favorite lodgings to which he returned year after year. Moishe Rabinowitz stayed in one of a variety of orthodox Jewish rooming-houses—a kind of rural ghetto, where he and his family rocked the hours away on the front porches when they weren't visiting the springs. Damon Runyon always stayed at the United States Hotel, where, an incorrigible gambler, he observed that "all horseplayers die broke"—except for his friend Johnny Buzzsaw, who after a disastrous day at the track attempted to hang himself on a fire-escape rope, only to fall three stories into the arms of a passing bookmaker when the cord broke. Mrs. Whitney had her own clapboard "cottage" (a forty-room mansion) which her daughter, Mrs. Charles S. Payson, now returns to each year. As did the Bostwicks, the Riddles, the Woodwards, the Wideners and the rest of the fast-growing racing aristocracy. Diamond Jim arrived with twenty-seven Japanese houseboys to attend him, and thirty sets of jewels containing twenty thousand diamonds (a fresh change of gems for each day of the month) to be distributed over his two hundred fifty-pound person, even down to the buttonholes of his BVD's. Brady, whose food intake (at least six times that of the average man) could serve as a symbol of the opulence of Saratoga at the turn of the century, would casually consume a ten-course dinner, with many of the courses served in multiple portions. In between courses, he devoured oysters, lobsters, crabs and shrimp by the dozens, spicing the seafood sometimes with sweetbreads, terrapin, pickled pigs' feet, boned goose with aspic, and saddle of mutton, all washed down with champagne, Benedictine and several gallons of freshly squeezed orange juice before he reached the desserts. (Years later he had to be rescued from the ravages of his diet, not by Saratoga mineral waters, but by the scalpels of intestinal surgeons at Johns Hopkins Hospital, where, in gratitude, he endowed the Brady Clinic.)

James Buchanan Brady, with his silver-plated rolling stock, his twenty-seven Japanese pages, and his mighty feats at various inns and casinos, was enough to spread the legend of Saratoga. But then there was also Lillian Russell. The maid with the golden hair, whose curvaceous limbs brought the entire male world to her feet, both at Tony Pastor's Music Hall and at Saratoga's racetrack, chose Sir Diamond Jim. For this he rewarded Miss Russell with trinkets such as her own black Victoria drawn by two matching black thoroughbreds, in addition to a gold-plated bicycle with her initials in diamonds and emeralds on the handle bars, which she pedalled among the admiring throngs in the lazy morning hours. At night the two could be glimpsed driving along the boulevards in their brougham—electrified for the occasion with a bank of marquee lights.

But it was the racetrack that now made Saratoga the legend that it was destined to become. If you belonged to the select group you were out to your stables in the early hours to watch your own thoroughbreds breeze through their workouts in the morning mists. Following this, there was breakfast at trackside or occasional bacon-and-eggs with the stable help in their own kitchen. Then back to the cottage for a respite.

After rest, or more play, or a few telegrams to Wall Street, you had lunch and then to the races. The races! Stroll through the green and shaded paddock, lady in arm, to admire the thoroughbred you had petted in the barn in the morning. Back to the box to consult with your trainer—and isn't that Brady over there with Lillian Russell? No, dear, it's not Brady, it's that even more vulgar "Bet-A-Million" or what-have-you-Gates . . . rejoin you presently, my dear. Order some more bubbly . . . must see what Gates is up to.

What John W. "Bet-A-Million" Gates was up to was what he was always up to: betting incredible amounts of money on horses. A tall, pot-bellied man whose squint-eyes glinted above a heavy, drooping mustache, Gates would bet on the outcome of any event, from a horse-race to the course of two raindrops running down a Pullman window. Before he was thirty he had made millions selling barbed wire to Western cattle-ranchers, and parlayed those proceeds, by daring speculation, into an immense fortune. He owned racetracks, had huge holdings in Wall Street and in railroads; his spectacular plunges made waves all the way from the bookie stands at the racetrack to the gaming rooms in Canfield's Casino. To Bet-A-Million Gates, $100,000 was a small bet—he once plunged $300,000 on the nose of a horse which ran out of the money.

In Wall Street he overwhelmed his rivals with the immensity of his gambles. So offensive were his audacious ways to conservative financiers that J. P. Morgan excluded him from the billion-dollar United States Steel deal, a project that Gates himself had conceived. Gates protested that he was guilty of nothing that anybody else, not even Morgan, did not do; except that he never hid behind closed doors. To which Morgan retorted, "What do you suppose doors are made for?"

John W. Gates operated on the theory that if a man could hold out in a gamble long enough the course of the game would turn and he would ultimately win. With his limitless resources and his colossal guts, he had the ability to put his theory into practice. "No man should bet unless he's sure he's right," he said. "And when he's convinced he's right, he should back his opinion with all he's got. Otherwise there's no excitement in gambling. I want to put up enough to hurt the other fellow—or hurt myself, if I lose."

In this spirit Gates made the biggest one-day gamble in resort history at Saratoga in 1902. First, he lost $400,000 at the racetrack by increasing his bets on one loser after another. At the Casino that night he played faro in the public room, losing $25,000 at stakes of $2,500 on case cards and $5,000 on doubles. Eventually bored with this, he went to the private rooms, where the stakes were higher, and by ten o'clock was out another $125,000. Then he prevailed on Canfield to raise the odds from $5,000 to $10,000. Now the Gates luck began to turn. By 2:00 A.M. he had won back his $150,000 faro losses, and by dawn, when the game closed down, he was $150,000 ahead. This, for Bet-A-Million Gates, was not a bad day. He had wound up losing only $250,000 instead of more than a half-million.

And so the story went, August after August up through the 1920s. Young Alfred Vanderbilt was now playing hide-and-seek behind the Saratoga racetrack elms, while his mother parasoled around the gossipy paddock. Jock Whitney was pulling the pigtails of sister Joan as they sat in the family box to watch Grandfather's horses run. Gladys Livingston Mills was perhaps already dreaming of the Bold Ruler she would one day own. And out on the track on that August 13th, 1920, the superhorse of the century was going down to the most stunning defeat in sporting history. Man o' War had tasted the dust from the heels of a horse named Upset (owned by H. P. Whitney) in the only loss he would ever know. The month of August! God seemed to cram the best of his universe into that all-too-brief moment which came each summer to Camelot in the Adirondacks.

With the arrival of the Great Depression in 1930, the nation fell into an unprecedented low of despair. Gone now were the days when tabloid readers would delight at discovering that Liz Whitney wore "emerald necklaces with her riding habit" or "came to the races straight from a night club wearing an evening gown and shepherding a pack of poodles." Or that Ella Widener had thrown an egg at a judge in night court. The hungry nation was in no mood for the antics of the horsey set. Austerity was now the watchword—hard times—for as far off as any but Herbert Hoover could see.

But life proceeded for Saratoga with the usual splendor, even during the season of 1930, seeming almost as a symbol of protest against the national obsession with hard times. "What hard times?" inquired the protesters.

In his book, *Saratoga, Saga of an Impious Era,* George Waller observed that:

> For the most part the protesters and displayers were members of the country's richest club, horse society—a coalition of high socialites, café celebrities and Hollywood aristocrats who had comfortably survived the financial crash and casually defied the aftermath. The posh Turf-and-Field veterans set the pace. In the luxurious summer cottages such leaders of the horsey set as William Woodward, Samuel D. Riddle, John Hay Whitney, Cornelius Vanderbilt Whitney . . . mounted a month-long series of parties. At the race track, in their fashionable boxes—which were as much a part of their personal estate as their permanent pews in the churches they supported—and in the picturesque paddock fronting their stables they entertained with still more open disregard of the national gloom. F. Ambrose Clark, who had engendered concern among his confreres by the number and variety of his falls as a steeplechase rider, won the sympathy and applause of every Saratogan who yearned for the past when, looking every inch a nineteenth-century country squire, he drove his old-fashioned but dashing four-in-hand coach to the track to see how his light blue and yellow silks fared in the races.

From the onset of the Depression, when private bookies were still catering to the betting whims of the rich, to the era of the pari-mutuel, when public machines serviced the masses at the racetrack; from the final years of Canfield's elegant legal Casino to the undercover game rooms of Lucky Luciano's Chicago Club; from the one-to-ten shot races of Man o' War in the 1920s to the "graveyard of favorites" during the 1940s, Saratoga saw relatively little change in its lifestyle, again as recorded by George Waller:

> The losses which resulted from society's tightened purse strings were largely offset, however, by some thirty thousand lower-status fun seekers who invaded the Spa each racing season free of inhibitions and plunged to the full extent of their holiday finances, whether sufficient for the entire month of August, a week or a week end. They crowded into hotels, boarding houses, restaurants and bars, spent the hours of darkness in the gaming establishments and night clubs in town and, if a flicker of energy survived, straggled off to catch the early morning workouts at the race track. There in the cool, ambiguous light, they watched the horses run, and at ten o'clock, when the track was cleared, they went to their beds for a snatch of sleep, or to the mineral baths for a quick pick-up. Or they simply hung on for another day, filling in the time before the races began by laying bets with the bookies who were positioned all along Broadway in the plaid suits and pulled-down panamas that had become the uniform of their fraternity. Around noon the sleepers and bathers emerged, and almost as one the entire assembly bolted down breakfast or lunch and a few drinks and hastened to the track. For three hours they concentrated on horses, jockeys, tip-sheets and picking winners; then, at twilight, the last race over, they surged back to Broadway, now abloom with prostitutes, to make the rounds again.

But the post–World War II years that saw so revolutionary a shift in the American scene: the great expansion of racing as a popular commercial sport with resulting income to state treasuries . . . the disappearance of the big-time spender in the face of more rigid tax laws . . . the puritanical reaction that closed casino gambling . . . all conspired to end an era. The State frowned on twenty-four days of upstate August racing at a small track that would yield far less to its treasury than the stadium-size Belmont and Aqueduct in New York City. It pressured for closing of the track. The lack of big-time spenders and bet-a-million gamblers put a damper on the need for pleasure domes such as the Grand Union. True, there were those who continued to sail their yachts up the Hudson to Schuylerville, where their chauffeured limousines waited to take them on the twenty-minute drive to their mansions. But that was hardly enough to underwrite twenty-four days of sparsely attended racing. So they solicited their fellow-patrician, Governor Nelson Rockefeller, to subsidize the Saratoga races for the sake of tradition. Rockefeller responded with pressure on the legislature to ease up a bit. The result was a financial arrangement that gave the old Queen of American Racetracks a new lease on life.

Still, the impression lingered that the end of an era was foreshadowed—especially with the closing of the Grand Union Hotel in 1952, after the last day of racing for the season—exactly one hundred fifty years after Gideon Putnam opened the original tavern which sent the Spa on its fabled way.

Three weeks later, the faded symbol fell to the auctioneer's hammer. Most of the hotel's furnishings were sold for $250,000 to the Siegel Brothers, textile manufacturers of New York and Albany. The rest, some five hundred rooms of Victorian treasure trove, went to dealers from all over the country. The ancient wealth of Camelot's public castle was redistributed to the four corners of the country whence it originally came. Victor Herbert's piano might now become the centerpiece of some rowdy San Francisco bar; the Tiffany lamps of Lillian Russell's suite could glow in the parlor of a Boston bawdy house. Beds which had supported the bulk of Diamond Jim, and bars which had known the elbows of General Grant, might end up as conversation pieces in *raffiné* apartments on the fringes of New York City's Sutton Place.

To many Saratogans the auction was a desecration. "Why, they had tears in their eyes when they came in here for the auction," said one of the Brothers Siegel to an interviewer from *Business Week*. "They're broken-hearted, believe me."

Nevertheless, the Grand Union Hotel will always linger in the American memory, if not by virtue of the strength of its legend, then at least through the effort of an unexpected benefactor. When nobody wanted to buy the building for operation as a hotel, a corporation stepped in to carry on the name. The Grand Union Company, which operates supermarkets throughout the country, bought it, razed it, and, on the site, built "the most modern shopping center in the East." Said the supermarket president at the time he made the gesture: "We bought the property because of the name. Purchase of the Grand Union Hotel by the Grand Union Company will carry on a tradition of names."

But all is not lost in Camelot; the ghost of Tiffany still returns each August. For, even if the carriage that now rolls by the Grand Union is a meshed-wire cart instead of a handsome black Victoria with Lillian Russell in it there is still the Tiffany of thoroughbred auctions.

During the second week in August, while The Jockey Club gathers for its annual "Round Table" on how to improve the breed, most of the horsey set find time to top a day of thoroughbred jousting with a game that is even more fun: the Saratoga yearling sales.

These auctions of young, unraced horses have been going on almost since the emergence of Saratoga as a racing center—during the last seventy-five years under the sponsorship of the Fasig-Tipton Company. Precisely at 8:30 P.M. on a Tuesday night—and for three successive nights thereafter—the microphone goes live in a $500,000 air conditioned amphitheater, the Humphrey S. Finney Pavilion, named after the world's best-known horse salesman. A moment later, American-born John Finney, in a voice more British-elegant than his British father, bangs a gavel and announces the start of the world's most expensive lottery. The players, some several dozen multimillionaires seated in choice locations, with another few hundred lower-bracketed participants distributed in the remaining seat and standing room, now flip through their catalogs. Outside, through glass windows and over loud speakers, thousands of the non-participating curious observe the spectacle.

The auction sale of thoroughbreds is a numbers game where the players are after something much bigger than a basketful of dollars. The participants in this lotttery, from Mrs. Marian DuPont Scott, who may quietly place as much as $235,000 on a number, to an obscure South American who can barely find standing room to plunge his $1,200, are all chasing the big dream.

"Hip Number One, ladies and gentlemen," announces the impeccably attired John Finney, as the first nervous yearling is led into the glaring light of the ring. "Hip Number One is the second foal of a winning half-sister to the dam of the stakes-placed So-and-So, by the rising sire Such-and-such. . . ."

Such is the verbiage that triggers dreams of another Mongo, winner of the Washington, D.C. International for Mrs. Marian DuPont Scott. It is the pitch that unleashes fantasies of another Canonero II for Pedro Baptista, who took the Derby and Preakness trophies back to Venezuela for $1,200. It is a siren song that, fortified by the vision of the young beauty prancing around the auction ring, calls up memories of the Man o' Wars and Alsabs and Hoop, Jrs., which brought immortality to their owners for a pittance and a nod of the head.

The odds in this lottery of dreams, as any of the initiated will confirm, are about as high as they come in any game. For every Canonero bought for $1,200, there are thousands of purchases that never get to the races, to say nothing of ever earning back their purchase price. Of all registered foals, about 25 percent never start in a race; only some 56 percent ever win a race and 2.64 percent win a stakes race.

"We are running a very elegant crap game," admits John Finney. "What appears to be wisdom in it is really a matter of how much you can lay on the line and still be prepared to lose."

And still the players come, year after year (in 1972 Fasig-Tipton, apart from the other auctions—which did as well or better—sold over $40,000,000 in horseflesh). At Saratoga the sale has many meanings. For the Whitneys, DuPonts and Phippses it is part of an old tradition, a kind of annual Equine Cotillion—fun, excitement and the possibility of adding another winner to their already superb family of bloodlines. On the other hand, there are the immensely wealthy entrepreneurs such as the Englehards and the McMahons (about a hundred big bankrolls are actually the mainstay of the auction) who can easily lay $500,000 on the line to edge one another out of an especially attractive bloodline. Then there are the newly prosperous junkmen, oil men and grocery men who want to join the sport of kings and enter domains where their immigrant parents could perhaps only scrub floors. Add to this both the moderate-sized working horseman who hopes to obtain bloodstock he could never afford to acquire by investing in enormous breeding fees, and the Christmas Club set who have been saving their pennies for another Canonero, and you have the American Equine Dream.

On the other side there are the sellers. For them—the commercial breeders and the "house"—the horse lottery is no dream. Fasig-Tipton and other auctions in 1972 sold upward of $40,000,000 in yearlings in North America at a gross commission of 5 percent. To the market breeder such as Cousin Leslie (who sells in Kentucky, but comes to Saratoga to observe and wheel-and-deal) the auction is hard-nosed business. "Hip Number 101, ladies and gentlemen," is a prize package that the commercial breeder has worked all year to supply for the pitchman's inventory. As for the big fashionable stables, in their role of seller they look upon the auction as a chance to unload whatever unwanted merchandise that can be slipped in between the glamorous brand names. The auction is a colossal game of hit or miss, hunt and catch—or lose—"to hurt you if I win," as Bet-a-Million Gates said, "or hurt myself, if I lose."

A Saratoga auction begins with the showing of the yearlings in the sales paddock in the morning, the big day being the Sunday before the sales. Spread out over a large grassy area behind the sales pavilion are clusters of stalls which house the two hundred-plus thoroughbred yearlings that will be auctioned off. It is a sunswept, glistening Saratoga morning. The smell of horse and hay blends in an intoxicating aroma. The horsey fragrance overwhelms the perfume of a passing lady down from Bar Harbor for a look at a Bold Ruler, and melds with the sweat of a mud-booted trainer hastening over from a morning workout. On the barns are posted the names of America's most prestigious breeders, together with pedigrees of the "Hip Numbers" they will show. Over there is the Nydrie Stud, of Virginia's Daniel Van Clief. Down here is the Mereworth Farm of Kentucky's Walter J. Salmon which bred Discovery. Across the way are the Windfields Farm and the Woodstock Farm of Canada's E. P. Taylor and Maryland's Mrs. Richard G. DuPont, owners of Northern Dancer and Kelso, respectively. Elizabeth Whitney Tippet, all done up in her fuschia and purple, down to the very collar of the dog that sits in her lap, is also a peddler of horseflesh at Saratoga, conducting it in the grand style and profit to which she is a accustomed. She nods at passing prospects as she hands out a fuschia-and-purple-bordered brochure that lists her thoroughbred holdings in Virginia, Kentucky, Florida, California, France, England, Ireland and Australia.

The fashion show begins. Horses that have been brushed, groomed, polished and braided for the last week (Liz's yearlings have four purple flowers in their tail) are led out by grooms from their 8′ x 10′ stalls, in which they have been sequestered all night. This is one fashion show in which you can touch the merchandise. Hands that might have squeezed the hocks of Secretariat now press the flesh of the young animal with "Number One" pasted on his hip. Eyes that could have peered under the flank of the yearling Man o' War now examine the abdomen of Hip Number Two. Lips are curled back for looks at teeth; hocks are felt for heat; hooves are lifted in search for cracks. If a yearling bucks or rears, "My! That's the Buckpasser in him! Should go for a pretty price. . . ."

The parade moves on through the ever-growing crowd.

"Say, did you have a look at that Sailor–Kiss of Death colt? Just the nick that Amy's had her eye on."

"That Gallant Man filly from the family of Turex looks pretty damn good to me."

"Well, I think the Forli filly . . . the one out of a sister to what's-his-name . . . would make a fine sprinter, don't you?"

"Taylor's the man to watch. He'll be after that Forli filly, damn sure. And don't know anybody'd outbid him, either. . . ."

And so the show goes on. Not only with the horses but with the people. There's Humphrey S. Finney, the peripatetic horse salesman with headgear that outdoes Bella Abzug's, walking-sticks that outflash Squire Abingdon Baird's, and spectacles that perch perilously at the finish-line of his nose. Whitney Stone of Wall Street's Stone & Webster and Virginia's Morven Stud stands guard at his barn in his bright red uniform of deputy sheriff for Albemarle County, Virginia. "Oh, it's really the only chance I get to wear it in public," the million dollar-a-year lawman explains. Glad it's not 1954 when Aly Khan was here to sell his daddy's horses, or who would look at me?"

Thursday night is the big night—the climax of the show. The bright lights go on. Rolls Royces and Bentleys arrive. Seats are at a premium; many are unoccupied, waiting for the late-arriving first families. Even standing space is in short supply, including outside the pavilion, for the longhairs from the performing arts rock concert are here to dig the scene, many of the bearded orthodox Jews have left their porch rockers, and the general population is out to watch the spectacle as did their fathers and grandfathers before them.

Down front in row one, seat one, sits, of course, Queen Liz. With her ermine-and-sable stole, she presides as the queen of the horsey set. John Finney peers out at the audience, then at his watch. He bangs his gavel and the lottery begins. Five, ten, twenty horses go under the hammer. Now the big one comes in.

"Here, ladies and gentlemen, is a filly that needs no talking about," says young John Finney in his most impressively formal tone. "I need only mention that she is by Hail To Reason out of Cosmah by Cosmic Bomb . . ." With that he turns the microphone over to the auctioneer. The big dream begins to unfold.

"Awright, whatidya give to starter? Anybody start her at a hundred? Willya give FIFTY for her?"

Over there in the fourth row, "Cee Zee" Guest, dressed in a green Iranian print, is calmly munching on a frozen custard—she comes for fun, not for buying.

"Do I have fifty? Anybody bid fifty?" calls out the auctioneer.

The yearling, agitated now, lets go droppings and a white-coated groom comes out with broom and shovel.

"Hup!" cries a bid spotter in evening clothes, and the first bid is up.

The two young Phippses, "Dinny" and Cynthia, still in racetrack clothes and mud-flecked moccasins, nod at each other. E. P. Taylor, richest man in Canada—also in moccasins and casual clothes—puffs on his pipe and blinks his eyes.

"Willya give a hundred for her? I've got a hundred over here—no, it's ahead of you, Bob. I'm bid a hundred thousand, now willya go two?"

Alfred Vanderbilt looks in, folds his arms, and stares at the yearling —he rarely buys. John A. Morris has his wife's scarf draped around his shoulders against the harsh air-conditioned drafts, but he too never takes his eyes off the horse in the ring. John Schapiro, Laurel's president, despite his elevator shoes a good bit shorter than his blond blueblood wife, enters; he seems to look at the people, not the horses. Jock Whitney drops into a seat with his English trainer and seems to doze off to sleep.

Up goes the bidding, from one hundred-thousand to one hundred and fifty thousand, while diamonds flash, cigars glow and heads nod in approving bids. Now the final hot stage is reached, bid against bid jumping one hundred fifty dollars a minute, until at last the peak is reached.

"At two twenty-five do you want her? At two twenty-five, six . . . do you want her? Are you all through? At two twenty-five *and*? . . . ALL finished . . . ?" Down goes the gavel and Elliot Burch, agent for Paul Mellon and Charles Englehard, has won the lottery on the beautiful filly by Hail to Reason out of Cosmah by Cosmic Bomb for 225,000 of the aforementioned gentlemen's dollars.

Hail to Reason's daughter was vanned out of Saratoga that night, delivered to the farm, trained and named Love of Learning. Eventually she went to the races, competed seven times and won once. With total earnings of $3,575, Love of Learning became known as one of the most cosmic of "bombs" ever. But the record price for a yearling sold at Saratoga to date was the $235,000 paid in 1971 by Mrs. Marian DuPont Scott for a yearling by Ogden Phipps's Buckpasser which never got to the races.

There are, of course, some who have hit the jackpot both at Saratoga and at Lexington. However, of the ninety-two selected yearlings which have to date been auctioned for prices in excess of $100,000 and had at least one year of racing, only seven have earned back their purchase price on the racetrack. At Lexington in 1968, a grocery-chain operator named Wendell Rosso decided he would like to cross swords with platinum magnate, Charles Englehard, for a Sea-Bird filly later named Reine Enchanteur (Rosso had fallen in love with the stallion Sea-Bird). The new-rich "banana salesman" traded bidding blows—at thousands of dollars a clip—with Englehard, who ducked out at the last second and left him with a $405,000 filly that was a complete washout.

"I felt sorry having pushed Mr. Rosso so hard," said Englehard, who died in 1971. "I consider that anything over $200,000 for a young horse is excessive. But I've always enjoyed competing with others for something I wanted, and occasionally one gets carried away and ends up with something one really did not want that badly. I must say I was greatly relieved when I realized I had not paid that enormous price for that filly."

Nevertheless, Englehard is a prime example of one player who consistently hit the jackpot. By 1971, in less than nine years, he had invested $7,000,000 in some 140 American-auctioned thoroughbreds (his total investment in the thoroughbred business was estimated at $20,000,000) and ended up with a considerable number of profitable horses. Nijinsky, named after the ballet dancer who believed he was going to be reincarnated as a horse, was a star on the race course like his namesake on the stage. He was also syndicated for $5,400,000—the highest price before Secretariat. Another, named Minsky—impresario of a different kind of dancer—is still racing and doing nearly as well.

As Cousin Leslie says, you don't go into racing in "some little itty-bitty operation," or you'll lose all your money. Englehard never had to worry about that. He was one of those few who, as the old-timers say, "could afford to play a numbers game with the odds heavily stacked against them." At Saratoga, the game still goes on, year after year, with the odds getting higher and higher.

CHAPTER 24

The New Crowd

. . . it was only from her French being so good, that you could know she was not born a woman of fashion.

—W. M. Thackeray, of Becky Sharp, in *Vanity Fair*

EVER SINCE CIMON, the great Athenian statesman, had himself entombed with his two mares that won the Olympic "Triple Crown" in 500 B.C., nothing has been more fashionable than to be associated with racehorses. "My kingdom for a horse!" cried Richard III—a call that has echoed down the ages—except that to the *nouveaux* it generally has been heard as: "A horse for my kingdom!" Men seem to feel that owning a racehorse creates some special kind of kingdom for them.

But for many groups, entry into the higher eschelons of horse-racing has been difficult. The history of the treatment of blacks in thoroughbred racing has been a shameful episode.

"Shameful treatment of blacks in racing? You must be kidding," Alfred G. Vanderbilt, chairman of the board of the New York Racing Association and a well-known liberal, told the author. "Why, my mother had a black jock. Besides, what do you think Angel Cordero is? He's one of the top jocks in the country and he's not exactly a Caucasian, is he?"

Mr. Vanderbilt was reminded that Angel Cordero, Jr., and the other dark-skinned jockeys who now ride for the most fashionable stables, are not exactly *American* blacks or non-Caucasians either. To a man, they come from outside the continental United States. And there is a clear difference between the social status of an American "nigger" and a "black" man from outside the States as is perhaps illustrated by this incident from the author's private recollections.

My father once operated a burlesque theater in Baltimore, not too far from a thoroughbred farm where Alfred Vanderbilt had installed facilities for his stable help. There was nothing fashionable about my father's burlesque theater, a place on Baltimore Street where white men gathered to watch white women strip. The guidelines for admission were the same as in the rest of white America: *no colored allowed.* But my father was not one to let a potential customer escape because the Supreme Court had made certain that the city provide an equal facility on Pennsylvania Avenue where black men could see their own women strip. If by chance a venturesome black approached the box office, my father always looked at him like a lawyer telegraphing a leading question.

"You know the policy here," my father would wink at the black. "We can't admit Negroes."

The black man, silent, would start to move off.

"Wait!" my father would call after him, "You look like a South American. Aren't you from Panama? Maybe Liberia? Ethiopia?"

The black man, never daring to implicate himself with an oral acquiescence, would simply stare cooperatively.

"Okay, then," my father would proclaim. "If you are a foreign Negro, it's okay. The law doesn't apply. The cops don't bother foreign Negroes. You can go in."

This is a policy with which African ambassadorial personnel in the U.S. have always been familiar and which, with few exceptions, has applied to the black in racing since the turn of the century. It still applies today, particularly with fashionable stables that race on the New York tracks. The only men of color who seem acceptable as jockeys are those that come from other countries. As of this date *there is not one American black jockey riding on The Jockey Club–controlled racetracks in New York.* With exceptions that can be counted on the fingers of one hand, the same situation prevails for black trainers—and in those instances where they can be found, it is almost invariably in the minor-league establishments.

On the matter of color, Alfred Vanderbilt had something further to say: "There just don't seem to be any capable black jocks around. But you can be damned sure I'd put any boy up on my horses who showed potential, no matter what the color of his skin."

Mr. Vanderbilt's comments constitute what is essentially the official position paper of the racing establishment on the role of the black in the sport. "Sure, we'd employ blacks–blues, greens–anything that would bring our horses in first. But where are they?"

Ironically, most members of The Jockey Club well know, as do most professionals around the racetrack, that one of the world's greatest jockeys–in the opinion of most, America's greatest–was a black man by the name of Isaac Murphy. This is an unknown name to the average white man. Even those who can tell you all about Tod Sloan, Earl Sande and a dozen other deceased white jockeys, have never heard of Isaac Murphy. Not even the well-informed black, when shown a photograph, can identify the man who was the first great American black athlete, as outstanding a champion in his own right as Jack Johnson, Jesse Owens, Jackie Robinson, Joe Louis, and Althea Gibson.

Isaac Burns Murphy was born of slave parents in 1860 on the plantation of the Lexington, Kentucky city treasurer, symbolically enough, on New Year's day, the official birthday of all thoroughbred horses. His father, James Burns (Isaac later added his grandfather's surname) became a "free" man by enlisting in the Union Army. He died in prison after being captured by the Confederates. Isaac's mother was left to support herself and young Isaac by working as a washerwoman for the owner of a southern racing stable.

Noticing Isaac's small size, the stable's trainer, "Uncle Eli" Jordan, as he was affectionately called, apprenticed him as a prospective jockey when he was twelve and put him to work breaking yearlings. Use of a young black boy to break thoroughbreds was nothing new at this time. All through the era of slavery much of the stable personnel in the south was black. Many of the jockeys, too, were black, some of them being deliberately stunted for this purpose. They bore names such as Mr. Hawkin's "Abe," or "Washington," or Warner & Company's "Hunchback." All of them were referred to as "boys" regardless of their ability or age–a name that to this day adheres to jockeys, even such a white millionaire as, say, Willie Shoemaker.

The war was over about ten years before Murphy, fifteen years old now, was aboard Glentina, his first winner for "Uncle Eli." He defeated the future Kentucky winner, Baden Baden, at the Lexington

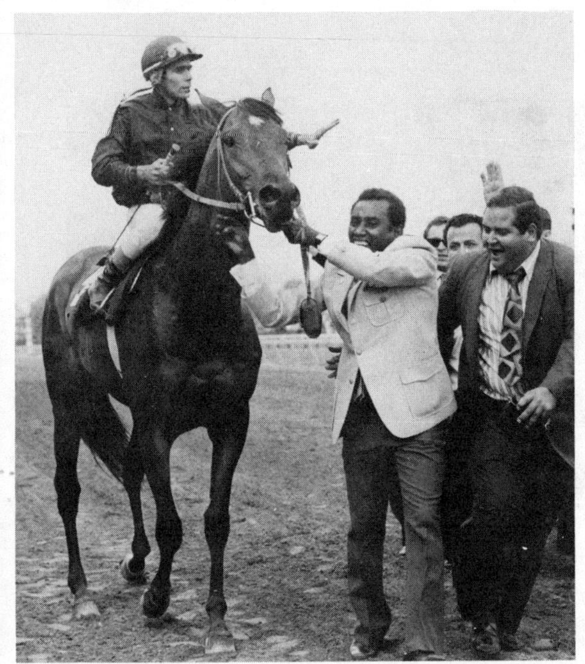

Above, left: Happy hordes of Venezuelans follow jubilant trainer Juan Arias (center) to the winner's circle after Gustavo Avila rode Canonero II to a sensational, record-breaking triumph in the 1971 Preakness.

Above, right: Humphrey S. Finney, world's best-known horse salesman, makes the rounds of the Saratoga Sales paddock to inspect some of the several millions of dollars in yearlings which wil be auctioned off by the Fasig-Tipton Company, of which he is chairman.

Below: Horse super-salesman Leslie Combs (right) receives The Jockey Club Gold Cup trophy from chairman George D. Widener. The presentation honors the victory of Nashua, a horse which Combs had syndicated. Eddie Arcaro (center) was in the saddle.

Above, left: A yearling goes on the block at the Saratoga auctions. The "tote board" at the top registers the progress of the prices bid. *Above, right:* John W. ("Bet-a-million") Gates, the most spectacular plunger of his day.

Below, left: James Buchanan ("Diamond Jim") Brady was a regular visitor at Saratoga. With trainer Charles Durnell (left) he looks over the scenery under the Spa's famous elm trees. *Below, right:* Lillian Russell, with banker Jesse Lewisohn, at Saratoga in 1906.

Top: Man o' War suffered his only defeat in the 1919 Sanford Memorial Stakes at Saratoga. The big red horse (center) was beaten by Upset. Golden Broom is at left.

Bottom: Revenge: in the 1920 Travers Stakes at the Springs, Man o' War trounced Upset. John P. Grier is at left.

Right: Laurel Race Course president, John D. Schapiro, with his wife, the former Eleanor Tydings, at a foxhunt outside Baltimore.

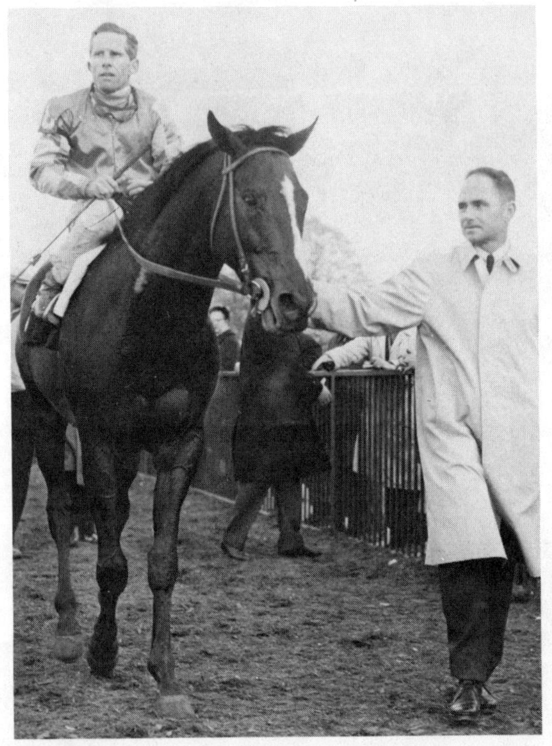

Left: Jack J. Dreyfus, owner of Hobeau Farms, leads his Beau Purple, William Boland up, to the winner's circle, after the horse defeated Kelso in the Man o' War Stakes. Beau Purple defeated the great Kelso three times.

Below: Hirsch Jacobs receiving a trophy in 1960 from Marshall Cassidy, executive secretary of The Jockey Club for his three-thousandth win. With him (left to right) are his son Tommy, Mrs. Jacobs, daughter Patrice and son John. Jacobs, an ex-pigeon trainer from Brooklyn, became the country's leading thoroughbred trainer, heading the list of winners for eleven seasons. One of his greatest accomplishments was claiming a non-entity named Stymie for $1500 and developing him into one of the world's most popular and greatest horses, noted for coming from way behind to cross the finish line first. Jacobs died in 1970. His wife and daughter continue in the sport as owners and breeders, and son John is a highly-regarded trainer.

Isaac Murphy (*left*), winner of three Kentucky Derbies, a record which stood for thirty-nine years, died at age thirty-six in 1896. The black rider was considered by many to be the "perfect jockey," but his memory, along with his body, mouldered in a weed-overgrown grave, as a result of the white backlash following the Reconstruction. His record of percentage of winners still stands today.

Ed ("Brown Dick") Brown (*right*), one of the great black trainers of the late nineteenth century.

Below: Isaac Murphy on Salvator winning a match race against Tenny, ridden by Snapper Garrison, by half a head at Sheepshead Bay, June 25, 1890.

Above: Mrs. Helen Chenery ("Penny") Tweedy, owner and later, syndicator of Secretariat.

Left: Secretariat is led by trainer Lucien Laurin to the winner's circle after his smashing triumph in the Preakness. In the saddle is jockey Ron Turcotte.

racetrack. Six days later he won the Blue Grass Stakes at Louisville and the next year was in Saratoga riding against the top white Eastern jockeys.

Isaac was ready for the bigtime. With Uncle Eli as trainer, he was retained by the powerful Fleetwood Stable and rode their Falsetto to the three-year-old championship of 1879. In one race, Saratoga's Travers Stakes, he pushed the horse to a two-length win over the eastern champion, Spendthrift, Man o' War's grandsire, a victory that most of the regulars regarded as merely a fluke. Many of the more sophisticated were less inclined to regard the black jockey as a flash-in-the-pan—particularly the professional gamblers. Some approached Isaac with inducements to "throw" his next encounter with Spendthrift in the Kenner Stakes. His response was characteristic: he brought Falsetto in again with a two-length margin over his rival.

"Isaac could have made enough to buy a Blue Grass farm, if he would have agreed to lose on Falsetto in the Kenner Stakes in 1879," Frank Talmadge Phelps reported in the *Thoroughbred Record* of May 13, 1967, many years after the event.

Murphy was the very opposite of the newly emancipated black man now free to make racing deals with the white man and complain about double dealings if he so chose. This was a sentiment expressed in verse by Albert Cooper, the black trainer of the great horse Domino, and quoted by Dan M. Bowman III in his book *Giants of the Turf* (*The Blood-Horse*, 1960):

> A naught's a naught
>   and a figger a figger
> All for the white man
>   and none for the nigger.

Isaac Murphy was his own man: independent, honest, overwhelmingly generous. "In person," wrote L. P. Tarleton, who owned Fleetwood Stable (quoted by Phelps in his *Thoroughbred Record* piece), "Isaac was about five feet in height, with short, straight legs and long sinewy arms; and in full life would weigh about one hundred thirty pounds. He had a brown skin with thin lips and a straight nose. His countenance was open, with a happy, intelligent expression, almost childlike in its innocence; and in talking he looked you straight in the face with large, wide-open eyes that seemed to say, 'You can trust me and I will trust you.'"

Isaac married in 1882 and later bought a house in Lexington. No one is quite sure where it was located but some think it was a vast Victorian mansion opposite Walton Avenue, until recently occupied by the YMCA. This is easily possible, for at the peak of his career, Isaac was earning $20,000 a year—a large sum at a period when the Kentucky Derby carried a purse of only $5,000.

But by 1882 Murphy had not yet won a Kentucky Derby. That occured in 1884, when, during a race in which his mount was almost left at the post, Murphy came from way behind and breezed Buchanan into a two-length victory.

This was the beginning of world-wide fame for the man whom his contemporaries called "the nearest perfect jockey." Other black men, on the crest of the Reconstruction tide, were also making names for themselves in racing. The first Kentucky Derby, run in 1875, was won by black Oliver Lewis on Aristides. In the period from 1875 to 1895, black jockeys won eleven Kentucky Derbies, Murphy himself won two in succession, only one white rider to date—Ron Turcotte with Riva Ridge and Secretariat—ever equalling that feat. In addition, black trainers were doing as well—and in the employ of top white-owned stables.

None of them—black or white—matched the record of Isaac Murphy. In his short life of thirty-six years he rode in every great stakes race in the country except the Futurity; he won three Kentucky Derbies, a record that stood for thirty-nine years until Earl Sande equalled it in 1930 on Gallant Fox and Eddie Arcaro surpassed it in 1948 on Citation. In addition, Isaac Murphy won four American Derbies and five Latonia Derbies. In all, he rode in 1,412 races and won 612, giving him a lifetime winning-average of 44 percent—a record which stands to this day, the closest approximation being the 25 percent of Willie Shoemaker and Avelino Gomez. At the peak of his riding career he was given the perhaps well-intentioned if dubious honor of being called "the colored Fred Archer," after a famous English jockey. Many believe that in view of their comparative accomplishments, Archer should have been dubbed the "white Isaac Murphy."

Isaac Burns Murphy died of pneumonia on Lincoln's birthday in

1896. His death was attributed to the rigors of a lifelong battle to maintain the low weight required of his profession. He had been in retirement for some time before his death and much of his earnings had eroded away, a good deal of it in generous gifts.

"He is an elegant specimen of manhood," wrote the eminent turf authority, Walter S. Vosburgh, in *Famous American Jockeys,* published in 1884 by R. A. Saalfield, "strong and muscular and as graceful as an Apollo. He sits his horse like a Centaur, and there is little flourish to his finish. He is, moreover, a great favorite—owing to his polite, modest and engaging manners, and his reputation is beyond reproach."

Perhaps Isaac Murphy's early demise was a blessing. It was not long after his death, just two years after the formation of The Jockey Club in 1894, that the writing of such words about a black man might have invited a visit from the Ku Klux Klan. The white backlash against blacks earning the honors and the high financial rewards associated with the fast-growing sport of kings was now raging unchecked, as it was in other areas of society. Not even the separate-but-equal doctrine would have been tolerated in racing—nobody was going to stage a separate Kentucky Derby so that the "niggers" could have an equal chance. Gradually black aspirants were phased back into the more menial aspects of turf life: grooms, exercise boys and stall-muckers. By 1911 the black jockey had ridden in his last Kentucky Derby.

"I am as proud of my calling as I am of my record," Phelps reports Isaac Murphy said before his death. "And I believe my life will be recorded as a success, though the reputation I enjoy was earned in the stable and saddle. It is a great honor to be classed as one of America's greatest jockeys."

There is no record of Isaac Murphy's life in the sports encyclopedias. Neither is it mentioned in the Encyclopedia Britannica, or any other. Even *The New York Times,* which, on February 13, 1896, reported the demise of William Fowles, Archie Warner and Alvin Rowley, who perished in a well they were digging in Milan, Ohio, did not find it fit to print the news of the death of the country's greatest jockey.

As for the resting places, the horses which Isaac Murphy rode did better than the jockey, who was buried in a "Negro" cemetery where, years later, it was impossible to find the grave because the wood marker had crumbled, and the ground was overgrown with weeds. His wife, who lived in poverty for fifteen years after his death, was not able to join him in death—she was buried in a pauper's grave.

Seventy-one years later, in 1967—about a hundred years after Lincoln's assassination, and just one year before Martin Luther King's—the coffin of Isaac Murphy was removed from the weeds and placed beneath the verdant greensward of Man o' War Park in Lexington, next to an heroic statue of the world's most famous horse. The ceremony was attended by Lexington's mayor, Fred Fugazi, and federal judge Bert Combs, the former governor of Kentucky.

"Honor and shame from no condition rise," reads the excerpts from Alexander Pope's *Essay on Man,* inscribed on Isaac Murphy's new monument, donated by Kentucky Club Tobacco Company. "Act well your part, there all honor lies."

Jack Johnson, the first black heavyweight champion of the world—even though he infuriated the white world by flaunting his prowess with white women—did not fare as badly as did Isaac Murphy. One can find his name in the Columbia Encyclopedia. Jesse Owens, too, has nearly three column-inches in the encyclopedia—a representative of the United States at the Olympics held in Nazi Germany, a black man who demolished Hitler's Aryan supremacy myth. Jackie Robinson is recorded in even greater detail in the encyclopedias, as the first black man in major league baseball. Boxing, broadjumping and baseball are one thing; apparently the sport of kings is another. Isaac Murphy had the misfortune not only to have made his mark at the high point of the Reconstruction backlash, but also to have done it in the most aristocratic and exclusive of all sports.

But it's really not that at all, reiterate the liberal apologists. There just *are* no black boys around. The black has grown too large to be a jockey. The present-day black is tall, big-boned and husky. That's because his slave ancestors were well-fed by their masters, while poor whites lived on the edge of starvation. Oh, the reason for it is a dastardly one, of course. The slave was a valuable property and needed to be well-fueled for hard work. But the fact remains that the present generation of black is much too big for the jockey profession.

"Yeah, I know," said a diminutive black groom for one of the major stables. "We're all Wilt Chamberlains. But I tell you one thing. Let somebody lay down some bread and I'll find you enough black midgets around here mucking out stalls to ride the horses in all nine races at Belmont tomorrow. Get with it, man. To go anywhere as a jock, you got to be pushed and nursed along by a powerful trainer. Now, can you imagine some bigtime white society trainer pushing along a little nigger from Harlem so's he has to be hugged in public by some Mrs. Tweedy on TV, like she did when Ron Turcotte won the Triple Crown?"

What about black trainers, then?

"Same thing . . . the leftovers. Bush-leagues, mostly. You must have looked in at the Saratoga auctions. Don't ever see a black man sitting there next to some white millionaire and whispering in his ear what to buy, do you? Some day, maybe. But not now. I'm missing two fingers, and even so, you can count the blacks in racing on both my hands."

The New York Times said it more emphatically. As late as 1967, the year of Isaac Murphy's official rehabilitation, that newspaper wrote: "In recent years, Negro jockeys could be counted on the fingers of one hand." In sum, the blacks have a long way to go to become a significant part of the New Crowd in racing.

There has always been some kind of a New Crowd clamoring at the gates of thoroughbred racing. At Maryland's Pimlico, forty years ago, even Alfred Gwynne Vanderbilt could have been considered something of an outsider: a "New Dealer" from the aristocracy shouldering aside the Dixie "Old Guard." Or, even further back in time, August Belmont II, a founder of The Jockey Club, the son of the Jewish upstart who had crashed his way into the Old Crowd as August Belmont I, a reconditioned WASP.

With few exceptions (notably Rent-a-Car John Hertz, owner of Triple Crown winner Count Fleet), the New Crowd of fifty years ago were non-Jewish *nouveau riche.* It was an odd mix. There was the Philadelphia butcher's son, Joseph E. Widener, the shoemaker Phippses from Barefoot Square in Pittsburgh, and a host of oilmen, grocers, and miscellaneous entrepreneurs (hustlers) such as Harry Sinclair, the Dwyer Brothers and James Butler. Even Christopher T. Chenery, whose daughter, Mrs. Helen Tweedy, would become the future syndicator of Secretariat, came late upon the scene. But none of them would have been found on the Board of Elders of Temple Emanu-El.

The New Crowd of the last twenty-five years, however, is largely a Jewish group—at least of Jewish parentage. Entry into the sport of kings as an owner is easy enough, especially since Jule Fink ended the power of The Jockey Club to license purely at its own discretion. Required are a few million dollars and a spiritual sip or two of Cousin Leslie's mint juleps. A roster of the names of owners would list Sigmund Sommer, building tycoon and owner of Sham, Secretariat's strongest opposition in 1973. Louis Wolfson, owner of Harbor View Stable and Wall Street manipulator, who served a term in jail for manipulation of stockholders' dollars, would also be there, both Sommer and Wolfson being major powers with strong stables. A few years back Louis B. Mayer of Hollywood spent millions trying to buy what he considered the best in racehorses.

As for racetrack ownership, positions of power in the turf, to a large extent, have come into the hands of the Jewish New Crowd, as in the beginning of this century they fell to the status-seeking new-rich WASP, and, in the next half century, may well be acquired by some members the new black bourgeoisie. But for the present this situation exists chiefly in the provinces. In the citadels of power—New York and the DuPont state of Delaware—their turf has remained firmly in *their* hands.

It is in places such as Maryland that the change is most evident. Pimlico, one of the oldest and most prestigious of the provincial racetracks, was surrounded by Alfred Vanderbilt almost two decades ago and ended up under the control of Herman and Ben Cohen, Baltimore entrepreneurs. Laurel, another Maryland track in which Vanderbilt also had an interest, came under the control of Morris Schapiro, a Baltimore immigrant who, with his brother Jacob, founded a metal-salvage empire with a pushcart. Two of the richest races in the world, the Preakness and the Washington, D.C. International, are now presented by Herman Cohen and Morris Schapiro's son, John, respectively. In New Jersey Dr. Leon Levy, a dentist who made millions in Columbia Broadcasting System stock, sits on the board of Atlantic City Racetrack with a Widener dynasty member, W. Eugene Dixon, Jr. Hialeah, Joseph Widener's "Belmont of the South," passed for a time out of The Jockey Club orbit and into the hands of another entrepreneur (this time non-Jewish) but is now back in the establisment fold. Churchill Downs itself almost fell into the hands of outsiders, but it, too, was finally secured again with a Jockey Club-oriented board.

Perhaps the two most interesting and, in many ways, most representative members of the so-called Jewish New Crowd are Jack J. Dreyfus of Wall Street and the New York Racing Association, and John D. Schapiro of the Boston Iron and Metal Company and Laurel Racetrack in Maryland.

Jack Jones Dreyfus, Jr., is a short, wiry man of fifty-nine who moves about in a tense, restless fashion. His grandfather was first cousin to the French Captain Alfred Dreyfus. Having become rich in a few years in association with a well-known lion (not Louis B. Mayer's but his own that came up the steps of New York subways selling mutual funds on television), Dreyfus retired from management of his $2,500,000,000 mutual fund to devote himself to his racing stable and his medical foundation. In less than twenty years, Dreyfus has worked himself up to the very highest level of the racing establishment as a member, then chairman, of the board of trustees of the NYRA, a job held at this writing by Alfred Vanderbilt, and as a member of The Jockey Club.

Jack Dreyfus seems to fit into none of the categories common to the Jewish New Crowd. He is the only Jew in The Jockey Club (John Schiff, grandson of Jacob Schiff, the Jewish banker, is a member—but he converted like Belmont, and further certified the change by marrying the daughter of George F. Baker, Jr). Schiff's father was one of the most powerful financiers in the country and left an estate of $140,000,000. Jack Dreyfus's father was owner of a small candy business.

"He sold candy canes," Dreyfus told the author, "those peppermint red and white sticks—out of Montgomery, Alabama, where I was born. He went up to the races in Louisville one day and lost all his money, so my uncle, his partner, sent him some candy samples and told him to work his way back. That's how badly my father liked to be with horses."

As for adherence to Jewish heritage, he seems to have ranged himself with other co-religionists admitted to The Jockey Club, from August Belmont II on through Harry Guggenheim and John Schiff.

"No sir, my parents were Jewish, but I don't think of myself as a Jew . . . I'm not un-Jewish . . . and I'm not un-Catholic . . . I'm not anything. I never particularly adopted that religion. Just because your parents happen to have a religion doesn't mean you have to adopt it. Besides the question of being Jewish never rises in The Jockey Club." (Dreyfus himself never sought admission to the Club.)

"Why they ever invited me to become chairman of the Board of Trustees of NYRA [all trustees are Jockey Club members] I'll never know. Because of my good looks, I guess," he said wryly.

In fact, Jack Dreyfus is a handsome man. He has all other and perhaps more compelling credentials. Jack Dreyfus had been a wonder boy of Wall Street, a managerial genius of the first order. He had a stock exchange seat at thirty-four—the youngest in his time—had taken a moribund brokerage house and turned it into a profitable company, made multi-millionaires of his friends many times over with his promotion of Polaroid stock, and built up, almost single-handedly, a quarter-of-a-trillion dollar mutual fund. He was the lion of Wall Street, and the lion was an apt advertising symbol for his fund. The cheetah ad related more to his racing interests.

"Yes, the cheetah ad ["the thoroughbred horse, not the cheetah, is the fastest animal alive"] was mine. Seems I identify with cats, doesn't it? But we also did other things not only to pull in customers at the tracks but to please them when they got there. We knocked down brick walls so people could see better, we put linoleum over the cement to soothe aching feet, made snack bars more available, that kind of thing. Also we tried to get more for the horseman. I'm on the side of the average man."

Dreyfus has been accused of being a snob in reverse by his practice of watching the races in the midst of the crowds in the grandstand, wearing a sport shirt and looking more like a two-dollar horseplayer than Jockey Club member. He doesn't have a private box and rarely wears a tie. When on August 4, 1973, his horse Onion upset Secretariat by a length in the prestigious Whitney Stake at Saratoga, he wasn't on hand for the trophy in the winner's circle. Once, when he was experimenting with an early Polaroid, he snapped a picture of a woman who apparently thought he was a street photographer. She gave him a quarter. "Of course I kept it. Handing it back might have hurt her feelings." On another occasion in the Roney-Plaza Hotel, in Miami Beach, a guest asked him where the ladies room was; apparently she mistook him for a busboy. Dreyfus obediently told her where he thought she might find it.

"Look, I believe in being relaxed," Dreyfus insisted. "There's no symbolism in the way I dress or where I watch the races from. I'm in racing to relax, not to prove anything. This business of rubbing elbows with the Whitneys and the Vanderbilts . . . well, they're nice people to rub elbows with, but that's the furthest thing from my mind."

There were, indeed, other and deeper dimensions to Jack Dreyfus. In 1967, there appeared in *Life* magazine a feature story under a banner headline that read: "10,000-to-1 Payoff." The story was a public statement made to *Life* writer Albert Rosenfeld that Jack Dreyfus, a name which made great waves on Wall Street, had for years been a victim of depression, fear, and anxiety. A full-page picture showed the manager of over a billion dollars of investments cupping his head in his hands, like a man suffering from psychic demons. An even more sensational *Readers' Digest* article on the same subject followed close on the *Life* story.

The details of how Dreyfus collected his "10,000-to-1 Payoff" were even more revealing. After having tried psychotherapy, tranquilizers, sleeping pills, psychic energizers, and other devices to relieve his agonies—all to no avail—he came, quite by accident, to what he considers the overwhelming event of his life. He discovered that, "I have too much electricity in my body."

This occurred as a result of touching a faulty vacuum cleaner and getting an electric shock, whereupon he exploded in a fit of anger when his wife reminded him he was always experiencing electric shocks. After consultation with doctors, Dreyfus concluded that an excess of electricity in his body—"hyper-excitable cells," he later explained—was causing his symptoms.

"Maybe," he said to his physician, according to the *Life* story, "some people are poisoned by too much electricity, while others have an electrical explosion which releases it called epilepsy." It was a 10,000 to 1 possibility, Dreyfus felt, but just maybe. When his physician informed him that . . . "epileptics *do* have an unusual electric [brain] pattern," the odds fell to 100 to 1 in Dreyfus' mind. And that was the beginning of his experience with the drug called Dyphenolhydantoin (Dilantin) that epileptics use to control seizures.

That was merely the beginning. Dreyfus became convinced that the malfunctioning of the human nervous system was in many cases a result of an excess of electricity and perhaps a key to many disorders of the mind and body. He began to take Dilantin regularly, and does so to this day.

"It only took me a couple of days to lose the need for psychotherapy." His excessive feelings of fear disappeared and the feelings of impatience and irritability and anger "also went back to what I view as normal." His mind instead of getting hooked onto a single subject, "was able to operate its switch-off mechanism as it should. I could think of things as much as I wanted, but I could drop them when I wanted to." The neck pains and stomach trouble disappeared. "I felt no sedative effect from the DPH [Dilantin] nor any elevating effect. On the other hand, because I was not worn out by my mind being so busy all the time, my energy returned full force."

Today, some seven years later, he heads the Dreyfus Medical Foundation, which he supports to continue research on the use of Dilantin, particularly in the area of non-epileptic behavioral disorders. In 1972 he was invited by a group of Soviet doctors to Leningrad, where the drug, he told the author, "has been widely used both for organic and behavioral disorders and found extremely successful."

Today, Jack Dreyfus's whole life is devoted to two things: thoroughbred racing as an owner and breeder, and running the Dreyfus Medical Foundation as the world's most enthusiastic proselytizer for Dilantin. Sitting in his suite on the twenty-seventh floor of a lower-Broadway tower with a fine view of the New York harbor, one has a feeling of being in the office of a hip J. P. Morgan with Jackson Pollack tastes. Pointing toward Battery Park in the direction of the Statue of Liberty is a huge antique brass telescope. A ten by eighteen foot abstract painting called "All Day Long" by Milton Resnick dominates a bright arrangement of pastel furnishings in which stock quotations, coming in on a closed-circuit TV, struggle to assert themselves in the sun-drenched room. A fat tabby cat—the only symbol of Dreyfus's feline-oriented days (the mutual fund lion is gone and the cheetah a memory of past racing-advertising campaigns) lopes lazily through the room—the only cat, one suspects, that roams about an executive suite of the Wall Street financial district. The cat blinks at the Dow Jones figures flashing on the TV, and Dreyfus, pausing over his boiled egg and toast, blinks along with him.

"Got to keep track of what money you don't give away," he says, looking first at the tabby and then at the flashing quotations, as though apologizing for both the fatness of the cat and the time spent watching a stock ticker. "I can't completely retire from the Street, else there'd be no money for Dilantin."

There is a feeling that here is a man of the turf that really fits into none of the traditional patterns. Certainly he is not one of Ortega's aristocrats, as Alfred Vanderbilt or George D. Widener, who need the thoroughbred to fill unoccupied time. Neither does he seem to be like Joseph E. Widener, who used the thoroughbred as a status symbol. If you look for Jack Dreyfus, you'll find him among the blacks and Puerto Ricans crowded up against Aqueduct's grandstand fence. Could it be that racing is for him, a game of destroying an enemy in a gentlemen's encounter?

"Jack Dreyfus has been said to be a fierce competitor in everything he undertakes, whether it be golf, bridge, tennis, Wall Street, or racing," a visitor reminds him, "the implication being that he is always out to demolish his rivals."

"Not so. I was out to demolish nobody. I couldn't have. I hadn't the resources to compete with any giants worth toppling. I was fascinated first by the mathematical intricacies of handicapping and betting. Then I fell in love with a filly named Belle Soeur, and when she was mated with Count Fleet I was intrigued by the possibilities. I was not yet well-off, but I persuaded Laudy Lawrence to sell me a 25 percent interest in the foal for all that I could then afford: 150 shares of Polaroid."

Those shares, incidentally, eventually became worth about $234,000 to Laudy Lawrence as Polaroid stock skyrocketed.

"The foal was named Beau Gar. He didn't get to the races until he was three and never had a chance to prove what he could do. He hurt his back and had to be retired after winning only $14,000. I was determined to give that horse a chance. So I bought the rest of him, and decided to take a chance on making him a stallion. Not because of his breeding . . . that's nonsense. You can have the best breeding in the world and have a horse who can't run out of his shadow."

He plunged into the endeavor with typical Dreyfus energy.

"I rented six mares . . . which is the tail-backward way of doing things. Usually you have a mare and you rent a stallion. Well, I was incredibly lucky . . . not knowing what a wild longshot I was playing. In Beau Gar's first crop I got three allowance race winners, a small race winner in Canada, one horse who didn't get to the races, and . . . Beau Purple!"

For a moment, hearing the sense of pride with which Dreyfus described how Beau Purple beat Mrs. Richard DuPont's Kelso (world's leading money-winning horse) three times, one wondered if, after all, it was not indeed a wish to topple the official giants that magnetized Dreyfus for racing. From penny-candy to outstripping a DuPont?—in any case, not a story to be ashamed to tell your grandchildren. Dreyfus went on to become the leading money-winning owner in 1967. And Beau Gar, even as late as 1972, at age twenty-two, ranked fourth on the General Sire List, above such stallions as Bold Ruler. The Hobeau Stable of Jack Dreyfus (the stable name in key with Dreyfus' ironic style) was now one of the top operations in the country, made even more so by the win of Onion over Secretariat in the Whitney.

"Racing is not a thing to go into as a business," said Dreyfus, in reply to a question about his real motivation for going into racing. "You could do much better almost anywhere. I really don't remember *any* motivation on my part. It was just to give Beau Gar a chance. I sort of was crazy about him . . . and I felt I didn't want to take the defeat which, for him, or for myself . . . was not that he was only winning $14,000 as much as . . . I just wanted to extend his possibilities . . . to give him a further chance."

Somehow one had the impression that there was some kind of an identification with Beau Gar—"I didn't want to take the defeat for him, *or for myself*"—(Ortega calls attention to this sort of natural identity between man and the animal he hunts [races]). Part of the hunter's feelings are always depressed by the killing of the beast—only the Cartesians had no compunction against it, because they considered lower animals machines. With the horse he races, man has an even closer communion than with the animal he hunts, and is therefore perhaps even more distraught at seeing him go down to defeat.)

The pleasantly fat cat, which at this very moment was sunning in the warm rays filtering through Dreyfus' office windows, was once an outcast that had been rescued as a homeless kitten on Lower Broadway by Dreyfus. Similarly, Dreyfus had once spotted through his brass telescope an abandoned puppy wandering in Battery Park and had rushed down from his Wall Street tower to help him. He has found homes for over fifty stray dogs and once, seeing fourteen cats cooped up in a cage in a swank hotel, he immediately arranged to ship them to his 1,200-acre horse farm near Ocala, Florida.

Jack Dreyfus is a man *dedicated* to something other than the pursuit of trophies. He might not inappropriately be reported as a modern Don Quixote mounted on his Beau Gar, hoisting aloft a standard reading "Dilantin." Except there is a difference: this Don Quixote seems to succeed at everything he does.

John D. Schapiro, the obscure son of an immigrant junkman, had imagination and a desire to move in exalted circles, which he did when he took over Laurel Race Course in Maryland and established his Washington, D.C. International Race.

Becoming the owner of a racetrack that can present an international race featuring horses from many nations gives a man a much quicker opportunity to hobnob with the Beautiful People than does the acquisition of a stable of racehorses. It is like the role of the "house" as compared to the player in a casino. The horse-owner—however big—is still one of a crowd, most of whom will never be lucky enough to get a good horse and gain access to the charmed circle; but the racetrack owner is *assured* of success. All of the owners of the world's top horses are immediate possibilities for invitation to John Schapiro's International.

Within about a year after his father—who had become a multi-millionaire scrap-iron tycoon—bought him a second-rate racetrack just outside the nation's capitol, a Jewish boy from Baltimore by the name of Schapiro was dreaming of being on the welcome list of Queen Elizabeth, Baron Guy de Rothschild, Sir Winston Churchill and American high society whose horses he intended to invite to his

International. But, like Napoleon (Mr. Schapiro is about the same height), he had to be content with a few minor victories at first. His first International in 1952 was, except for the German Baron von Thyssen's entry, almost entirely a campaign among the English-speaking countries—including two rather insignificant horses from Great Britain, one of which—fortunately for his hopes for keeping it international—won, and a racehorse from Canada. People might joke and mock the Schapiro International—but this "little corporal" had a most ambitious master plan that, in its context, was as ambitious as the Corsican member of the New Crowd of 1789. Having, in his very first campaign, adorned his program with the name of a personage such as Baron von Thyssen, Schapiro had already tasted some heady fruit. Now he was preparing for much bigger game. Within a few short years he would snare for his International Lady Bury, Sir Percy Lorraine, Le Comte de Chambure, Sir Winston Churchill, Prince Aly Khan and Queen Elizabeth herself, in addition to Whitneys, DuPonts, and Vanderbilts from the local scene. John D. Schapiro had created —not so much with a horse as with a horse race—his very own kingdom. And like the "upstart" who crowned himself emperor in 1804, Schapiro bestowed upon his own race the title of "third leg of the Triple Crown of Internationals"—to perhaps as much chagrin on the part of the thousand-year-old aristocracy who currently rule the revered King George VI/Queen Elizabeth Stakes and Le Prix de l'Arc de Triomphe as their ancestors felt at the self-anointment of the Corsican. Along the way, with his entry into the higher circles of aristocracy, Schapiro also exchanged a Jewish wife from Baltimore for a blue-eyed "shiksa" from Baltimore.

Had it not been for his father, Morris, all of this might not have been possible—a fact which brings to mind the way other racing dynasties were founded. Like Cornelius Vanderbilt, Henry Phipps and Peter A. B. Widener I, Morris Schapiro had to work and fight hard for the first few pennies that made him a millionaire. In addition, he was a Jewish immigrant—one who fled Russia in 1902 in the wave of migration away from the Czar's anti-Semitic terrors. After two years of wandering from Boston to Georgia in search of a living, the non-English speaking refugee arrived in Baltimore at the time of the great fire which leveled the city. In his pocket was seventy-five cents, enough to hire a pushcart in which he immediately started to haul junk metal and lumber from the ruins for two cents a load.

"It was much better than what I was doing in Georgia," his obituary in the Baltimore *Sun* quotes him as being always proud to say. (A distant cousin had set him up as an itinerant country peddler, with a mule, a stock of soap and a supply of dry goods, plus an earful of good advice.) "That lasted one day, because I couldn't see myself for the rest of my life pushing that stuff on *landsmen*."

By the end of the year, Morris Schapiro had thirty dollars and the determination to set up a salvage business. With two relatives recently arrived in Baltimore from Latvia, he pooled $200 and established the Boston Metals Company—named after the city where he had spent his first night in the United States. In the sixty-five intervening years until his death at eighty-six, Schapiro was one of the great scrap-metals kings, specializing in worn-out ships, of which he salvaged more than fifteen hundred. Among his customers, spread from Hong Kong to Genoa, were D. K. Ludwig, world's largest shipowner, and Aristotle Onassis, to whom he sold the Canadian frigate that eventually became the yacht, *Christina.* In addition to the pride he took in seeing the elegance to which the latter piece of junk was dedicated, he also had the rather perverse pleasure, in the course of his long career, of acquiring the U.S.S. *Pennsylvania,* and personally scrapping the ship which had brought him in steerage to this country.

Morris Schapiro also became a pillar of the local business and religious community, never, however, losing his immigrant sensibilities. Like the founders of most dynasties, he made the traditional connections with powerful politicians. Again, according to his *Baltimore Sun* obituary of May 4, 1969, "Mr. Schapiro was accused of spending 'outrageous sums' in the re-election campaign of United States Senator Millard E. Tydings in 1938, but was cleared of the charge." He was also a longtime member of the Oheb Shalom Temple, and had the usual charitable foundations associated with dynastic money. Like the earlier industrial titans he bitterly fought government regulatory agencies when he could not do business with them—particularly the U.S. Maritime Commission, in connection with his policies for buying old ships—but he passed out crisp new hundred dollar bills to employees on his birthday. Always a controversial figure, Morris

Schapiro was considered the racing czar of Maryland because of his extensive holdings in the state's four major racetracks. His interest in horseracing, however, was principally one of investment. Schapiro's concern for racetracks that went beyond the area of money was soon to be taken care of, for in addition to children named Joseph, Doris, and Jerry, he had a son named John.

John D. Schapiro, at fifty-nine, is a craggy-faced balding man who goes hatless in all weather, except when horsey protocol calls for one. Then he wears a derby or a top hat as befits either the racetrack ceremony or the foxhunt in which he is participating. Schapiro compensates for his lack of physical height by wearing a French custom-made version of what was once known in vernacular as "Adler Elevators." Otherwise he clothes himself in the most conservative of Savile Row fashion.

"Well, you know," he said to the author, "for the last twenty years since the International started I've been getting over to London regularly. So my tailor has things ready for me. It usually takes three fittings to get a good job but I manage to do it in two. That gives me time for other things. If you have access to markets like these, it's very easy to build your taste around them."

The ring on the left pinkie finger? Does it have any special significance?

"That? No, it's just a ring I picked up in France. It's bloodstone, my birthstone, March."

John D. Schapiro, president of Laurel Racetrack and impressario of the Washington, D.C. International, seems to be a man interested in exchanging his background for a "classy" cut, although until his father's investment in the Maryland racetracks, he manifested little interest in the horsey set. He had, in fact, never been on a horse, except a childhood pony, until he acquired Laurel.

His first marriage, in 1938, was the fairly expected sort of liaison for a promising young man of his background—a Jewish girl from a good neighborhood, catered reception in a good hotel, religious ceremony according to orthodox tradition. John D. Schapiro, twenty-four, of 907 Lake Drive, Baltimore, married Jeanne Miller, twenty, literally the girl from around the corner, in a June wedding at the Waldorf-Astoria in New York.

After two sons it was not long before the marriage fell apart. John was now a free-wheeling bachelor, president of a racetrack and running with Maryland's horsey "valley" crowd, thereby making acquaintance with a horse.

He also made connection with the foxhunting crowd, by joining the Elkridge-Harford Hunt—an organization not especially notable for its Jewish membership.

"Sara [Secor, the club's joint master] convinced me I should give it a try," he told Snowden Carter, of the *Maryland Horse,* in December 1972. " 'We'll just go hill-topping,' " she said. " 'I'll stay back with you, just in case you have trouble.'

"Well, she had me come out on Thanksgiving Day in 1957. The meet was at St. James Church, and I showed up in jodhpurs and a soft cap. Completely incorrect, of course, but I didn't know any better.

"The field went off from the church and turned into George Constable's place, where we had our first jump. I was on my Irish import. I hadn't taken any riding lessons since I was a child. I had told Sara that I didn't know how to jump. But there we were, cantering into this fence. I didn't have any place to go except into it. So that's how I jumped my first fence. My good old Irish hunter simply took care of me."

About this time John also acquired a townhouse in the city to do the kind of entertaining appropriate to his developing role in society.

"I remember when John was still being bachelor-stylish around what was then the elegant Mt. Vernon Place area in Baltimore," recalled one of his old acquaintances. "He had this classy *pied-à-terre* which featured this immense fireplace that he seemed to think good taste demanded should not go unused. He'd appear at his parties dressed in riding britches, and in the middle of July light a fire in that damn thing and then turn up the air-conditioning."

It was during this "valley" period of transformation that John first saw Mrs. Eleanor Tydings (Gillet), a hard-riding member of his Elkridge-Harford Hounds; she was fair-haired and blue-eyed. She was above him both in height and in social position. She was the daughter of U.S. Senator Millard E. Tydings and granddaughter of Joseph E. Davies, first U.S. Ambassador to Moscow. At her wedding to F. Warrington Gillet, Jr., son of Mrs. George Eustis of Aiken, South Carolina, and Mr. Gillet of Baltimore, the guest list included governors, senators, ambassadors and high commissioners—all that kept

Supreme Court Chief Justice Vinson away was his sudden demise.

It took John about five years to win Eleanor, despite the fact that his father had been close enough to the ex-Mrs. Gillet's father to have been accused of excessive contributions to his senatorial re-election campaign. In 1964, John made his second marriage. This time the political and diplomatic corps were not in attendance. Neither was the marriage a catered affair at a hotel with a rabbi officiating. The wedding took place aboard an ocean liner, the *United States,* with at least one representative from Washington present: the Reverend Dr. Lowell Ditzen, who performed the ceremony.

Now he had a hostess most capable of supporting him when he was required to stand alongside the ambassador and his wife in the receiving lines of foreign embassy promotion parties for his International. No longer would he feel it necessary to engage a professional hostess with the right social connections to preside over functions such as his party in 1954 for Aly Khan at Saratoga. The big question was, now that he had arrived at this dizzying height, how to keep from falling off-balance.

John Schapiro hung onto his International—his lifeline to the world of the Beautiful People. He thought of his race as being not merely "mentioned in the same breath as the King George VI and Queen Elizabeth Stakes and the Prix de l'Arc de Triomphe," as a reprint from *Baltimore Magazine* in one of his brochures describes it, but, also "regarded in determining the 'Horse of the World.'"

Up until the seventh running of the International in 1958 there was only modest interest on the part of both the American public and racing stables here and abroad. The first two runnings, won by England and France, respectively, had horses only of middling merit, and certainly no names, except that of Baron von Thyssen, of international social importance. In 1954, Queen Elizabeth sent a mediocre horse, over the vocal protest of British breeding groups, who feared a bad showing would harm local bloodstock interests—and her horse finished last in a race won by Sonny Whitney's Fisherman. The fourth, fifth, and sixth runnings saw a little improvement in the kind of name-entering horse. Comte de Chambure sent a horse in 1955, Sir Winston Churchill (whose horse also ran last) sent one in 1956, and Prince Aly Khan sent one in 1957, with the score standing at two U.S. wins against four by foreign countries. Not much in the way of top horses

—not even one winner of any leg of the American Triple Crown. Despite vast promotional efforts few people outside of veteran racegoers had ever heard of the Washington, D.C. International.

In 1958 Schapiro managed a coup that immediately put the International not only in column one of the sports pages but on the front pages of newspapers throughout the world. That was the year that the Russians came.

John D. Schapiro had sensed the publicity value of breaking the Iron Curtain in horseracing. No Soviet thoroughbred had ever raced this side of the Iron Curtain. To the vast majority the very idea of horseracing in a communist country seemed inconceivable. How could anybody own a racehorse there? Did they gamble in a communist regime?

John Schapiro did not personally make the trip that implemented arrangements for the Soviets to enter their horses. Visiting the offices of the Ministry of Agriculture, which oversees Soviet racing, was nothing like hob-nobbing with the lords and ladies of the British Jockey Club or France's Société d'Encouragement. Instead he sent Joseph Cascarella, a one-time professional baseball player who had married his sister Jerry and turned racing dandy as executive vice-president of Laurel. Nobody had any idea of what the Russians would look like on arrival in the U.S., but Cascarella doubtless looked very much like what the Russians expected. Red Smith, who accompanied Cascarella on his Russian mission, reported in the *Baltimore Sun* of February 22, 1961: "If there is an unoccupied niche in the racing Hall of Fame in Saratoga, it might be a fitting gesture to rescue it for the heliotrope bowler with the cocoa band which Joseph Thomas Cascarella wore to Moscow in 1958. . . . Wrapping his shapely torso in a belted trench coat of the style affected by all secret agents in all films of intrigue, and cocking his iron skimmer at a rakish angle, he took flight for Moscow. . . . Competition would have forced the exhibit [Lenin and Stalin mausoleum] to shut down if Mr. C. had lingered longer than he did. For four days, kulaks in peasant garb queued up outside this bone-bowl, turned to gaze, transfixed, upon an apparition from another planet, so bedazzled by the crease in the trousers, that they forget why they'd come."

By the time the plane landed at Friendship Airport that autumn with two Russian thoroughbreds named Garnir and Zaryad, along with a retinue of trainers, jockeys, grooms, and technical personnel, public interest had skyrocketed. Crowds of photographers, reporters, and broadcast men were present at the unloading. The two Russian horses looked like any other thoroughbred at Belmont (although as mentioned earlier The Jockey Club had, in a sense, to declare them "honorary" thoroughbreds in order to comply with the rigid conditions of its Stud Book.) The director of the Moscow Hippodrome, the Moscow racetrack, Yevgeni Dolmatov, who had been an aide to Marshall Budenny, the famed Russian cavalryman, obviously had never visited Saville Row. The jockeys, except for the distinctive Russian fur hats and greatcoats, could have walked out of the Aqueduct jockeys' room and been mistaken for Eddie Arcaro or Ron Turcotte. And the trainer, a short gold-toothed, felt-hatted man in a casual business suit, might well have been taken for Hirsch Jacobs. Indeed, his name was Yevgeni (Eugene) Gottlieb. Later, at the welcoming ceremony, when a visitor, failing in Russian, ventured an alternative language, Yevgeni Gottlieb replied:

"Sicher! Gottlieb iss ein Yiddishe numen. Feyrde haben nisht anti-Semiten, ihr vayst? Ihr hat Yiddishe feyrde-leyhrners in America, nein? Vus sieht ihr a soy ibberascht in Russland sennen oyich du feyrde-leyhrners?" ("Certainly! Gottlieb is a Jewish name. Horses are not anti-Semitic, you know? You have Jewish horse-trainers here in the United States. Why are you so surprised that there are also Jewish horse-trainers in Russia?")

While the other foreign jockeys were quartered at fancy hotels (Laurel pays the expenses of all foreign trainers and jockeys), the Russian riders preferred to remain with their horses in a shack in International Village. Vodka, which the Russians carried in Coca-Cola bottles, flowed in mutual toasts at a press party in the Village. *Life* magazine came, TV came, *The New York Times* came, and dignitaries —curious and official—including anyone who could wangle a pass, came. American jockeys also came, to the great delight of the Russian jockeys, particularly Nikolai Nasibov. Some years later, when Nasibov had become a trainer in the USSR, he told visiting reporter Whitney Tower of *Sports Illustrated,* "Eddie Arcaro was a most elegant man. I also admired Shoemaker and Ycaza, but it was Arcaro I tried most to copy, and it is Arcaro's crouch and seat that I try to teach these boys. But it is difficult for me and especially for them. In America a jockey has a chance to ride and improve his style every day. Our jockeys race once a week, and you cannot acquire style when there is such little opportunity. We pick up boys at stud farms and teach them as best we can. I am luckier than most because I know what I want to teach them."

On International Day, November 11, 1958, after jockeys Nikolai Nasibav and Vladimir Kovalev had worked their horses for days to acquaint them with the track and the starting apparatus, and trainer Yevgeni Gottlieb and Director Yevgeni Dolmatov had been generously exhibited to the press, the crowds came. Mostly they came to see the two thoroughbreds owned by Soviet Horse Factory No. 33, the name of the official owner. (In the USSR, racehorses are at least theoretically owned, bred, trained, and ridden on a communal basis. A collective farm—loosely translated into English as "factory," a place where things are produced—owns the horses, and stable personnel share in their earnings. There is also a Russian Derby.)

Australia won the 1958 International with Sailor's Guide, the United States taking second with Tudor Era, and Ireland third with Ballymoss. Garnir, one of the Soviet horses, did not come off too badly, running sixth, while the other, Zaryad ran last. The crowds loved it, and John D. Schapiro's International, thanks to the Russians, was a popular success.

For the next eight years, except for 1965, the Soviets were there, and almost always sent two horses. They did better—getting a second with a horse named Anilin, and a third with Zabeg. John Schapiro was doing better too. People such as Mrs. Richard C. DuPont were now racing horses such as Kelso along with the Russians. The Aga Khan, Baron Guy de Rothschild, Irish President Eamon de Valera, Jock Whitney, Charles Englehard were also coming into the competition.

In 1972, after an absence of five years, the Russians once again accepted a request to enter the race, being, in fact, the first to be invited that year. They again submitted their customary two horses—Herold, a colt which had won the Russian Derby, and Skala, a filly of lesser accomplishment.

This was to be one of Schapiro's most prestigious years. As the season advanced, an acceptance was received from Jockey Club member John Schiff, who would be sending Droll Role, one of the best turf horses in the country, down from New York. The sensational

Cougar II was coming from California. Riva Ridge, 1972 Kentucky Derby and Belmont Stakes winner, was entered. And, most important, San San, a Prix de l'Arc de Triomphe winner, owned by Countess Margit Batthyany, was coming from France.

But the picture suddenly changed. Schapiro informed the Russians that he would not accept their second horse, the filly Skala. At that moment the two horses were en route to Cologne for transshipment to the U.S.

" 'We could not make them understand that the International was designed for classic horses, not ordinary runners,' Schapiro declared," reported Gerald Strine, turf writer for the Washington *Post*. " 'Skala finished fifth in the Grand Prix von Europa in Cologne about a week ago, and we already turned down the winner of that race, a German horse, Prince Ippi.'

"Cascarella said, 'It's unfortunate this had to happen. But in fairness to those owners who were turned down because of their horses' past performances we felt it was the only thing to do. It is our policy to keep the International as the grass championship of the world.'

"Who is kidding whom? And why?" asked reporter Strine.

The Russians, having invariably sent two horses, retaliated by pulling their Derby winner, Herold, out of the race. John Schapiro had, in effect, erected a Berlin Wall of his own.

Said Shirley Povich, sports editor of the Washington *Post:* "But Schapiro's concept of the International as a race for quality horses only is a brand-new and confounding one. During the previous twenty runnings it has been populated by some of the most hopeless starters ever invited into any race, a fact that suggests Schapiro's excuse for the rejection of the Russian filly—to preserve the integrity of the race—itself deserves rejection.

"In previous years the only excuse for the presence of some foreign horses in the Laurel race was a threatened scarcity of foreign entries. Their embassy connections were also useful, helping Schapiro to flesh out the Upper Turf Club teas he conducts for the odd collections of socialites, positive and putative, in his aerie above the clubhouse.

"Gerald Strine, The Washington *Post*'s turf columnist, noted the importance of social connections, when he suggested the other day that the Russian filly might have her invitation to Laurel were she owned by a czar or a prince, instead of by Moscow Horse Factory No. 33."

But this year, John Schapiro's Upper Turf Club victory celebration was going to be well-packed with Schiffs, DuPonts, French countesses, English lords, and miscellaneous nobility. The Russians were really not needed.

For the racing public it was another matter.

"The Russians . . . would have added considerable interest to the race," wrote Gerald Strine. "They always did. Usually they came in pairs: Garnir and Zaryad in 1958, Garnir and Flang in 1959; Zabeg and Zadorny in 1960, Zabeg and Irtysch in 1961, Zabeg and Liven in 1962, Ivory Tower and Bryansk in 1963.

"Could Skala have been worse than Bryansk? Or Irtysch?

"Nyet.

"As it is, the International is evolving into a showcase for the selling of foreign bloodstock, with transportation charges paid in advance. Owners and trainers come here more interested in getting a good price for their horse than in winning the race. . . .

"Meanwhile, rest well in the knowledge that Soviet horses won't squat on Laurel's doorstep in '72. Horse history probably will record that Kutuzov checked Napoleon's cavalry at Borodino, and Fischer captured Spassky's knights at Reykjavik, but that Schapiro and Cascarella stopped the Russians cold at Cologne."

The twentieth running of the Washington, D.C. International went ahead without the Soviets.

At a West German embassy party given to honor Mr. and Mrs. John D. Schapiro two nights before the race, the two honored guests stood in the receiving line, next to Ambassador Rolf Pauls and his wife, smiling and accepting congratulations. The West Germans had been invited and had qualified two horses, but in the end they could not make it. This, however, in no way damped enthusiasm for the reception on the part of either Schapiro, whose father had been a member of Temple Oheb Shalom, or for the ambassador, who had been a major in Hitler's army. Said the ambassador ". . . . beaming on the diplomats, horse breeders, socialites, sportswriters and jockeys massed at his embassy evening," as reported by Diana McLellan in the Washington *Evening Star*, "diplomats and horse breeders have much in common. We must both have patience. And we must both know how to pick the moment."

The ambassador raised his glass in toast to the creator of the Washington, D.C. International, and everyone joined in.

"What a scene!" a visitor overheard one guest remark. "Here's a Jew being toasted by a guy whose commander-in-chief not so long ago was roasting Jews!"

As the race turned out on Saturday, November 11, 1972, there might have been cause for rejoicing on the part of both the Germans and Russians that their horses never appeared. First, the International is run on a grass (not dirt) course, and a downpour had softened it so much that the favorite, Cougar II, was scratched. Trainers, owners, management, and sportswriters walked the course the morning of the race. Some considered it raceworthy only for a short distance out from the rail, which obviously all the horses in the race cannot get close to at the same time. Others felt that the hard crust of an inch or so that management had created by rolling the top would not support the weight of 1200-pound horses when even some of the 180-pound walkers were breaking through.

The race went off at the appointed time. Shortly after the field got off, Boreen, the Irish entry, third in the backstretch, fell into a hole, which, according to his trainer, Dermot Weld, and as reported in the Washington *Post*, ". . . was eight inches deep. If you don't believe me, you might want to go over there, look at and measure it yourself." Just behind was Jumbo Jet, from Singapore, which stumbled over Boreen and also fell. This disjointed the favorite, San San, and Riva Ridge, another heavily backed horse, and caused a great uproar among the bettors. The final result was that although no horse was apparently fatally hurt, there was much resentment against Laurel on the part of jockeys, and trainers and owners who had shipped horses thousands of miles only to wind up on what they considered a dangerous track.

But the pageant proceeded according to the traditional scenario. In the Upper Turf Club victory celebration that followed the race, John Schiff, whose Droll Role had won the race, was toasted by John Schapiro. The tall aristocratic-looking gentleman whose grandfather, Jacob Schiff, had been a member of the New Crowd in American banking, looked down on the upcoming member of the New Crowd in American racing. They clinked glasses, Mr. Schiff rather impatiently, for his car was waiting downstairs to take him to the airport for his return to New York. There was just time for the host to complete the ceremony. "You know," John Schapiro said to John Schiff, "there is something more we have in common besides racing, something dear to both our hearts. Both of us are interested in the Boy Scouts of America."

CHAPTER 25

The Phenomenon of Secretariat (1970-)

"Oh, Lord, he's perfect."
—Pat Putnam, *Sports Illustrated*, March 26, 1973

FOR ALMOST A YEAR the United States had been caught up in the Watergate affair—but on June 9, 1973, for two minutes and twenty-four seconds, the nation held its collective breath as it watched the running of the Belmont Stakes on television, more concerned with the hope of a horse breakthrough than a human break-in. Secretariat, a big chestnut three-year-old, had captured the heart of America with spectacular victories in the Kentucky Derby and the Preakness. No horse had gone on to win the Belmont Stakes and capture the Triple Crown of thoroughbred horseracing since Citation had swept to victory in 1948, almost a quarter of a century ago. So intense had been the public interest in the series of steps leading up to Secretariat's ultimate test that, in the week preceding the Belmont Stakes, he practically monopolized the entire news media.

Secretariat did not let his fellow Americans down: he won the Belmont in a breathtaking operation, a 31-length victory in world-record time. Excellence in the performance of a trust was not dead in America.

With his capture of the Triple Crown, people began to relate to Secretariat as a kind of new culture hero. Not even Senator Sam Ervin, the head of the Watergate Committee, Joe Namath, Mick Jagger, nor even the most charismatic Hollywood star, had ever appeared as had Secretariat, simultaneously on the covers of three national news magazines, while also commanding the attention of television, radio, newsprint and wire services throughout the world.

Secretariat has become a star of the first magnitude and a culture hero to countless millions who have never even been near a racetrack. A performer, whose "act" usually takes less than two minutes—quicker than a comet's flash, briefer than an Ervin quip, faster than the set-up, completion and run to daylight from a Namath pass, shorter and most certainly less noisy than a Jagger song—had become a legend in his own brief lifetime. It was the kind of thing that, whatever else one might say about the sport of kings and some of the people exploiting it, made it all, in the end, worthwhile. Such beauty in one of nature's most magnificant creatures, such excellence in the performance of a mission might well have been enough to have made Vaslav Nijinsky think twice about deploring his reincarnation as a horse. For believers, considering the corporeal evidence, Secretariat might even *be* the world's great dancer reborn as a thoroughbred.

The records show that whatever his otherworldly antecedents might have been, Secretariat's terrestrial progenitors were the stallion Bold Ruler, owned by the Phippses of New York, and the mare Somethingroyal, property of the Chenerys of Virginia. He was foaled at the Virginia farm of Christopher T. Chenery (under the same astrological sign, Aries—in case someone wants to make something of it—as that under which Nijinsky died.)

Even from the moment of birth, the foal with the three "white-stockinged" legs was already involved in a game of chance. The ownership of most thoroughbreds is generally decided well in advance of the moment they set foot in this world. Mr. A breeds his mare to Mr. B's stallion, and the resultant foal is generally the property of Mr. A. Not so with Secretariat. As previously mentioned, his fate was decided by the toss of a coin between Christopher Chenery's daughter, Mrs. Helen Tweedy, owner of his dam, and Ogden Phipps, chairman of The Jockey Club, owner of his sire.

This arrangement came about because of an agreement the parties had for breeding two Chenery mares each year for successive years to Phipps's Bold Ruler. By flipping a coin the winner would have his choice of the resulting foals the first year, with the loser having first choice the following year. Mrs. Tweedy, the loser in 1969, automatically got Secretariat in 1970, since only one of the two mares had foaled that year.

So, the question of whether, as a yearling, Secretariat would romp in the Kentucky sunshine on Bull Hancock's Clairborne Farm—where Phipps boarded his thoroughbreds—or munch the bluegrass at The Meadow in Virginia, was decided by the direction in which John F. Kennedy's likeness faced in the palm of a human hand.

Like most heroic individuals, Secretariat's life was spent confounding the experts and shattering existing standards. Ogden Phipps, in making his choice of the 1969 foals, selected the one by Bold Ruler out of Somethingroyal, and the horse turned out to be a dud. Secretariat, on the other hand, from exactly the same parents, became the superhorse of modern times. In addition, because of his male parentage, it was considered his destiny never to be a distance runner, i.e., a "classic" horse. "One of the clichés of the American turf in recent years," wrote Dan M. Bowmar III, in *The Thoroughbred Record,* "has been that Bold Rulers were not to be considered by anyone who was interested in a 'classic' horse." Nevertheless, Secretariat swept all three of the classics in the Triple Crown. Not only did he win the great classics but he also shattered track records as well. In the three years from the time that two people were deciding his fate with a fifty-cent piece, Secretariat had become a $6,080,000 phenomenon, of which thirty-two people had acquired a part.

What is the background of this modern fairy tale?

In a sense the story is the paramount example of making a fortune in the racing business and in many ways parallels Henry Phipps's turning an $800 investment into a $50,000,000 steel fortune.

Christopher T. Chenery was born of an old American family in Richmond, Virginia, in 1886. After the Civil War most of the Chenery possessions, including its ancestral home near Doswell, Virginia, built in 1818, had been lost. At sixteen, Christopher became an assistant surveyor for the Virginia Railway and, with his earnings, managed to attend Washington and Lee University from which he graduated with a Bachelor of Science degree in engineering. He worked as a civil engineer on projects in Virginia, in the Northwest and in Alaska, where he helped build a railroad with the aid of packhorse trains. Chenery was not a stranger to horses. In addition to his work with packhorses, he hunted and played polo. One of his early photographs shows him mounted on a horse being swept downstream in a river, like the early pioneers of the west.

By 1936, Chenery had become chairman of the Southern Natural Gas Company and a wealthy man, and that year he bought back his ancestral home and founded Meadow Stud on the 2600-acre Virginia farm.

Chenery was a bargain hunter supreme. At an auction sale, he bought a seventeen-year-old mare for $125 which, as a four-year-old, had sold for $125,000. Whiskaway gave him his first two stakes-winners and set the pattern by which he was to acquire a thoroughbred fortune: bargain purchases—two in particular—that produced offspring which paid off handsomely both at the track and in the stud.

The first of these bargains was Hildene, which his trainer bought for $750 along with two other fillies at a sale in Kentucky. Hildene won back only $150 of her purchase price at the races. But she produced Hill Prince, winner of $422,140 for Chenery, in addition to the Horse of the Year Award for 1950 and the Jockey Club Gold Cup.

Seven years later, Chenery paid $30,000 for Imperatrice, a bargain for a horse of her quality. She gave him three stakes winners. She also gave him Somethingroyal, who, although she never raced, produced Secretariat.

By the time Secretariat was born, Christopher T. Chenery had long been a leading member of the racing establishment. He played a major role in the reorganization of the old New York racetracks into the NYRA. He was a member of The Jockey Club and he was also the father of Mrs. Helen "Penny" Tweedy, Mrs. Margaret Carmichael of Tuscon, Arizona, and Dr. Hollis Chenery, chief economist of the World Bank. Christopher T. Chenery died in 1973 at the age of eighty-six after a long illness that had compelled him to turn over management of Meadow Stable to daughter Penny—"Boss Tweedy," as she is known to some around thc racetracks.

"Wow!" was the one word that Penny Tweedy is said to have inscribed in the notebook she keeps on her horses, when for the first time she saw the colt which the flip of a coin had won for her.

"The colt was big, bright-eyed, barrel-chested, a picture horse," reported *Time*. "His legs promised to be straight and flawless; knees and ankles—often soft spots on a thoroughbred—were trim and tight. As he grew, a purist determined not to give him 100% on looks, might have argued that his rump was on the skinny side. He was and still is, as the track people say, 'just a touch goose-butted.'"

This was not the kind of a son to expect of Bold Ruler. That thoroughbred was a sickly horse which was so miserable-looking as a yearling that Bull Hancock had to conceal him from the sight of visitors. A good part of his life was spent in battling all kinds of ailments. In addition, he was arthritic and carried his family's tendency to unsoundness, a fact that presaged lameness at an early age. He died of cancer at the age of seventeen.

"But Penny Tweedy has a breeding theory based on the belief that every horse, male or female, has some defects," said *Time*. "The trick is to cross bloodlines so that the dam's virtues cancel out the sire's flaws and vice versa. According to this theory, [her father] had the ideal mate for Bold Ruler—a mare called Somethingroyal, daughter of a very different kind of sire, named Princequillo.

"Horses sired by Princequillo are usually the exact opposite of Bold Ruler foals," the *Time* writer pointed out. "They have proved to be tough, durable, and able to go almost any distance, though seldom blessed with early speed. Mrs. Tweedy had never forgotten what another horse-breeder once told her: 'The Princequillos will run all day—and if the races get long enough and the other horses get tired enough, sooner or later they'll win for you.'

"The theory that you can breed a brilliant sire of young speedballs with the daughter of a line of gallant and tireless plodders, and thereby produce a superhorse, may be entirely wrong. Indeed many people think that all breeding theories are wrong. 'What you really need to get a good foal,' one expert has said, 'is a male horse, a female—and a lot of luck.'"

In any case, the Chenery family got themselves a horse whose healthy red chestnut coat glistened over 1,100 pounds of powerful bone and muscle. At maturity, his neck reminded one of a buffalo, and his back approximated the width of an elephant's. So deep was his chest and wide that in order to get a saddle on him, he required a custom-made 75¾-inch girth to encircle his body. With his 25-foot stride he is the Primo Carnera of horses, except that he has the grace of Muhammad Ali and the intelligence of Gene Tunney.

What was the lady from Denver, Colorado, whose education had been in Business Administration—not in racehorses—to do with a phenomenon whose designation at the moment was not Secretariat, but simply "Wow!"?

As a daughter of Christopher Chenery, she had inevitably been exposed to the goings-on at The Meadow. She had done her share of riding, hunting and the like, but as for the practical end of the racing and breeding business, she knew little more than the rest of the Smith College classmates with whom she spent her undergraduate years.

"I was born in New Rochelle, New York, and grew up in Pelham Manor," she told the New York *Post,* "and, well, I was a tomboy and tagged around with my father. . . .

"My mother"—Helen Bates Chenery, who died in November, 1967—"was from Portland, Oregon, and from a large family of homeopathic doctors. Her father was a Congregationalist minister. My mother and dad both wanted to rise above their own situations. My father wanted to recoup the family fortune, so he bought back the family farm, which is what The Meadow is. . . . My father didn't start Meadow Stable until 1936, and that was when I was away at boarding school. So I wasn't around the track, I mean, regularly, until [with a laugh] I was 45."

This is the background that tall, blue-eyed Penny Tweedy from Denver—where she lived with her lawyer-husband and four children—brought to the horse business when she was called by her incapacitated father to take over operation of Meadow Stable in 1967.

In the ensuing four years Penny Tweedy plunged into an educational blitzkrieg that matured her "horse sense." She read the horse journals from page to page, followed the auction sales like a professional bloodstock dealer, perused the veterinary literature as though she were an intern. Daily she was in telephone contact, both with Howard Gentry, Meadow Farm manager, and with Mrs. Elizabeth Ham, her father's longtime secretary—a lady who still oversees the financial side of the business. And finally, "when I got up the gumption," she told Martha Duffy of *Sports Illustrated*, "I decided to replace Casey Hayes, my father's trainer for 20-odd years. He had trouble transferring authority to me," she said. "In fact, he didn't."

She sought Bull Hancock's advice about a new trainer, and her father's longtime advisor recommended one of the Laurins, either the French-Canadian ex-jockey Lucien Laurin or his son, Roger, both trainers of high reputation. Mrs. Tweedy retained the son. But, in early 1971, he resigned to take over the training of the Ogden Phipps stable on the death of Eddie Neloy. The horses of the chairman of The Jockey Club are not exactly third-rate platers, but young Laurin's move was like abandoning a property that next year would have a fortune in oil gushing out of it. Riva Ridge was about to start his spectacular two-year-old career, and a yearling, now named Secretariat —after Chenery secretary, Mrs. Elizabeth Ham, who once worked for the Secretariat of the League of Nations—was ready to get his first lessons as a racehorse. Generally it is a father who recommends a son for a job, but here the situation was the reverse. Young Laurin, on leaving Meadow Stable, suggested that his father be hired to succeed him. Mrs. Tweedy accepted the advice, with the result that, between them, Laurin & Son now train two of the most powerful stables in the world.

Lucien Laurin, a gray-haired, chubby man of sixty-one, is the diametric opposite of the horses he set out to train for Meadow Stable. He has a tiny ex-jockey's frame of some 140 pounds, as against Secretariat's huge mass of 1,100 pounds. He came up, not in the bluegrass luxury of Chenery thoroughbreds, but the hard way—a struggling jockey making the rounds of Canada's second-rate tracks. After twelve years of trying to overcome his appetite and mediocre mounts, he came down to New England and began his career as a trainer. Soon he had a reputation for bringing sore-legged horses back to good form. By 1958 he was a top-drawer professional, having developed Quill, the champion two-year-old filly of that year, and in 1966 Amberoid, a winner of the Belmont Stakes for Reginald Webster. At the time he joined the Meadow Stable team, he was training for Bull Hancock's Claiborne Farm, one of the most powerful operations in the country.

With him, he brought along his compatriot, the French-Canadian jockey, Ron Turcotte, who had been Canada's top rider before he moved to the United States in 1964. Since that time Turcotte has annually won more than $1,000,000 in purses. Turcotte's move to the top is also a story of privation and hard work. Genetics being the mysterious thing that it is, Ron was a 5-foot, 128-pounder in the company of eleven siblings, one of whom stood 5′10″ and weighed over 200 pounds. Nevertheless the diminutive young man started his work life as a lumberjack in the Canadian woods, the traditional occupation of his family. When a deep snow closed down the New Brunswick lumber camps, Ron went to Toronto in search of other work, and wound up as a hot-walker at E. P. Taylor's Windfields Farm. He went on to groom, to exercise boy and finally to jockey. When he joined the Meadow Stable team he was, in terms of stakes won and dollars earned, one of the world's leading riders. Despite the fact that he is the first jockey since 1902 to have won a Kentucky Derby back-to-back, "he has never captured public imagination in the style of an Earl Sande, an Eddie Arcaro or a Willie Shoemaker," says Whitney Tower of *Sports Illustrated*. "'. . . Ronnie isn't the kind of fellow who makes headlines,' one of his associates has said. 'He's just a level-headed, down-to-earth, hard-working country boy without charisma.'"

This was the team that took over the development of the biggest star, in terms of audience volume, in the world today.

When Lucien Laurin first inspected Secretariat as a yearling, he is reported by *Horsemen's Journal* to have said to himself, "This horse is too good-looking to ever amount to anything."

Good looks, that is, conformation—such as size, strength and breeding—is no guarantee of speed, stamina or heart. Many large horses, particularly, are often not ideally structured for excellence in racing: hind legs are sometimes malformed, or backs are too long. Most successful racehorses are medium or even small-sized. In this connection, Secretariat at first elicited "Wows!" only on the basis of his excruciatingly good looks.

Then there was the problem of his appetite. Jockeys eat themselves out of their professions and so can a racehorse. Secretariat could easily have been in this class. He presently eats sixteen quarts of oats daily, four more than an above-average male, in addition to nibbling constantly on hay.

Also, many horses hardly touch food after a hard race. After the Derby, according to *Time*, "Laurin watched the groom prepare Secretariat's usual supper—oats cooked into a mash, plus carrots and some vitamins and minerals plus some 'sweet feed': grains coated with molasses to provide the rough equivalent of a candied breakfast cereal. The mixture filled the better part of a big tub, and Laurin said, 'He won't finish that in three days.' An hour-and-a-half later the tub was empty."

In getting Secretariat ready for his debut, Laurin was confronted with the same problem that caused his own retirement as a jockey: a spreading waistline. And the horse had not yet even been trained.

"Training a fat horse requires even more forbearance than working with a skinny one," *Time*'s reporter pointed out. "The fat has to be exercised away, without unduly straining the muscles, before there can be any thought of trying to find out whether he has any speed. The months went by. Other two-year-olds were getting to the races starting to make names for themselves. When Mrs. Tweedy asked how her wow horse was doing, Laurin's answer for a long time was, 'He hasn't shown me much.' Then the bulletins were amended slightly —but only slightly—to 'He's coming along.' "

Finally, the big day came and Laurin advised his boss that the horse was ready, with a sly look in his eye that suggested, "Madam, be prepared for witnessing a spectacular." The debut had to be postponed because Mrs. Tweedy, unavoidably detained out of town at the time, reasonably insisted on being present at the race.

On July 4—a most apt debut day for a future American hero—Secretariat made his first start, in a 5½ furlong maiden race at Aqueduct. Hopes were set back a bit. He was slammed at the start and, but for his great strength, might have been thrown. He made up ground in the last quarter, coming from tenth position to be beaten only by 1¼ lengths.

From then on, throughout his two-year-old career, it was no contest. He swept the season. No runner ever finished in front of him. But he was not permitted to keep first money in the Champagne Stakes, having borne in and bumped Stop The Music, and as a result was disqualified and placed second. His 1972 record was nine starts, seven official wins and two seconds, with earnings of $456,404 and the Horse of the Year award—first time a two-year-old colt had ever received it.

Meantime, his stable-mate, the three-year-old Riva Ridge, had himself become something of an heroic figure, having won the Kentucky Derby and the Preakness but missing the Triple Crown with his defeat in the Belmont Stakes. Penny Tweedy had become a national celebrity. Two horses like this in a row was rare as an elephant having twins. As the year 1972 came to a close, the Meadow Stable barn at

Belmont was being daily overrun with the press and the curious from all over the world.

"Here he is," said Lucien Laurin to *The Blood-Horse* writer, Art Grace, who was visiting Secretariat, now wintering in his Hialeah barn and awaiting his three-year-old debut in New York, "here's the boss. Isn't he something? You think he looks good now? Wait until you see him under tack!"

"He pushed the colt backward," wrote Grace, "to get a better view. 'Look at that rear end, will you.'

"Secretariat turned and put his head out of the stall. 'Better move back,' Laurin said. 'He'll take your arm off.'

"In the next breath, Laurin added, 'he's a real good-natured colt.' Which, of course, is not necessarily a paradox. A colt can be good-natured and high-spirited.

" 'This is positively one helluva horse,' Laurin said—without fear of contradiction, at least not from anyone who had seen Secretariat perform. 'He gives you heart failure, the way he drops out of it, but there's nothing you can do about it. That's his game.

" 'I said to Ronnie [jockey Turcotte] after one race, 'Look, I don't know if you're putting on a show, or what. But why do you have to be so far out of it?

" 'And Ronnie just shook his head and said, "Honest, there is nothing anybody can do to make him run before he hits the half-mile pole. Nothing. But once he gets there, all you got to do is steer him where nobody will get in his way . . . and then hang on." ' "

When Secretariat came north for his first start as a three-year-old —in the Bay Shore Stakes at Aqueduct on March 17—it was the same old story. All Turcotte had to do was to "steer him where nobody got in his way . . . and hang on." He won by 4½ lengths over Champagne Charlie, showing all of his old ease and confidence, his old power and finishing punch, and most of his old zest for the race.

Next came the Gotham Stakes, where Secretariat suddenly changed his style and, instead of loping behind his opponents, dashed immediately into the lead—seeming to enjoy toying with his opponents. As soon as Champagne Charlie began to close in, Secretariat let out again and danced away from him to win by three lengths and equal the track record.

By this time many were beginning to suspect that a superhorse was in the making. In the upper eschelons of the racing establishment, heads began to wag together, and in the winter of 1973, even before he had won the Kentucky Derby, came the sensational syndication—the $6,080,000 deal that put a horse, now literally worth nearly four times his weight in gold, into the hands of the owners of 32 shares.

The wires buzzed even louder than ever with news of the world's most expensive performer—a star insured for perhaps a greater sum than Elizabeth Taylor—a horse whose stud fee was the equivalent of $190,000 and might even have reached $300,000 had the syndication waited on his winning the Triple Crown. Some horsemen were soon to clamor for freezing his semen and preserving it for use after his death. "This horse is syndicated for $6,080,000," Dr. Harry Sweig, president of the Harness Horse Breeders of N.Y., Inc., told Steve Cady of *The New York Times.* "Suppose something happened to him and he never got to the breeding farm. You wouldn't have a drop of semen from a horse some people say might be the greatest in racing history." The possibility of the failure of Secretariat to reproduce himself was in fact nightmarish enough to cause the horse to be insured against impotency and homosexuality. So heavy was the weight of all those dollars, moreover, that Mrs. Tweedy had to work overtime "helping the people who have to do with the horse to exist and function," she told Martha Duffy of *Sports Illustrated.* "At night I had dinner with Ronnie, who really feels the pressure of that $6 million syndication. By day I'd tell Lucien, 'I want to see such-and-such a stud'. . . ." They would get into Laurin's car and go looking. It took their minds off the huge responsibility.

Then, suddenly and shockingly, a dark cloud settled over the picture. In the Wood Memorial, a nine furlong (1⅛ mile) race just two weeks before the Derby, Turcotte asked his horse for the burst of speed he had always given, but it was not forthcoming. Secretariat came in a badly-beaten third, trailing his stablemate, Angle Light (owned by Edwin Whittaker, but also trained by Laurin) and the new threat, Sigmund Sommer's Sham, who placed second.

Was it the old Bold Ruler syndrome again—the inability to go a distance? Was this to be another flash-in-the-pan, a $6,080,000 flash, no less?

To make matters worse, Laurin had come under considerable criticism to the effect that he had entered Angle Light as a "stalking horse" to undo Sham for the benefit of Secretariat. Frank "Pancho" Martin, Sham's trainer, had in turn responded by entering two other horses—Knightly Dawn and Beautiful Music—in addition to Sham. This was the beginning of something that resembled a feud, fired even more by Charles Hatton, veteran columnist for *The Racing Form,* who had written that, "The Wood is supposed to decide who has the most horse not the most horses . . . we can't think he [Martin] wants to run three or even two." Both Martin and Sigmund Sommer, Sham's owner, were furious, and on the morning of the race had withdrawn their two other entries. Sham went it alone and in fact outplaced Secretariat in the Wood Memorial, but the grudge persisted.

On May 5, 1973, 134,476 people (the largest crowd ever to attend a horse race in this country) came to the Kentucky Derby at Churchill Downs to see for themselves. This was a Kentucky Derby that no one considered would now be a "walkover." There was the big question mark of the Wood Memorial and Sham, in addition to the unknown possibilities of any of the other twelve entries. Pancho Martin, still fuming from the accusations that he had been using "rabbits" to knock off Secretariat, responded by again scratching his two "stalking horses," Knightly Dawn and Beautiful Music. "Sham will go out and beat Secretariat alone—with no help," he told his critics.

The result was history, or "MURDER," as Whitney Tower of *Sports Illustrated* headlined his report of the race. It was Joe Louis come back to avenge his defeat by Max Schmelling, it was Man o' War returned to break the heart of Upset, his one and only conqueror.

In a field of thirteen horses, including Angle Light (which in all fairness to his owner, Edwin Whittaker, trainer Laurin had to keep in the race) Secretariat roared down the track from eleventh place at the quarter-mile pole, to 6th at the ½ mile, 5th at the ¾, 2nd at the mile, and then, swallowing up his opposition in the stretch, plunged across the finish line 2½ lengths ahead of Sham, to one of the greatest crowd roars in sports history. He also smashed, by three-fifths of a second, the track record of 2:00 flat set by Northern Dancer in 1964.

TURCOTTE: (raising his cap in the winner's circle on a perfect May afternoon): "Wood Memorial? Throw that race out. We've seen greatness today."

LAURIN: (after the race) "Well, I was mighty nervous going into

> that first turn. We were last again, and I said to myself, God Awmighty, don't tell me it's gonna be another one of them!"

TWEEDY: "Well, that's *one* Bold Ruler who can go the distance!"

THE PUBLIC: SECRETARIAT! WE LOVE YOU!

On to Baltimore and the Preakness. New doubts. It was here that Secretariat's stablemate, Riva Ridge, in his own try for the Triple Crown, had bitten the dust—or, more exactly, tasted the mud, for on that day the track was a virtual quagmire. Contenders for the past twenty-five years since Citation's Triple Crown in 1948, had gone down to defeat in one or more of the trophy's three legs. Pimlico was a tricky course with very tight turns.

Another record crowd was on hand for the 1³⁄₁₆ mile race, one reason for the 61,653 people who swarmed over clubhouse, grandstand and grassy infield being the continuing controversy between Pancho Martin and Lucien Laurin. Egged on by the press and professionals, Martin was still claiming that Sham would have won the Derby had it not been for the rumpus in the starting gate which caused his horse to lose two teeth.

"This time will be different," he informed the press. "I think from the three-eighths pole home my horse will outfinish any horse in the country. Never mind the tight turns; they still have nearly a quarter-of-a-mile of homestretch. Sham should be laying second most of the way and can go to the front anytime the leader tires."

This was a perfectly feasible race plan. Sham, in third position at the quarter—3½ lengths in front of Secretariat —did move up to second at the ¾ pole and lay there into the stretch. "The only hitch," said *Sports Illustrated*, "was that the leader, who [now] happened to be Secretariat, forgot to tire. In fact, by the end of the mile-and-three sixteenths, Jockey Ron Turcotte had neither used the whip on Secretariat's massive backside, nor even bothered to shake it at him. The pair of them, in perfect harmony as they coasted to the finish line, looked as though they could have gone around again and then set off cross-country."

In some quarters, Secretariat is considered to have also broken Canonero's track record of 1:54 in the 1971 Preakness. The track's electric timer showed Secretariat's final time to be 1:55, and that is recorded as the official time. But two *Racing Form* clockers, operating independently, both showed 1:53⅖ on their stop-watches. This may well be as much a cause for debate over the years as has Gene Tunney's "long count" in the Dempsey fight. And it added more fuel to the Secretariat fire.

After the Preakness victory, the tension mounted to enormous proportions. It seemed that everybody in the world was talking horse.

The Belmont Stakes appeared a foregone conclusion, despite its more demanding distance of 1½ miles. Sham had been effectively eliminated as an opponent in the two previous races. Only five other owners could be induced to enter horses against Secretariat and these chiefly to capture second, third or fourth shares of the purse, which would be substantial. Nevertheless, the three weeks until June 9th seemed an unbearably long wait, for the Belmont Stakes represented more of a coronation than a competition.

It was just that. An exhibition, a pageant, indeed a coronation—a romp, in which the rider had to look back 31-lengths, practically a city block, to see the escort—led by an animal called Twice A Prince—that would accompany his horse to the crowning. The conquest of the Triple Crown had been completed in 2:24, the fastest time for the distance run on any dirt track in the world.

This was indeed "The Ultimate Superlative," as Arnold Kirkpatrick of *The Thoroughbred Record* dubbed Secretariat. "There's absolutely no doubt in my mind," he wrote, "that he is the finest athlete of any race, color, family, genus or species ever to have lived." Mrs. Tweedy, less volatile, said, "I am in absolute awe of him. His size, his good looks, his astounding speed—he must be frightening to other horses."

Secretariat was a star of the first magnitude. All kinds of offers were pouring in for Secretariat: movies, television, books, offers from Las Vegas (to parade the horse before an audience for fifteen minutes for a flat fee of $25,000 a day), a $200,000 performance against stablemate Riva Ridge for Marlboro cigarettes and CBS, Secretariat T-shirts, jewelry and what-not. Secretariat signed with William Morris, one of the world's biggest talent agencies, complete with his own agent, Steve Pinkus.

Whether or not Secretariat is actually as great or greater than Man o' War is really of little significance. The fact is that he is a star in his own right, a phenomenon—beloved of the people, and an authentic culture hero.

George Plimpton, no stranger to stars, specialist on culture heroes, wrote in *Sports Illustrated* on July 9, 1973, "The largest Arlington [Chicago] crowd in three decades—41,223—was on hand for the exhibition (Penny Tweedy and her trainer, Lucien Laurin, had brought the great horse to the Midwest, keeping their promise to let the people watch him run), and there was applause from the moment the horse appeared on the track. There were many young people on hand, including college girls with bare midriffs and painful-looking sunburns, and in the infield, opened for the first time in memory, bands played, a large group had a beer keg set on a wheelchair, and as Secretariat turned into the stretch, the infield crowd roared him home and hundreds of arms shot up in the power salute . . .

"At the Arlington barns his fans came by the hundreds to look at him.

" 'Where's the Big Horse?'

" 'Where's the one that did it?'

"They aim their Instamatics past the guards lolling in the beach chairs at the end of the shed row and whistle for Secretariat to peer out of his stall. They ask for souvenirs, a clip of chestnut hair from his mane. They gossip about him like a movie star.

" 'How does he sleep?'

" 'Horses sleep standing up a lot of the time.'

" 'No kidding?'

" 'He's a star. He sleeps in the nude, standing up.'

" 'G'wan!'

" 'Hey, look! He's looking out.'

"Secretariat likes to peer out of his stall from underneath the protective webbing across the open door, so that looking down the shed row one sees the line of horses' heads at the normal eye level, and then beyond, a horse peering out of his stall at kneecap level.

" 'What's wrong with that horse? He's either lying down or he's got awful short legs.'

"The guard leans forward. 'That's Secretariat.'

" 'Oh.'

"The Instamatics click."

On August 4, 1973, Secretariat ran his seventeenth race: the Whitney Stakes at Saratoga, named after William Collins Whitney. In a mortal sort of way, Secretariat joined an illustrious roster of acknowledged superhorses. For the first time, the three-year-old "unbeatable" was taking on older horses, and a four-year-old Jack Dreyfus gelding, named Onion, beat him by a length. At least this served to prove that Secretariat, like all living things, was mortal—but a superhorse indeed. Because now he was a peer of Man o' War, who was defeated by Upset at Saratoga; he was in the company of Gallant Fox who fell victim, also at Saratoga, to a 100 to 1 shot named Jim Dandy, he was one with Native Dancer who lost his only race, the Kentucky Derby, to a horse named Dark Star.

If there were any valid excuses—and in racing it is only getting to the wire first that counts—it might have been hitting his head on the starting gate just before the break. That is one of the imponderables of racing luck—but it is no fun to get banged on the nose and then have to run a mile-and-an-eighth.

But Lucien Laurin made no real excuses. "I think he would have been better off a little more out from the rail (the track was less heavy there)" he said after the race. "Hitting the gate didn't help any, either. But I just don't think he could handle the track today."

So the mortal Secretariat entered the company of the immortals with his upset at Saratoga. And it is only by reference to Secretariat that Onion will be remembered.

Helen Tweedy and the estate of C. T. Chenery became rich from the phenomenon known to the world as Secretariat. So did Lucien Laurin and Ron Turcotte. In addition to Mrs. Elizabeth Ham, after whom he was named, and Howard Gentry, manager of the farm where he was foaled, and Eddie Sweat, his groom, and all the people who played a part in the development of this star, all are the richer for his presence on this earth. Even the members of the princely families over whose turf he has run are enriched by contact with this culture hero. But, by far, those who are the richest as a result of the two years during which he has flashed through our consciousness, are the millions of Americans whom he dazzled by his appearance (up to his Chicago race) on *their* turf.

Index